Hogan Lovells | Our Story

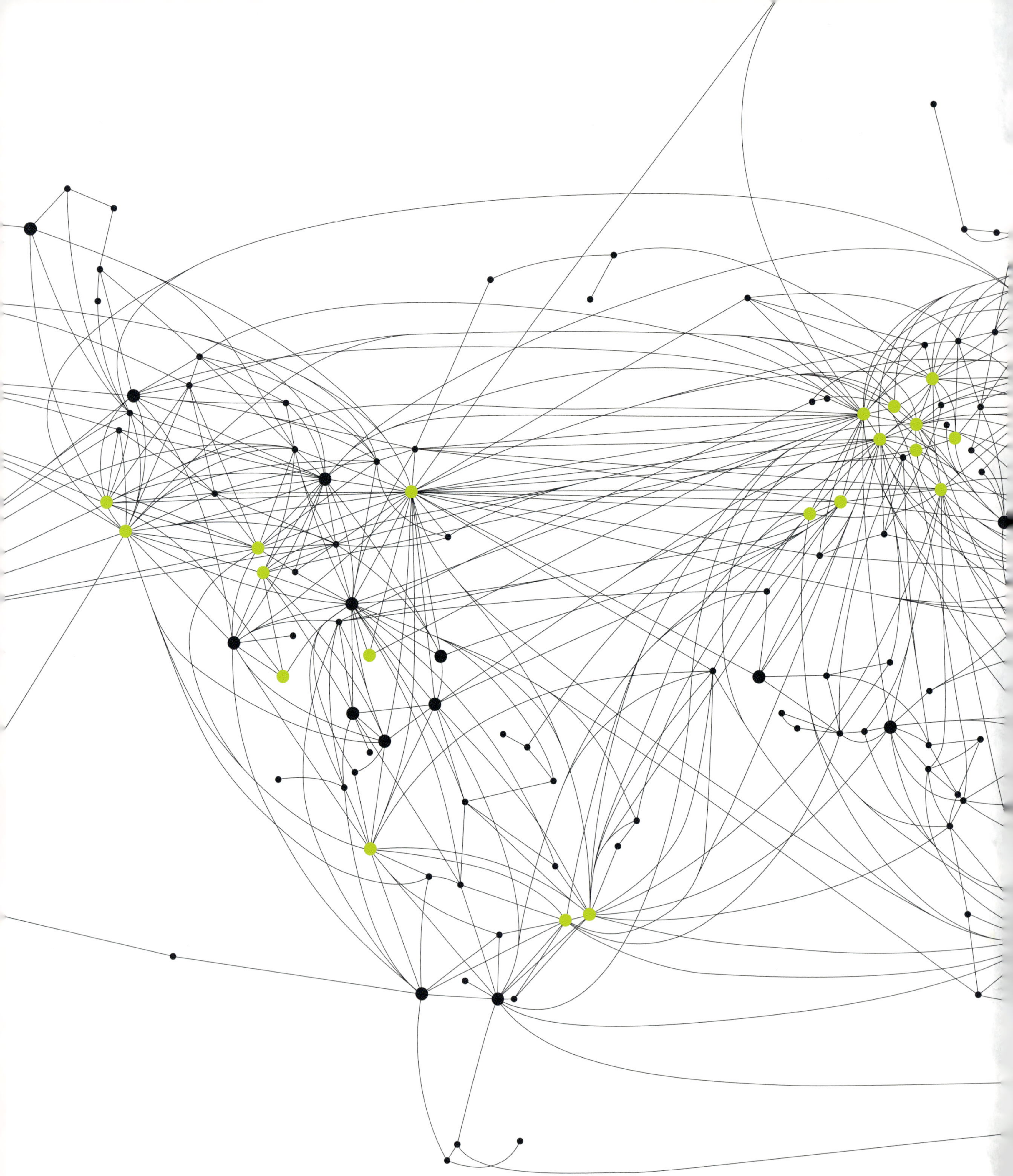

Hogan Lovells
Our Story

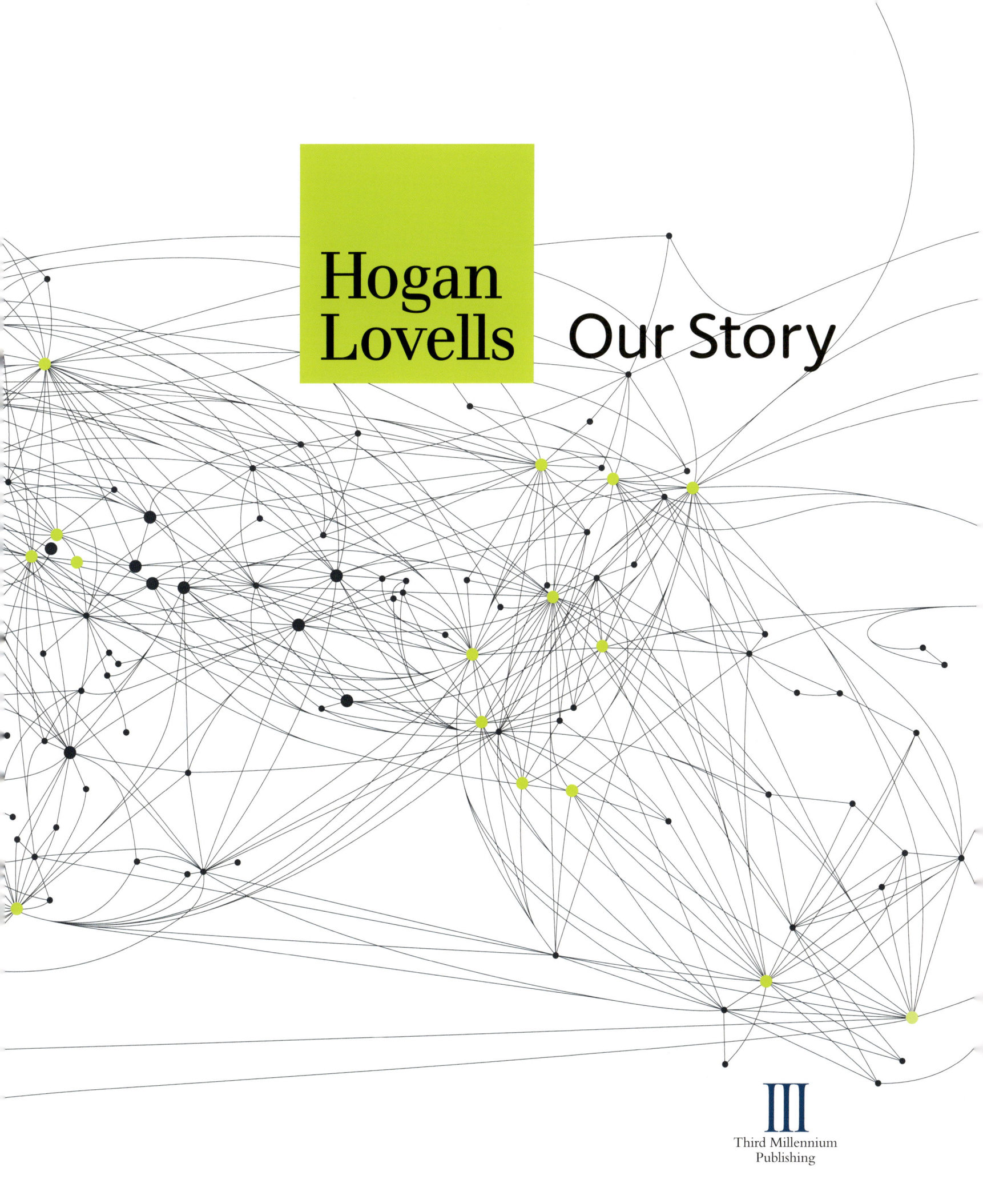

Third Millennium Publishing

The artwork used on the previous page is *Air Routes of the World (Day & Night)* by Langlands & Bell, 2002.

First published in Great Britain in 2016 by
Third Millennium Publishing, an imprint of Profile Books Ltd

3 Holford Yard
Bevin Way
London WC1X 9HD
United Kingdom
www.tmiltd.com

Copyright ©Hogan Lovells International LLP and Hogan Lovells U.S. LLP 2016
and Third Millennium Publishing, an imprint of Profile Books Ltd 2016

The rights of ©Hogan Lovells International LLP and Hogan Lovells U.S. LLP 2016 to be identified as the author of this work have been asserted in accordance with the Copyright, Designs and Patents Act of 1988.

All rights reserved. No part of this publication may be reproduced, stored, or introduced into a retrieval system or transmitted in any form or by any means (electronic, mechanical, photocopying, recording, or otherwise) without the prior written permission of both the copyright holder and the publisher.

A CIP catalogue record for this book is available from the British Library.

ISBN: 978 1 908990 62 4

Project manager: Susan Millership
Designer: Susan Pugsley

Reprographics by Studio Fasoli, Verona, Italy
Printed and bound in Italy by L.E.G.O. Spa

Contents

	ACKNOWLEDGMENTS	6
	INTRODUCTION	8
CHAPTER 1	OUR FOUNDERS	12
	Frank Hogan	12
	Lovell, White & King	28
	Montagu Piesse	34
	Guy Hambling	36
	Martin Wassermann	37
CHAPTER 2	OUR GROWTH	44
	London	44
	Washington, D.C.	64
CHAPTER 3	OUR COMBINATION	86
CHAPTER 4	OUR BUSINESS	106
	Corporate	106
	Finance	112
	Government Regulatory	115
	Intellectual Property, Media and Technology	118
	Litigation, Arbitration and Employment	122
	Business Services Teams	126
CHAPTER 5	OUR CITIZENSHIP	136
CHAPTER 6	OUR WORLDWIDE TEAM	152
	Asia	152
	Europe	156
	United States of America	162
	Latin America	168
	Middle East	169
	Australia	169
	Associated Offices	170
	OUR PEOPLE, OUR FUTURE	172

Acknowledgments

This book owes a great debt to a great many people. We mention a few of them by name here.

Judy Slinn was the author of a Lovells history predating our firm's historic combination. Adrian Kinnane authored *The Heart Of It All*, a history of Hogan & Hartson's first hundred years. We enlisted Adrian again in this effort, and John Young drew from Judy's past work, in order to knit together our firms' founding narratives.

Elizabeth Lockwood and Rebecca Umhofer gathered and contributed significant material in this volume—Liz, for the Citizenship chapter, and Becky, for the chapter on Our Business. Peter Mosback did the detailed work of assembling the many origin stories of our offices all over the world for the chapter on Our Worldwide Team. We owe them all great thanks for their tremendous effort.

Warren Gorrell and David Harris provided pivotal anecdotes and insights into the formation of Hogan Lovells, from its initial vision to the intense work of carrying out that vision. We are grateful to Nick Cray for using this wealth of material to author Our Combination chapter.

Kay Hart, Head of Knowledge and Research, worked tirelessly on every stage of the book's evolution, from initial idea to its hardcover binding. Her guidance, together with that of our editor, Susan Millership, has been invaluable.

We also are grateful to Steve Immelt and Nicholas Cheffings for their thoughtful leadership on this and every endeavor.

There are many hundreds of people not named in this volume—associates, staff, and partners, past and present—who over the past many decades have contributed to our firm's work, its successes, and its values. Their names may not be written here, but their contributions are reflected in every chapter of our firm's story.

Leo von Gerlach and Cate Stetson

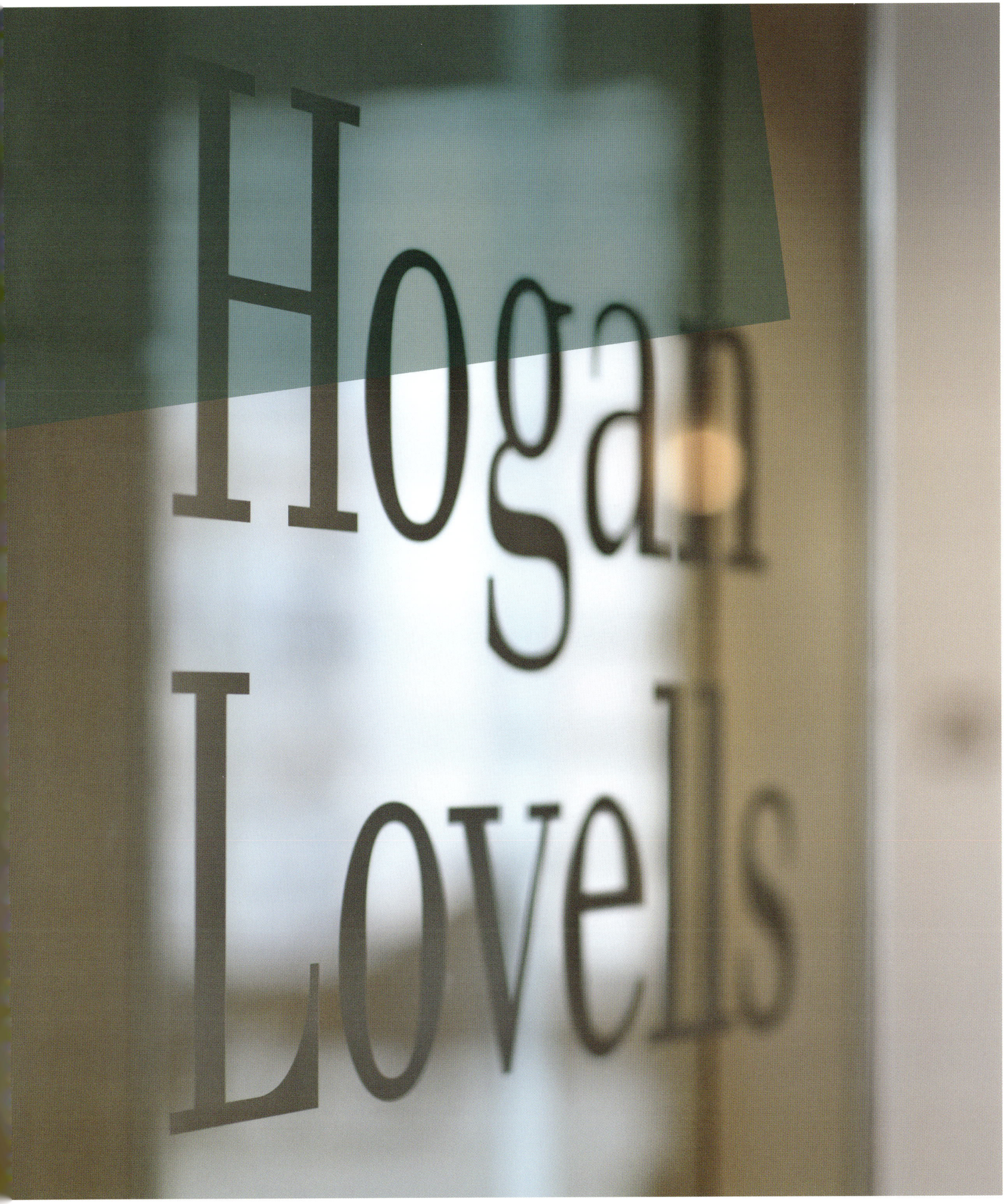
Hogan
Lovells

Introduction

The creation of Hogan Lovells on 1 May 2010 brought together two firms, each with more than one hundred years of rich history. We spoke then of what the two firms brought to our combination. Now, some five years later, we speak with pride of the unified Hogan Lovells that we have created, and we plan—with great optimism—for the future of our worldwide firm.

But our past—our history—is a vital part of what we are. Hogan Lovells would not exist were it not for the many individuals who created that history of which we are so proud. The purpose of this book is to recount a small part of that history. As you read, you will find that our past is also a prologue; our firm's founders and our early partners carried with them the same values that we prize today. They were bold, ambitious, and passionate about their work. They were imaginative: embracing new approaches where others saw barriers. They looked out for each other: forging deep and true friendships across practices and offices. Over the years, our partners and their teams built, collegially and collaboratively, the foundations of our firm's present success. The values we emphasize today have deep roots in the firm, which we are privileged to now lead. We have been entrusted with a rare and special legacy. It is our responsibility—and the responsibility of all of us who are currently a part of Hogan Lovells—to build upon this legacy for future generations.

As you turn the pages of this book, you will learn about our offices and our work, and of how our firm developed from modest beginnings in London, Washington, D.C., and Hamburg to a firm with about 6,000 people working across the globe in almost fifty offices. The success of our firm has depended, and will always depend, upon all of our people and all of our clients, across the world. We have been blessed in both respects and no history of our firm can do adequate justice to the thousands that have contributed to our success over so many years. By selecting just some of the many anecdotes from our past, however, this book seeks to tell "our story." With such rich material from which to choose, we are dedicating a chapter of this book to our good citizenship—which is, and always has been, an essential part of what makes Hogan Lovells. *Our Story* would not be complete without it.

The legal profession is facing a period of immense change. We relish the opportunities that this presents, and the challenge of finding better ways to work together, to communicate better with each other and with our clients, to continue to improve the exceptional legal services for which we have been known for so long, and to make a difference in the lives of others by working to effect positive change in the world. That is no small undertaking. It will demand the very best of all of us. But we are more than capable of it; look at what we and our predecessors have already built together. *Our Story*, past, present, and future, is an enduring one of boldness, vision, individual and collective endeavor, humility, and humanity. Those attributes have served us well for over a century, and they will take us forward with optimism, determination, and confidence.

The process of capturing *Our Story* on these pages has reminded us of just how fortunate we are, as individuals, to stand on the shoulders of those who came before us. We must never lose sight of this fact and, in many ways, this book serves not only as a tribute to them but also as a thank you.

We hope that you will enjoy reading *Our Story*. We have greatly enjoyed being a small part of it and we look forward to many future chapters being written by those who follow in the footsteps of our founders.

Nicholas Cheffings,
Chair

Steve Immelt,
CEO

Lawyers and summer associates at the U.S. Summer Associate Retreat on the Washington, D.C. office roof deck, 2013.

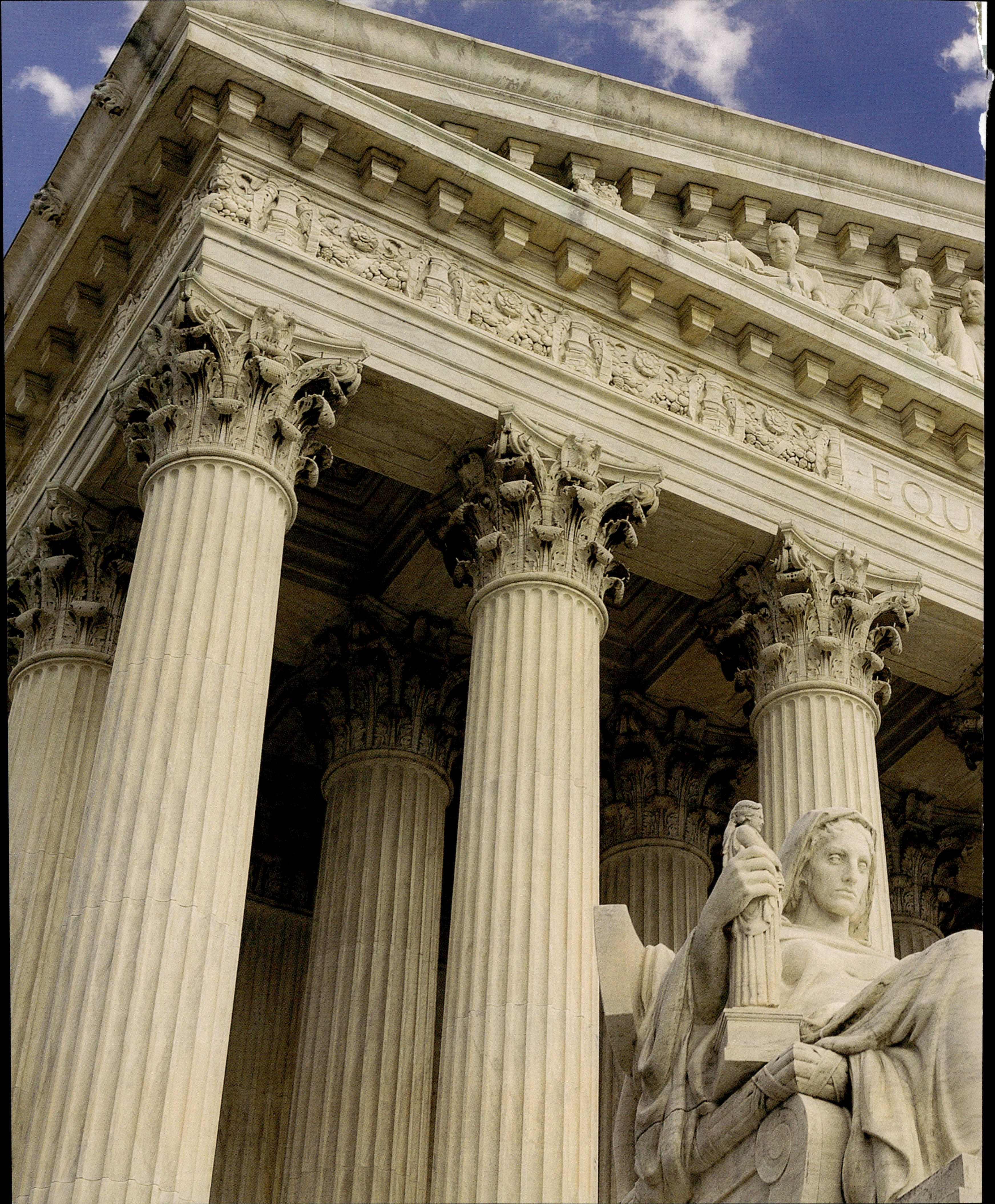
EQU

Chapter 1

Our Founders

Chapter 1
Our Founders

PREVIOUS PAGES: The Supreme Court of the United States, Washington, D.C.

BELOW: Frank Hogan experienced great hardship as a child, and left school at the age of twelve.

FRANK HOGAN

At the age of eleven, Frank Hogan's recitation of an Irish poem at St. Patrick Church's school graduation ceremony in Charleston, South Carolina, elicited comment from a local paper that the youngster "probably will become some day a noted orator." But the next year the budding speechmaker left school, his formal education finished. He was lucky to have made it that far. In fact, he was lucky to be alive.

From Poverty to Practice

Frank was born in Brooklyn, New York, on 12 January 1877. His father, Maurice, tried to support his growing family on a tailor's earnings, but the money did not stretch far. His wife, Mary—the family called her "Mollie"—helped with some sewing work during the few hours she was not attending to the couple's five children. The burden of hungry mouths to feed gave way to a heavier one of grief when two of the children died of tuberculosis. The family tragedy deepened in 1882 when Maurice also died from the "wasting disease." Mollie carried on, stitching handkerchiefs and making children's clothing, but her meager earnings could not support five-year-old Frank, his older sister, then seven, and his new baby sister.

The baby soon died, another victim of tuberculosis, which at the time was the leading cause of death in the United States and Europe. Weighed down by grief and penury, Mollie could no longer keep her family afloat. With resources dwindling away, she took Frank to a nearby orphanage run by the Sisters of St. Joseph. One of the children needed refuge, and perhaps the boy could weather a separation better than his sister. But Frank's health had never been robust and the nuns turned him away, suggesting that a warmer climate might help him more than they could. So Mollie packed up a small bundle for Frank and put him on a train to Charleston, South Carolina, to live with her sister Elizabeth Byrnes and her son Jimmy, two years Frank's junior. Frank proved no burden to his widowed aunt and was a good playmate for Jimmy. Before long, his mother and sister followed him to Charleston where Mollie and Elizabeth took on sewing jobs to support the household.

The Hogans averted calamity, and Frank was now determined to endure. When he finished the fourth grade there was no question that he would leave school to earn money for the family. He started work as a "cash boy" at Kerrison's department store, bringing home two dollars per week. Within a couple of years he had moved on to a messenger job with the South Carolina Railway, where his duties included perusing the newspapers to clip out pertinent railroad items. While he honed his reading skills he gained perspective on the important events of the day. He also brought in extra money by selling newspaper subscriptions in the evening.

But heartache returned to the Hogan household when Frank's remaining sister died. Her loss further strengthened the bond between Frank, now the sole surviving child, and his mother. Frank made the most of his opportunities, learning shorthand from another railway employee, Marian Little, and steeping himself in the English classics—Shakespeare, Macaulay, Byron, Tennyson, and others—under the tutelage of John Austin, who also worked for the railroad. Young Hogan could read whatever he wished, as long as tutor Austin selected it for him.

In 1895, at age eighteen, Hogan went to Savannah, Georgia, for a better-paying railroad job (thirty dollars a month). Anxious to fill gaps left in his education, he burnished his arithmetic by taking private instruction after hours from William H.

ABOVE: Hogan started work as a "cash boy" in Kerrison's department store in Charleston, South Carolina. On the right of this photograph of King Street, Charleston, a sign points the way to Kerrison's.

RIGHT: One highlight of Hogan's time at the *Savannah Morning News* was interviewing the legendary baseball player, John "Muggsy" McGraw, who was playing for the Baltimore Orioles at the time. McGraw is shown here at the start of his career with Olean, New York, 1890.

Baker, superintendent of Savannah's schools. He also tried his hand at sports reporting for the *Savannah Morning News*. A highlight was his interview with the quick-tempered and later legendary Baseball Hall of Famer, John "Muggsy" McGraw, in town with the Baltimore Orioles. The two had much in common. Only four years older than Hogan, McGraw also was the son of hardscrabble Irish immigrants, and had lost his mother and four of his eight siblings to disease. Professional baseball had offered McGraw a way up. Hogan's own path, however, was still unclear.

When the United States went to war with Spain in April 1898, Hogan recognized a personal opportunity as well as a national cause. He enlisted, but failed

LEFT: Hogan was very close to the women in his life. Shown here is Mollie, his mother, with Mary Cecile, his wife (on the right) and Dorothy, his daughter (on the left). They are pictured in front of the Doheny Mansion in Los Angeles.

BELOW: Georgetown University Law School, c. 1900 and now, and (inset) Frank J. Hogan, Class of 1902, Georgetown University Law School.

the physical, so he answered a call by the War Department for civilian volunteers to work with the Quartermaster Corps in Cuba. Although officially a stenographer with the Corps, Hogan undertook additional risky duties by assisting the medical officers during a virulent yellow fever epidemic among the troops. His courage was rewarded with an assignment as a salaried stenographer for General J. B. Bellinger. At the end of the brief war the following year, Hogan followed Bellinger, now Quartermaster General of the U.S. Army, to a permanent civil service position in Washington, D.C. Hogan stopped in South Carolina to marry Mary Cecile Adair and then escorted his new wife and his mother to new lodgings in the nation's capital. Ensconced in the War Department, he soon spied a route by which he could rise.

Hogan may have been exaggerating years later when he reflected, "In my day, every male stenographer in the government departments at Washington tried to study law," but this self-deprecating assessment of Washington, D.C.'s civil service aspirants at the turn of the last

Georgetown University

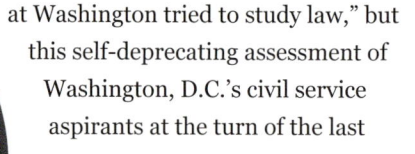

Founded in 1789, Georgetown is the oldest Catholic and Jesuit institution of higher learning in the United States, with the law school opening in 1870. The first twenty-five students came from twelve states and Cuba. The course of study required two years of evening classes. In 1890, construction began on a new law school building at 506 E Street, N.W., where the law school remained until 1971 when it moved to its present location at 600 New Jersey Avenue.

Hogan attended Georgetown between 1900 and 1902, working in a government post during the day. He continued his involvement in his professional life, teaching classes in evidence, partnerships, and wills between 1911 and 1917, and becoming president of the Alumni Association in 1923–1924. He went on to receive both an honorary doctor of law and honorary doctor of letters degree from the university. The firm's link with Georgetown continues: at the time of writing, over 160 Georgetown alumni work at Hogan Lovells.

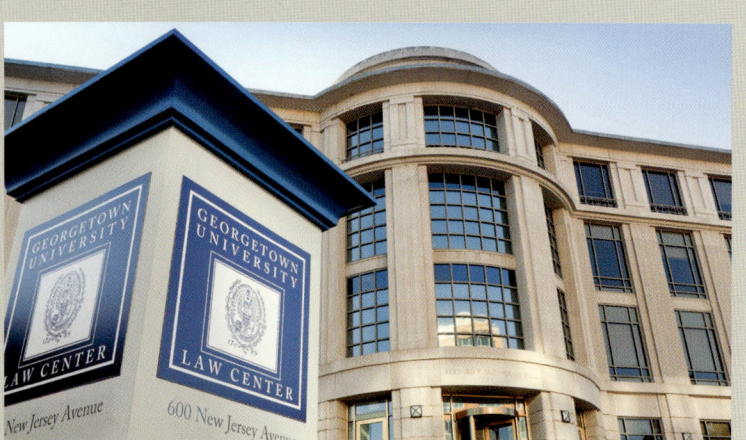

century was not far from the mark. Like doctors, social workers, engineers, and others at the time, lawyers were busily professionalizing, setting higher educational standards and entrance requirements for prospective practitioners. Hogan observed his peers enrolling in night classes at Georgetown University's law school, where an openness to the capital's cadre of upwardly mobile government workers—and to the many Catholics, Jews, ethnic immigrants and formally "undereducated" applicants rejected out of hand by some well-established schools—made it the country's largest law school in 1900. Fewer than 10 percent of Americans completed high school in those days, and a meager 1 percent graduated from college. The doors of Georgetown's law school were open to all and Frank Hogan hurried inside.

Local Success

He also hurried out, earning his law degree in record time in 1902 with the highest grades in the school's history. He held onto his War Department job for a time, "sundowning" after hours among the city's "Fifth Street" lawyers who represented indigent clients before the D.C. courts on Fifth Street, N.W. His first client was a local ne'er-do-well, Augustus "Gus" Wilson, charged with burglarizing a women's clothing store that had recently employed him as a porter. Wilson admitted to Hogan that he had pilfered a few blouses to sell but denied having returned to the store after hours for a break-in. Contesting this claim, however, were three prosecution witnesses who claimed to have seen the defendant lurking outside the shop on the night of the burglary. Wilson's future behind bars looked certain.

Hogan did his homework and discovered that two of the three witnesses had, in fact, been behind bars themselves on the night of the burglary, and could not possibly have seen Wilson outside the store. The third witness had been even further away that night, serving on a chain gang for assault with a knife. The charge crumbled, and since the indictment had been for burglary rather than the larceny to which he had admitted, the astonished Wilson left the courthouse a free man.

Such diligence, combined with Hogan's affability, wit, and enthusiasm, won friendships and garnered referrals from some of the city's veteran trial lawyers. By the summer of 1904, Hogan's practice had reached the tipping point and on 31 August he resigned from the War Department, surrendering, as he wryly put it, "the certainty of a government job for the well-established uncertainty of a law practice." Hogan combatted the uncertainty by raising his reputation in Washington, D.C. He solicited donations for churches and charities, and gave stereopticon travel lectures on exotic destinations such as Yellowstone Park, the South Pacific, and the Philippines, the latter being of note since it had fallen to the U.S. in the Spanish-American War. "This bright young man," proclaimed one press announcement, "held the intense interest of his audience for more than an hour, and, after

ABOVE: Hogan's first office after qualifying as a lawyer was on F Street, N.W. In the early years he had to "sundown"—representing his clients after a day's work in the War Department or by using his vacation.

his beautiful peroration, was the recipient of a spontaneous ovation."

Given the harshness of his childhood, which would have tilted many toward the security of the civil service, Hogan's willingness to take risks with his and his family's future—he and Mary now had a baby daughter, Dorothy—bespeaks an unusual confidence. At the same time, young Hogan's efforts over the years had consistently drawn encouragement from every quarter. What others saw in him he seems also to have recognized, with neither inflated pride nor debilitating doubts.

Something of that determination also may have driven President Theodore Roosevelt, who warmed to Hogan during an encounter at the White House over a military procurement dispute in 1905. A Pennsylvania shoe manufacturer had been found guilty of selling "paper sole" shoes to the Army, whereupon U.S. Secretary of War William Howard Taft banned the company from any further government contracts. The shoe company, however, had managed to win a U.S. Navy contract, narrowly asserting that the ban applied only to its dealings with the Army. The Herman Shoe Company of Boston, which had lost the Navy contract to its Pennsylvania competitor, cried foul and hired Hogan to seek a reversal of the decision. Hogan knew the intricacies of military procurement procedures from his days in the Quartermaster Corps. Armed additionally with a stellar record of service in Cuba, he was confident he could engage that war's most illustrious "Rough Rider," now in the White House. He headed straight for 1600 Pennsylvania Avenue.

Hogan made it inside, not difficult in those days, but getting past Presidential Secretary William Loeb was another matter. Loeb had nearly succeeded in deflecting the lawyer's incursion when the president himself arrived. Hogan seized the opportunity to make his case, but Roosevelt was not easily convinced. "Your story is preposterous," he barked. Prepared for an uphill climb, Hogan stiffened his stride. "Will you at least direct an investigation, Mr. President?" Hogan asked. "If you find that

RIGHT: The official White House portrait of President Theodore Roosevelt by John Singer Sargent, 1903. Hogan first met President Roosevelt in 1905 when he was representing the Herman Shoe Company of Boston and the two men became firm friends.

BELOW: The Herman Shoe factory.

Hogan's showmanship and adversarial style is shown in this cartoon from 1926. The lively courtroom antics took place before the House Judiciary Committee when Republican John Rankin threw a bottle of ink at Hogan, and Hogan replied in kind by hurling a glass of water at him.

the facts are not precisely as I state them, then I wish you would issue an order barring me out of the government departments." That kind of spunk appealed to Roosevelt and he agreed to conduct an inquiry. A few days later Hogan was summoned back to the White House, where the president announced that he had found Hogan's account to be correct and had ordered the Secretary of the Navy to cancel the Pennsylvania company's contract. The exchange started a friendship, cemented Hogan's political loyalty to Roosevelt and, usefully, boosted Hogan's reputation as a man who could "get things done" in Washington, D.C.

Hogan's legal and courtroom skills, and the warm regard his collegiality earned for him among his peers, continued to advance his practice, as did some highly visible local cases that kept his name regularly on the front pages of Washington, D.C.'s newspapers. He seemed never to lose a case and, in fact, had never lost one during his nine years of representing personal injury claims against Washington, D.C.'s streetcar company. Indeed, when the Capital Traction Company gave up in 1913 and hired Hogan as its lawyer, he established an equally impressive record, now on behalf of the company. Hogan also routinely prevailed in cases involving allegedly corrupt city officials, and in disputed wills of the wealthy, most famously that of *The Washington Post*'s deceased owner Stilson Hutchins in 1915. That matter, which Hogan won for Stilson's youngest son Lee, gave the rising lawyer a chance to demonstrate his prowess before a jury—and a highly interested press corps.

Hogan began by asking an expert witness, a psychiatrist, to answer a single question with a "yes" or a "no." He then delivered the question, which turned out to be a three-hour-long, 27,000-word précis of the entire case, delivered without notes and without interruption, in an astounding display of memory that was duly noted, and professionally appreciated, by the reporters on hand. The witness gave his one-word response, and after just one hour of deliberation the jury returned a favorable verdict.

LEFT: Grandstand in front of the U.S. Treasury on Pennsylvania Avenue, 1913. Hogan's reputation as a gifted lawyer spread nationally during a series of lawsuits between Riggs National Bank and the U.S. Treasury in 1915–1916.

National Prominence

Shortly afterward another high-profile lawsuit, by Washington, D.C.'s venerable Riggs National Bank against the U.S. Treasury, lifted Hogan to national prominence. The background for the matter was the Federal Reserve Act of 1913, a banking reform measure promulgated by the new president, Woodrow Wilson, to help stabilize the national economy. Many bankers, however, saw the Act as a federal usurpation of local control and objected, for instance, to what they saw as an underrepresentation of bankers on the new Federal Reserve Board. In 1915 things got personal between Treasury Secretary (and Wilson son-in-law) William McAdoo and Riggs Bank officials, whose respective institutions faced each other across Pennsylvania Avenue just east of the White House. McAdoo summoned Riggs president Charles Glover and other bank officers across the avenue to accuse them of planting newspaper articles critical of him as well as of U.S. Treasury policies. Vigorous denials failed to convince McAdoo, and the Treasury stepped up its demands on Riggs for report after report, imposing fines and deadlines that the bank could not meet and, most pointedly, undermining depositor confidence. The bank sued, alleging a conspiracy to destroy its business.

The trial began in mid-May 1915, before Judge Walter T. McCoy of the Supreme Court of the District of Columbia. Hogan was the junior lawyer for Riggs, assisting chief counsel and former U.S. senator from Texas, Joseph Bailey. Lawyers for the U.S. Treasury included notables such as crusading New York reformer Samuel Untermeyer, Assistant Attorney General Charles Warren, and Louis D. Brandeis, soon to become an Associate Justice of the Supreme Court of the United States. Brandeis, a progressive, had just authored a critique of the banking business titled, *Other People's Money and How the Bankers Use It*. This illustrious team would counter Riggs's allegations by asserting that bank officers had used depositor funds to engage in illegal stock speculation. The proof was clear, they believed, for the officers' signatures were on more than 3,000 stock transactions conducted through Riggs Bank.

The trial was barely underway when Bailey and Hogan submitted a bold affidavit, crafted by Hogan, in which the Riggs officers swore that they had never been party to any of the stock dealings on which their own signatures were clearly visible. This gambit confused Treasury lawyers, who asked Judge McCoy to reject it. McCoy denied the request. In the process, however, counsel Bailey managed to shred his good will with the judge. After McCoy interrupted him during what the judge felt to be a rambling repetition of a prior point, Bailey replied sarcastically, "The court has taken more time in correcting me than

I would have taken in argument." When McCoy threatened to remove him from the case, the former senator only compounded his offense with a deep bow and an exaggerated apology. McCoy took no action but the damage was done. Thirty-eight-year-old Frank Hogan was now Riggs's lead advocate.

After a summer break, the trial resumed in October but quickly headed down a side road when Treasury lawyers obtained grand jury indictments for perjury against Riggs president Charles Glover, vice president William Flather, and his brother, cashier Henry Flather, all of whom had signed Hogan's daring affidavit. Unable to puzzle out why Hogan had introduced it in the first place, the prosecution decided on a frontal challenge to its veracity.

Clearly, the bankers must have lied in signing that document. During the subsequent perjury trial—a separate matter from the conspiracy lawsuit Riggs had brought against the Treasury and that was now on hold pending resolution of the affidavit-related perjury charges—Hogan argued that Riggs Bank itself had never speculated or traded in stocks; instead, it had simply followed customary bank practice prior to the 1913 Federal Reserve Act, which was to assist customers, as a courtesy, in *their* placing of stock orders. Therefore, Glover and the Flathers had not been, strictly speaking, "parties" to the transactions.

Hogan's argument helped make the case that spiteful government officials were abusing their authority and harassing private citizens. But the affidavit strategy was meant to do more than exploit a technicality. The perjury charges that it elicited enabled the defense to summon character witnesses for the Riggs officers; and, as it turned out, Charles Glover was very well connected. On the morning of 15 May former U.S. President William Howard Taft, now a Yale law professor, entered the D.C. courtroom as a surprise witness for Glover, whom he had known for twenty-six years. Taft soon rushed to catch a train back to New Haven, but the effort by the ex-president just to support his friend Glover left an impression on the jury.

A week later Hogan was sitting in the courtroom when a messenger brought him a telegram. It was good news. There would be an additional surprise witness. But this time Hogan managed things differently—he pivoted in his chair and passed the telegram to some reporters. Now the whole world would know that another former U.S. president, Teddy Roosevelt, the most charismatic figure of his time, would be "dee-lighted" to show up in the morning to testify for the defendants.

Hogan's revelation of Roosevelt's appearance proved inspired. A tumultuous throng of several thousand fans, including law students from a class Hogan was teaching at Georgetown, surrounded Teddy the next day when he arrived at the

Hogan was able to call on his friend, former President Teddy Roosevelt, as a character witness in the Riggs/U.S. Treasury lawsuit in May 1915.

ABOVE: Hogan was an ardent Republican throughout his life and served as Washington, D.C.'s delegate to the Republican National Conventions in 1916 and 1920. He is pictured here (in the center holding his hat) with a group of well-wishers as he departs for the convention in Chicago in 1916.

RIGHT: Hogan's successful defense of war surplus contractors such as the U.S. Harness Company in the early 1920s helped spread his reputation as a talented litigator.

courthouse. Their cheers, Hogan recalled with satisfaction years later, "could have been heard by the jury even if they were confined in a hermetically sealed room." Presiding over the perjury trial, Judge Frederick L. Siddons tried bravely to maintain decorum amidst the excitement bubbling around the irrepressible witness. Unable to keep the ex-president within the prescribed generalities about the defendants' characters—Roosevelt kept wandering into specific incidents illustrating their worthiness—Judge Siddons was beside himself refereeing a barrage of objections from the prosecution and a matching flurry of apologies from the witness. Soon Roosevelt finished his testimony. He strode out of court to another shower of hurrahs on the street, also not lost on the jury, one of whom exchanged his own chair during the lunch break for the one Roosevelt had used. "Thereafter," noted Hogan wryly, "he drew in his inspiration in a way theretofore unthought of by counsel."

Around midday on 27 May, the jury retired to consider its verdict. It took just nine minutes. Judge Siddons, who had begun eating lunch in his chambers, had to leave it on his desk and return to the bench. When asked for their decision, all twelve jurors rose as one to thunder, "Not guilty!" Pandemonium swept through the courtroom. Siddons called for order but was left distractedly shuffling papers while Frank Hogan turned toward the press with a fulsome conclusion. "The shafts of malice," waxed the once boy orator of St. Patrick's school, "have failed to reach their targets."

In this and subsequent matters, Hogan often represented clients who believed they had been unfairly treated by federal authorities. As he added partners and diversified into tax, communications, and other aspects of administrative law, Hogan's own practice crystallized around the representation of wealthy, high-profile clients in complex civil and criminal matters before the federal courts. After World War I ended on 11 November 1918, for instance, a backlash set in against that conflict's appalling slaughter and against companies suspected of reaping excessive profits during the nation's mobilization and afterward, when surplus equipment was sold. Hogan defended several clients prosecuted by the government for profiteering from a variety of war-related contracts.

Hogan and his team prepared thoroughly for trials that often included dramatic showdowns, as when federal troops dispatched to West Virginia to seize a harness plant in Charles Town were turned away by a local sheriff with a machine gun mounted on his truck—"as is customary in that state," noted a reporter from *The New York Times*. Hogan defended six such clients—businessmen involved in the sale or distribution of horse harnesses, saddles, blankets, and bridles; gunpowder; lumber; and barracks construction—and won acquittals for all of them, prompting the *Washington Daily News* to note the government's "perfect record in war graft prosecutions here, 100 percent of the cases having been lost" to Frank Hogan.

The most widely known of Hogan's corporate trial cases followed hard on the heels of his war graft victories. In March 1924, federal prosecutors accused wealthy oilman Edward Doheny and his son, Ned, of conspiring with U.S. Department of the Interior Secretary, Albert Fall, to permit Doheny's Pan-American Petroleum Company to extract oil from federal reserves in Elk Hills, California, and ship it to tanks that Pan-American was constructing for the Navy at Pearl Harbor, Hawaii. When prosecutors brought identical charges against Harry Sinclair and his Mammoth Oil Company regarding the transfer of oil reserves at Teapot Dome in Wyoming, the entire scandal was dubbed "Teapot Dome." It was the "Watergate" of its day, generating near-continuous headlines and mounting revelations of widespread corruption in President Warren G. Harding's administration. "I have no trouble with my enemies," the president once complained to reporter William Allen White, "but my damn friends, my goddamn friends, White, they're the ones keeping me walking the floor nights."

The Ideal Advocate

Edward Doheny made for an unlikely tycoon. In 1892, at the age of thirty-six, the former schoolteacher and lawman was in Los Angeles looking for work. Numerous prospecting trips, including one he had just finished in the Southwest, had led to nothing. Nearly penniless, as he sat brooding on the front stoop of a rooming house, his eyes wandered toward a passing wagon filled with a load of odd-smelling brown dirt. Suddenly alert, he jumped to his feet and rushed over to the driver. What was in that wagon? "Brea," came the reply in Spanish—"Pitch." "Where'd you get it?" "Over at Westlake Park."

Doheny caught the next streetcar west to investigate and soon returned to the site with digging equipment. Before long he struck "liquid gold" in what would become the famous La Brea Tar Pits of Los Angeles. But the bonanza was bittersweet— Doheny's daughter died while he was digging and his wife divorced him, committing suicide shortly after, and leaving Doheny with his son Ned.

Almost a quarter century later, when the sixty-eight-year-old Doheny showed up for his civil conspiracy trial in Los Angeles, the magnate possessed all the trappings of success—the yacht, the mansion, the furnishings. But inside there was a pervasive sadness that his lawyer detected. Hogan empathized as he had carried his own burden through life: losing his sisters and father at a young

ABOVE: Edward Doheny, Hogan's wealthiest client, made his fortune initially in the 1890s when he struck "liquid gold" in the La Brea Tar Pits of Los Angeles. In 2007 Daniel Day-Lewis played Daniel Plainview in the movie *There Will be Blood*. His character was loosely based on that of Doheny.

ABOVE LEFT: Cartoon from 1924 showing Washington officials racing down an oil-slicked road to the White House, trying desperately to outpace the Teapot Dome scandal.

ABOVE: Cartoon highlighting the confusion caused by two very different court rulings in virtually identical cases in 1925. In California the court ruled against Doheny, whereas in Wyoming the court found in favor of oilman Harry Sinclair.

age. In a rare moment of self-revelation, Hogan vividly described the profound impact that his father's death had had on his life:

All through one night when I was five years old I listened to two sounds that through the years have re-echoed in my memory. One was the drip, drip, drop of the water from the ice on which my father's dead body lay; the other was the moaning of my young widowed mother as she kept vigil …

Hogan had once quipped before a gathering of lawyers in New York that the ideal client was "a rich man who is scared." The epigram was only half right, as Hogan, in a moment of wit, had omitted the qualification of some genuine pain in a client—not the whining of the entitled or the grousing of the inconvenienced, of which every trial lawyer hears full measure, but the deeper scars of loss and injury, the kind that the poor might elide on their way up.

Ed Doheny walked into a Los Angeles court for the opening of his trial on 20 October 1924, accompanied by a wealth of legal talent—Frank Hogan, Henry W. O'Melveny, "dean of the Los Angeles bar," and other seasoned lawyers. The oilman needed their skills, of course, but in chief counsel Hogan he had also acquired something beyond price or purchase—the empathy of an ideal advocate.

Hogan set forth a two-pronged argument in Doheny's defense. First, he explained that the $100,000 that his client had arranged to be delivered to Secretary Fall in "a little black bag," as prosecutors put it, was not a bribe but a gift. Second, Hogan argued that Pan-American Petroleum's pumping oil out of Elk Hills had not been motivated by private greed; on the contrary, it had been necessary on military grounds.

On 28 May 1925, U.S. District Court Judge Paul McCormick rejected Hogan's arguments and found for the prosecution. Interestingly, the next month in Cheyenne, Wyoming, Judge John T. Blake ruled in favor of Harry Sinclair's Mammoth Oil Company, reaching a conclusion directly opposite that of Judge McCormick in a similar case also involving Albert Fall. Hogan appealed on Doheny's behalf to the U.S. Court of Appeals in San Francisco, but on 5 January 1926, that court affirmed Judge McCormick's ruling, as did the U.S. Supreme Court a year later after hearing Hogan's arguments.

Doheny lost many millions over the scandal, including the $10.5 million that Pan-American had already spent on Pearl Harbor tank construction and that the company would now have to return to the government. And he still faced two trials on criminal charges, one for conspiracy and the other for bribery. So did Albert Fall, who was represented by an Ivy League patrician, William Lambert. Hogan would try to keep his own client, at least, out of jail.

Doheny's criminal conspiracy trial began on 22 November 1926, before Judge Adolph Hoehling in Washington, D.C.'s Criminal Court No. 1. The jury would be sequestered throughout the Thanksgiving holiday. Members looked anxiously at the calendar,

LEFT: Edward Doheny, Frank Hogan and Estelle Doheny celebrate another victory on the courthouse steps in Washington, D.C., 1930.

fearing they might even miss Christmas with their families. On 15 December, the jury heard summations from both sides and then retired to their cots in a makeshift dormitory on the court's third floor. The next morning they filed into their seats to announce their verdict. "Not guilty," intoned the foreman for defendant Doheny. And for Albert Fall? Again, "Not guilty." There was a riot of shouting and hugging on the defense side and an avalanche of jaw dropping by prosecutors. Doheny headed back to Los Angeles, but not before stopping to give his lawyer a Christmas gift of a million dollars. The moniker "Million Dollar Hogan" stuck. Hogan never tried very hard to shake it off. Ironically, he had never asked his client for a fee. Unlike other lawyers involved in the defense, he had made a deliberate decision never to mention the subject.

Once again, though, success mixed with tragedy for Edward Doheny when a mentally ill valet murdered his son, Ned, in Los Angeles, and then turned the gun on himself. Soon afterward, an ailing and aged Albert Fall, whose bribery trial had preceded Doheny's, was found guilty of taking a $100,000 bribe and sentenced to jail. In March 1930, Hogan won Doheny an acquittal, having convinced the jury that the offering to Fall had been only a gift. Fall's jury had concluded just the opposite—that the offering had been a bribe. This apparent paradox was partially explained by Judge William Hitz's instructions to the Doheny jury that bribery could be in the mind of the receiver without being in the intentions of the giver. A grateful Doheny, who regretted that Fall's jury had not received the same instructions, dispensed lavish "gifts" of money and fine automobiles to Hogan and the other five lawyers in Hogan's growing practice.

Frank Hogan entered the 1930s as an illustrious trial lawyer and a wealthy man. His many years of defending clients against federal charges pushed him to favor limited government. The Great Depression notwithstanding, he could not support Franklin Roosevelt and the New Deal. With the exception of his support for Theodore Roosevelt's "Bull Moose" reform candidacy in the 1912 election, Hogan was a lifelong Republican and active in party affairs. Ever sensitive to extensions of government authority, he was also astute enough to recognize the inevitability of a larger regulatory role for the federal government in a complex economy. "Administrative law is here," Hogan reminded a meeting of the Washington, D.C. Women's Bar Association in 1939, "Acceptance of its place in carrying out the functions of a modern government is plain common sense."

How Hogan Earns Million Fee

Page Five

By John Billings Jr.

Washington Lawyer Who Began Career as Newsboy Tells Secret of His Success

THE practice of intensive preparation of every case, down to the most trivial detail, has combined with a photographic memory to make Frank J. Hogan, of Washington, one of the most successful and distinguished trial lawyers in the country.

It was recently reported—a report he refused to discuss on ethical grounds—that Mr. Hogan received a check for $1,000,000 from Edward L. Doheny as a fee for defending him successfully against the charge of conspiracy to defraud the United States in the leasing of the

In 1899 he married Miss Mary Cecil Adair of Savannah, and, continuing in his capacity as an Army clerk, was transferred to the War Department in Washington. Hogan always has had a natural gift for speech-making, a capacity to put his easy flow of thought into words.

courts. In 1924 the oil cases broke over the country, and Doheny, "the ideal client," frantically sought out the best and most successful lawyer obtainable to defend him against the charge of criminal conspiracy. The rest is legal history.

"I'm not a criminal lawyer at all," said Mr. Hogan, seated in his luxurious office in the Colorado Building in Washington. "Probably not more than 10 percent of my cases are criminal. I've never had a murder case. But I will admit that most legal reputations are made on the criminal side, because there you have the human

Hogan Lovells ■ Our Story

Nelson Hartson joined Frank Hogan in private practice in 1925 and was a founding partner of Hogan & Hartson in 1938. He retired in 1972 after forty-seven years with the firm.

Citizen and Partner

Hogan's wealth distinguished him among the capital's citizens but it did not isolate him. He taught classes at Georgetown law school, headed fund drives for local orphanages and charities without regard to religious affiliation, and was a popular speaker at numerous civic events and meetings. He was president of the Georgetown University Alumni Association in 1923–1924 and in the following year gave the commencement address at Georgetown after receiving an honorary doctor of law degree. In 1927 Hogan and three other Washingtonians contributed $10,000 each to cover a shortfall in funding for foster child programs when the U.S. Congress ended session without passing the required appropriations bill. Like many others in the 1930s, Hogan believed that private sources could provide adequately for the poor until the economy improved, and he took to the radio to encourage generous donations to the District of Columbia's Community Chest. He also went on the air in December 1938 to excoriate the anti-Semitism of Detroit's "radio priest," Father John Coughlin, and to remind Americans that "the United States will not remain free for any of us unless it remains free for all of us."

Two weeks later, on Christmas Day, Mollie Hogan passed away, having lived to see her son elected earlier that year as president of the 12,000-member American Bar Association (ABA), the first Washington, D.C. lawyer to hold that office. Mollie had lived through much hardship and despair, but she spent most of her adult years free from care. Frank had seen to that with great satisfaction. He never tired of presenting his mother as a great celebrity to guests visiting the Hogans' limestone mansion, "Adair," on the District's Sheridan Circle.

Just before Frank Hogan was elected president of the ABA in 1938, he and six colleagues formalized their practice as a true partnership. Nelson Hartson, who had left the federal Bureau of Internal Revenue in 1925 to develop a tax practice in Hogan's office, was among this group. According to long-time partner Lester Cohen, then an associate with the firm, the newly organized partnership had to have a new name. Hogan's would be first, of course. Adding "Donovan" (William), "Phelan" (Arthur) or "Patrick" (Duke) would make the firm sound too Irish, while Hogan & "Jones" (Edmund) sounded too . . . well, ordinary. Hogan & "Guider" (John) had a nice ring, but Guider had married Hogan's daughter and putting his name alongside the founder's would look like nepotism. The only option left—"Hogan & Hartson"—was alliterative, euphonious, and fitting, for Hartson had the kind of government experience and patrician bearing that appealed to commercial and banking clients, while Hogan's name was associated with high-profile criminal trials. Hartson's low-key brand of regulatory practice nicely complemented the electric aura surrounding litigator Hogan.

After his term as ABA president ended in 1939, Hogan spent more time at home with his precious collection of English and American literature, which

Chapter 1 ■ Our Founders

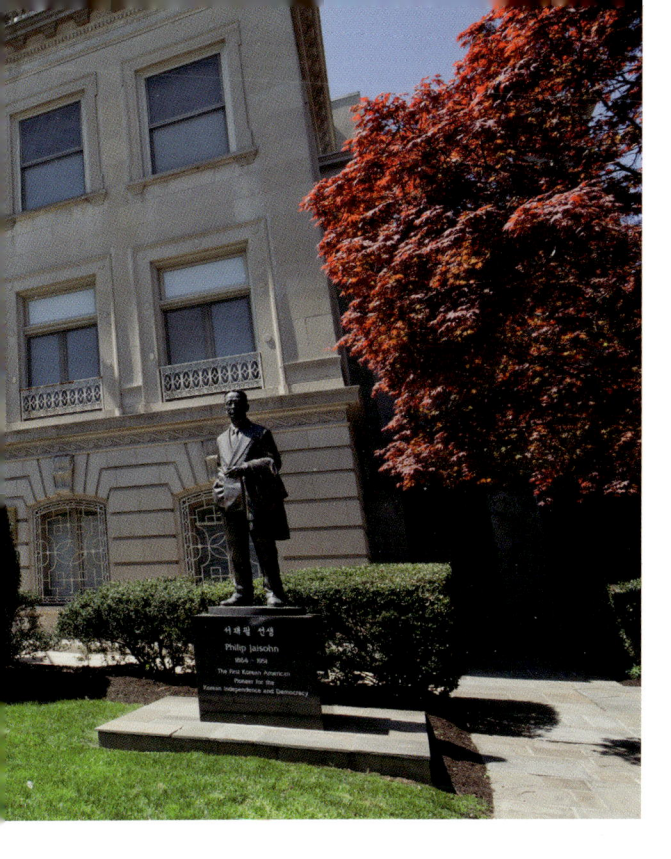

Hogan had a wide circle of friends and entertained frequently at his house on Sheridan Circle. (His house is currently the South Korean Embassy.) The cartoonist Clifford Berryman, whose trademark was a little bear, was a frequent guest.

included rare copies or first editions of Shakespeare, Chaucer, Bunyan, Longfellow, and many others. John Austin's tutelage had taken deep root. Georgetown University recognized Hogan's dedication to literature by awarding its alumnus another honorary degree, doctor of letters, in 1939. After the United States entered the war in 1941, Hogan aligned himself with the American National Conference Against Racial Persecution in Germany in order to encourage President Franklin Roosevelt to use his influence on behalf of Jews.

During the next few years Hogan's health declined as an incipient Parkinson's disease began to take its toll. He died at home on 15 May 1944, at age sixty-seven, surrounded by his books and his family. Among them was Hogan's cousin from Charleston, James "Jimmy" Byrnes, who also had moved from stenography to law, won election to the U.S. House of Representatives, and been appointed Associate Justice of the U.S. Supreme Court by Franklin Roosevelt in 1941. At the president's request, Byrnes had resigned from the Court during the war to take on numerous war-related positions with the government. He went on to serve President Truman as Secretary of State (1945–1947) before joining Hogan & Hartson as "of counsel" until 1951, when he was elected governor of South Carolina.

Father Joseph Moran administered the last rites and heard Hogan's final words. No doubt the always prepared lawyer had given them due forethought. After thanking God for the blessings of his talents, Father Moran told the press that Hogan had declared, "Now that my usefulness is over, I am resigned." It was another rare occasion when Frank Hogan was only half right. He may have been resigned to his own passing, but his usefulness was just beginning—as a model and inspiration for generations of lawyers to come, and for countless clients the world over.

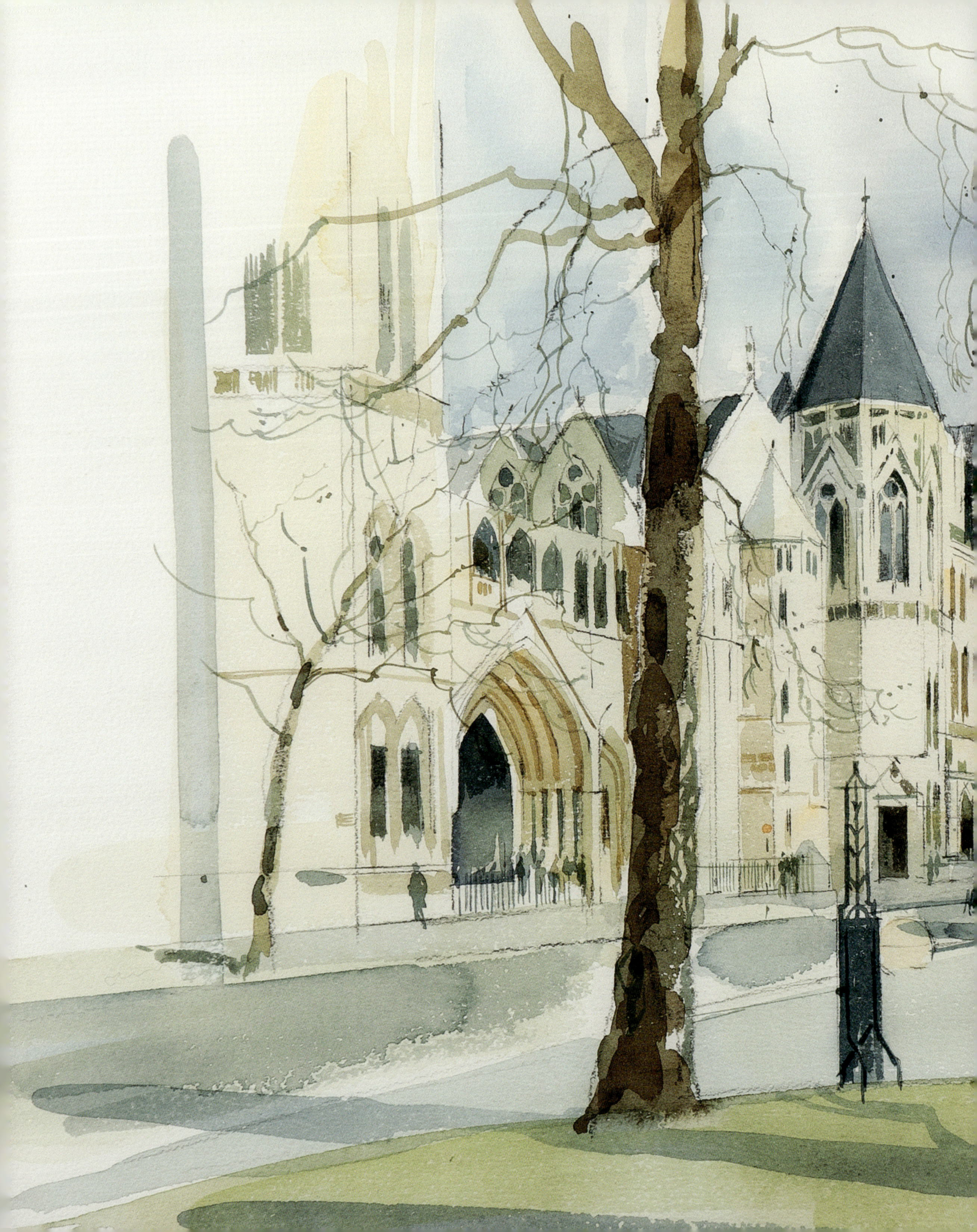

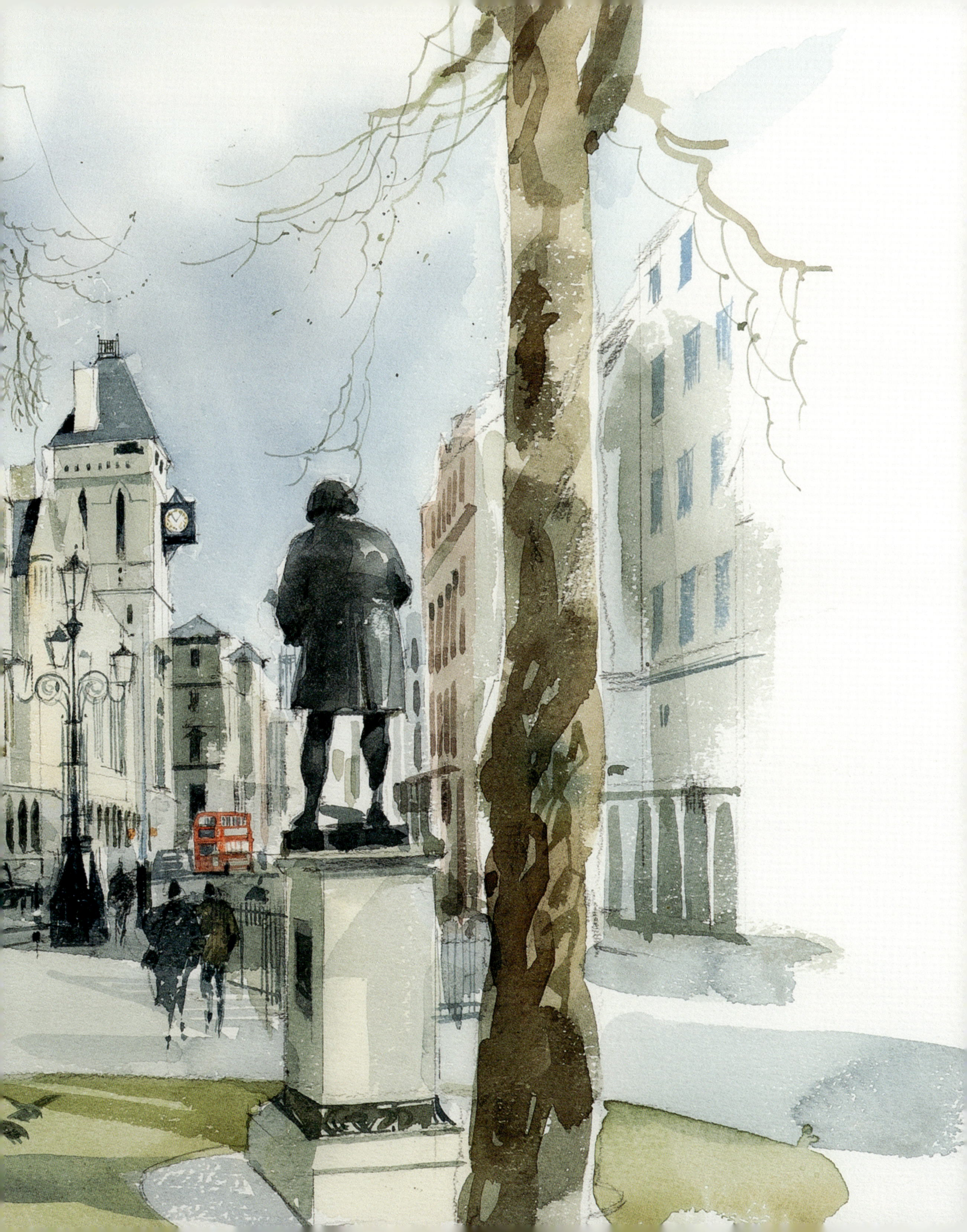

PREVIOUS PAGE: Watercolor of the Royal Courts of Justice, London used in the first brochure published by Lovell White Durrant in 1988.

ABOVE: The firm has remained close to its roots in London. Its first office in 1899 was on Snow Hill, very near to Holborn Viaduct.

RIGHT: John Cary Lovell (center with beard) formed a cricket team composed entirely of family members. This photo taken in 1911 shows Spencer Lovell (back row, second from the left), and William Lovell (seated, second from the right).

LOVELL, WHITE & KING

John Spencer Lovell (known to his contemporaries as Spencer) was born in 1869. He was the second son of a large family born to John Cary Lovell and his wife, Eliza. By origin, the Lovells were a farming family from Somerset, in the west of England, but in 1848 Spencer's grandfather, William Lovell, gave up his Somerset farm and moved his family to Smithfield in London, the home of the UK's largest meat market. There he established the family business of Lovell & Christmas, selling produce from Somerset, but it was his sons, particularly the youngest, John Cary, who built and expanded the business of the provision merchant. Self-educated, energetic, and able, John Cary was also a keen sportsman and "a born leader." His commercial interests ran well beyond his own business, extending to Hodgson's Kingston Brewery and Thomas Wallis's department store. While Spencer's brother William joined the family businesses, Spencer was destined for the law.

After graduating from Clare College, Cambridge in 1893, Spencer began his training as a lawyer at Pontifex, Hewitt and Pitt near Smithfield, a firm that acted for many of the businesses in the area. He went

Chapter 1 ■ Our Founders

RIGHT: Smithfield Central Avenue by Ian Ribbons.

BELOW: Lovell & Christmas delivery trucks in Smithfield, early twentieth century.

on with a fellow trainee to found Lovell & Broad in 1899. In the early days its staff consisted solely of an office boy. "We had, at first, no telephone and no typewriter, and our letters were press-copied by the water method—very messy and unsatisfactory." Lovell went on to say that "in the early days of the firm we longed for more clients and more work. Our clients consisted almost entirely of my relations and friends and the firms whom they represented."

Lovell & Broad represented Hodgsons' Kingston Brewery in its "first really big case" in 1900. The brewery owned the Red Lion Inn and it had been the practice for more than forty years to allow the business next door, which had no direct access from the road to its own yard and stables, to use the inn's yard to reach them, "paying each year fifteen shillings to the owners of the inn yard." In 1898–1899 the brewery gave notice to Miss Gardner, the occupant of the next-door business, "requiring her to give up the use of the yard of the Red Lion and to close the gate." She took the brewery to court, arguing that she was entitled to the right of way. Miss Gardner initially won her case, but the brewery appealed successfully to the Court of Appeal. Miss Gardner's lawyers then took their argument to the House of Lords, where the appeal was heard in 1903. Central to the argument was the question of the purpose of the annual payment of fifteen shillings, claimed by Miss Gardner's lawyers to have been for repairs rather than rent, but the Law Lords found this unproven: as Lord Davey noted, "there is a scintilla of evidence in favour of this allegation,

Smithfield

Smithfield started life as a "smooth field" just outside the walls of the medieval City of London. From the twelfth century until the mid-nineteenth century it was a livestock market. In addition, the site was used for large public gatherings and spectacles, including fairs and public executions. William Wallace, the Scottish patriot, was hanged, drawn, and quartered there in 1305.

In 1855, the cattle market moved to Islington, and, in 1868, a new wholesale meat market opened in Smithfield. By the time the Lovell family were active in the area through their various provisioning and legal businesses, the market was not only the largest meat market in the country but one of the largest in the world. It remains so today, although as this book goes to press plans have been announced for the market to close and its unique Victorian buildings to be put to new use as offices, shops, and restaurants.

Hogan Lovells ■ Our Story

RIGHT: Agreement on the incorporation of Lovell & Christmas, witnessed by Spencer Lovell and signed by several family members. In the early days, the firm, briefly known as Lovell & Broad, drew most of its business from friends and family.

BELOW: The firm, then known as Lovell & White, moved to Thavies Inn near Holborn Circus in 1912. Then as now, it was a busy traffic hub.

but nothing which approaches proof of it." Commenting that "the facts in this case are meagre and inconclusive" the House of Lords found in the brewery's favor—a good start for a fledgling firm.

By 1902, Broad had left the firm and Lovell was in partnership with Reginald John White. White was skilled in attracting and retaining clients. A newly qualified solicitor who joined the firm in the 1920s remarked:

He was a difficult man to get to know. He was small in stature, with a sardonic mouth and though he may have smiled occasionally I certainly never saw him laugh. ... The most amazing thing about him was the hold he seemed to have on his clients. There never seemed to be any friendship between him and them and he appeared deliberately to keep them at arm's length. But they also had the greatest respect for him and the advice he gave them.

Thanks to the energy and commitment of the two partners, the number of clients and the work picked up in the years before World War I. Lovell observed:

We worked very long hours every day, from 9 a.m. to 6 p.m. with a break of twenty minutes for lunch at Holborn Viaduct station and very often worked all Sunday. As I lived in the country and spent about two hours travelling every weekday, life was strenuous, and I occasionally took work home which occupied me until three or four o'clock in the morning.

White's acquaintances, clients, and connections were both numerous and geographically widespread. It was through White's contacts that the firm started to act for two large American companies, which established UK subsidiaries: Woolworth's and Ford. As clients they were to prove highly significant in the development of the firm for much of the twentieth century.

Chapter 1 ■ Our Founders

Frank King joined Lovell & White before the war but left the firm to join the army. He returned in 1925, became senior partner and retired in 1935.

White's flair for spotting influential contacts led to the firm's introduction to Ford. White became acquainted with Percival Perry (later Baron Perry of Stock Harvard, 1878–1956) when the young Perry was running a bicycle shop in Oxford. By 1909 Perry managed Ford's London showroom and had organized a national network of Ford dealers. At the same time he supervised the construction of a new assembly plant in Manchester, which began production in 1911. The Ford Motor Company (England) Ltd was formed in 1911, with Lovell & White appointed as its solicitors.

In the same year, Lovell and White were joined by an ambitious and brilliant young trainee from Australia, Charles Francis King. With war looming, Frank King qualified as a lawyer in April 1914, little realizing the impact that the war would have on his world.

With the outbreak of war, commercial work in the City, London's main financial district, slowed down. Most offices were left with skeleton staffs as the young men disappeared into the armed services. Women took their place in offices as well as factories; the number of women office workers doubled during the four years of war.

F.W. Woolworth & Co Ltd

The American entrepreneur and retailer Frank Winfield Woolworth established his first successful "five and dime" store in Pennsylvania in 1879 and subsequently a chain of stores across the U.S. in the late nineteenth century. Woolworth visited the UK in 1890 to source china and glassware and noted in his diary: "I believe that a good penny and sixpence store, run by a live Yankee, would be a sensation here."

It was not, however, until nearly two decades later that the first Woolworth's store in Britain opened in Liverpool, on 5 November 1909. Legend has it that Woolworth was unhappy with his legal advisers and, on overhearing this, a local decorator working on the new store recommended the firm he used—Lovell & White. A fruitful relationship was born with Lovell & White becoming solicitors to the British Woolworth's company. The relationship continued until the 1980s. (The last remaining Woolworth's stores closed in the UK in 2009.)

ABOVE: Lovell & White became the solicitors for the Ford Motor Company when it came to England in 1911.

Lovell joined the Royal Garrison Artillery where he became captain and served in France until he was wounded in 1917. He returned to the front line but in late 1918 was gassed and hospitalized as a result of his injuries. When he was finally demobilized in 1919, he was serving with the postwar military governor in Cologne.

King served with distinction throughout the war, being wounded three times and awarded both the Distinguished Service Order (DSO) and the Military Cross (MC) and bar. Extracts from King's medal citations highlight his leadership and determination—qualities that would later serve the firm well:

He organised the defence of a village, held it against heavy attacks, and over and over again led forward his small reserve to drive out bodies of the enemy who had obtained a temporary foothold. Throughout the subsequent withdrawal he was the life and soul of the defence and his example and complete disregard of danger instilled the greatest confidence in his men.

He led several bombing attacks and cleared out at great risk a bomb store which had been set on fire. All of this happened after he had been wounded. He refused to leave his post till ordered.

King returned to Lovell & White as a partner in 1925. The firm became Lovell, White & King, a name it retained until its merger with Durrant Piesse in 1988.

The postwar economic boom that began in 1919 was short-lived and was followed by a slump. However some businesses thrived, even in the difficult conditions of the 1920s. Notably, Woolworth's continued to expand and by 1923 the company was running 130 shops across Britain. Ford too continued to grow, and through the connection with Perry, the firm began to act for Firestone Tire and Rubber Company, continuing to do so until the 1980s.

A young, newly qualified solicitor, Geoffrey Hutchings, joined the firm in 1926. Hutchings

ABOVE: The Law Society's World War I memorial. Nearly a quarter of all British solicitors served during the war, with 588 being killed and a further 669 seriously wounded.

RIGHT: The firm acted for the Firestone Tire and Rubber Company until the 1980s. This Art Deco building on the Great West Road (A40), London, opened in 1928.

Partners and staff at the firm's Christmas dinner held at Oddenino's, 1939. John Spencer Lovell is at the head of the table with Geoffrey Hutchings standing behind him.

trained in Liverpool at a firm founded by his grandfather and then decided to look for a position in London. His own account of what followed is interesting, not least for the speed of events:

> I heard the result of my final examination on Friday afternoon and I immediately wrote to Mr John Roberts. Mr Roberts received my letter on the Saturday morning and happened to meet Lovell in the street and mention my letter to him. On Monday, King telephoned me in Liverpool. I had an interview with him in London on the Tuesday and started work on the Thursday.

With three partners and a growing staff, the firm appeared well placed for a successful future. But further progress was not destined to be smooth. The early 1930s proved difficult. In 1930, White died suddenly and Lovell retired a year later. Hutchings recalled that Lovell had told him that he "found things rather dull when he returned to the office at the end of the war in 1918." Lovell "was a most likeable and kind person who enjoyed life," despite suffering from shell shock and his wartime injuries. In retirement he maintained his links to the firm by visiting the office regularly. By the year of his death in 1952, when he was over eighty years old, he was still held in high esteem and regarded fondly by the staff.

Frank King succeeded Lovell as Senior Partner and, with Hutchings, he established a branch office in Liverpool, principally for the benefit of Woolworth's. It was the only office outside London that the firm, or its successors, had in the UK until the Hogan Lovells Birmingham office opened in 2014. King retired in 1935 due to ill health, partly because of the injuries he had sustained during the war.

Geoffrey Hutchings became Senior Partner—his was a meteoric rise, for in less than a decade, he had gone from newly qualified lawyer to partner and then

Hogan Lovells ■ Our Story

to Senior Partner. The new partnership agreement of 1936 included five partners: Hutchings (with half of the partnership capital); and four junior partners, David Jackling, Roger Slade, Pat Herron, and Alan Maby. There were also a number of non-partner solicitors, reflecting the growth of the firm's practice in the previous decade.

When war was declared in 1939, three of the partners, Hutchings, Jackling, and Maby, together with most of the assistant solicitors, Oliver Huntley, Ben Hutchings (brother of Geoffrey), Roger Jackling, and John Shankland, joined the armed services. The other partners were left to run the practice. In 1940 they were joined by Sir William Shenton, who had returned to England after a long and distinguished career with Deacons in Hong Kong. Although there was relatively little new commercial and corporate work, private client work on trusts, wills, probate, executorships, and divorce continued. There was enough, given the difficult conditions of the war, for the partners to keep the firm going until 1945.

TOP RIGHT: Montagu Piesse, known as "Monty."

BELOW: Esso was the largest client of Piesse & Sons. The advertisement dates from 1939.

MONTAGU PIESSE

The second London firm that brought key clients to the firm that eventually became Hogan Lovells was Piesse & Sons. Montagu Piesse, known as "Monty," joined the family law firm in 1896. Monty's strong leadership, drive, and passion for international affairs attracted a number of prestigious clients, particularly in the U.S.

There are many stories within the firm about how Piesse & Sons came to be involved with the Standard Oil Company of New Jersey (Jersey Standard), now known as the Exxon Mobil Corporation. According to Piesse family legend, John Henry Usmar, the London director of Anglo-American Oil Company, was a neighbor of Monty's father, Francis. Having been successful in a small case for Usmar, the relationship began to grow and then, in the 1890s, Francis Piesse received a cable from Jersey Standard asking what the firm's charges would be to send a partner to New York to discuss their UK subsidiary, Anglo-American—later known as Esso. The firm replied that it would charge 500 guineas for the Senior Partner or one hundred guineas for the junior partner; to which there came the brisk reply, "send junior partner." Monty departed on what was to be the first of many transatlantic journeys to New York.

While chance and serendipity played a significant part in the first work the firm did for Jersey Standard, there can be no doubt that Monty's ability and acumen ensured that the company's legal work in the UK and Europe stayed with Piesse & Sons, shaping his firm's development well into the twentieth century.

Following World War I most of Monty's time was spent on the affairs of the oil industry in which

Chapter 1 ■ Our Founders

LEFT: Map showing the extent of the territory defined by the Red Line Agreement.

BELOW: Calouste Gulbenkian, "Mr. Five Percent," head of the Turkish Petroleum Company, was rarely photographed but is shown here, at Lisbon airport, with his secretary in 1953.

he was deeply involved on behalf of Jersey Standard, particularly in the Middle East in the negotiation of what became known as the Red Line Agreement.

Monty's travels to the United States and the connections he made there brought other clients to the firm, including Elizabeth Arden, the beauty business founded in 1910 by Florence Nightingale Graham. Elizabeth Arden's London offices were in Bond Street and produced a variety of work for the firm, including debt collection and litigation. The Hughes Tool Company, the business inherited by Howard Hughes and on which he built his subsequent fortune, was another such client.

Piesse & Sons went on to merge with London firm Durrant Cooper & Hambling. As Durrant Piesse the firm merged again this time with Lovell White & King to form Lovell White Durrant in 1988.

Monty Piesse and The Red Line Agreement

World War I had shown the increasing importance of motor-driven vehicles, whether tanks, motor-bicycles, ships, cars, or—the most recent development—aeroplanes. The significant discoveries of large deposits of oil in the Middle East in the years immediately before the war stimulated a period of intense activity and "business diplomacy" by the international oil companies. The U.S. was particularly anxious to gain a foothold in the Middle East, a region where the dominant powers, politically and economically, were Britain and France.

Jersey Standard, headed since 1917 by Walter C. Teagle, was instrumental in bringing together a group of U.S. oil companies in 1921 to create the Near East Development Company. The Development Company, headed by Jersey Standard, and legally represented by Monty Piesse, then embarked on five years of "corporate and diplomatic wrangling" with the French and British oil companies and Calouste Gulbenkian, who headed the Turkish Petroleum Company, to gain access to the oil reserves of the Middle East.

This was achieved with the formal establishment in July 1928 of what came to be called the Red Line Agreement. Its name was derived from the red line on the map defining the area in which a newly formed consortium agreed to produce, refine, and market petroleum together; it took in most of the Arabian peninsula and extended north to include Turkey and Iraq, the latter including the recently discovered large reserves of the Kirkuk field. Each of the four members of the consortium—the Development Company, Anglo-Persian Oil, Shell, and the French Compagnie Française des Petroles (the ancestor of Total)—took a shareholding of 23.75 percent in the Turkish company, with Gulbenkian keeping the remaining 5 percent. (He was referred to as "Mr. Five Percent" for the rest of his life.) The parties met again in London and Paris for another three years of negotiations over a long dispute about the route of the Mosul-Haifa pipeline, a 940km pipeline through northern Iraq.

In all these negotiations, the historian of Jersey Standard has described Monty as "wise and conservative ... attributes that were particularly valuable at many points." With the company's American lawyer, he "helped to maintain the diplomatic *entente* which was so vital for success." The French government appreciated Monty's contribution and, in October 1928, awarded him the *Légion d'honneur*.

RIGHT: Sir Guy Hambling, Senior Partner of Durrant Cooper & Hambling. His father, Sir Herbert Hambling (far right), was a director of Barclays Bank, and this connection led to the firm becoming the bank's sole legal advisors. Barclays remains a key client of Hogan Lovells today.

GUY HAMBLING

The third London firm that ultimately made a significant contribution to the development of Hogan Lovells was known for most of its life as Durrant Cooper & Hambling. In June 1907 they were joined by a newly qualified solicitor who was to have a more lasting influence on the fortunes of the firm, Guy Hambling. Herbert Hambling, his father, was a successful banker through whom the firm came to act for Barclays Bank.

Herbert Hambling joined London & South Western Bank (L & SW) as a clerk in 1875, when he was eighteen years old. He subsequently became a branch manager, a City manager in London's financial district, assistant general manager and in 1911 general manager, a swift progression that owed much to his "industry, ability and personality. ... He was essentially a practical type of man, with a great fund of common sense." In 1917, Hambling was knighted, one of the highest honors bestowed by the monarch, and brought a long-cherished project to fruition: the amalgamation of the L & SW with the London and Provincial Bank. Sir Herbert became general manager of the merged bank. Less than a year later, the bank merged again, this time with Barclay & Co. Ltd. Sir Herbert Hambling became the deputy chairman of Barclay & Co. with Durrant Cooper & Hambling as its legal advisers.

The firm's work for the newly merged Barclays banking group was demanding and varied. Alongside routine corporate and property work for the bank, its senior managers and staff brought their private client affairs to the firm: property, wills, trusts, and probate. Barclays continued to expand the group so that, by the 1930s, it was "almost certainly the largest bank in the world, measured by the size of its consolidated bank sheet."

By the time of Sir Herbert's death in 1932, Guy Hambling's firm was established as legal representatives for the Barclays group. Barclays continues to be a key client of today's Hogan Lovells following Durrant Cooper & Hambling's merger with Piesse & Sons.

MARTIN WASSERMANN

The foundations of the modern firm of Hogan Lovells were also being laid in Germany when in 1896 a young lawyer, Martin Wassermann, joined the firm that Ruben Pels, his brother-in-law, had set up in 1884. From the beginning, Wassermann focused their practice on intellectual property (IP) law—an area of law which was still in its infancy at the close of the nineteenth century, but which went on to form one of the leading practice areas of the firm today.

On 1 March 1906, Martin Wassermann published the first edition of his new journal *Markenschutz und Wettbewerb* (*Trademark Protection and Competition*). His editorial "Trademark Battles" highlighted his passionate interest in intellectual property and his intention to inspire others to follow. *Markenschutz und Wettbewerb* soon became the most influential intellectual property publication in Germany.

Wassermann's good reputation spread fast and in 1908 Wassermann started to lecture in patent, trademark, and competition law at the Hamburg Scientific College, a predecessor of Hamburg University. In 1911, he published the influential *Basic Principles of Patent Law*, and in 1910, the similarly groundbreaking *Unfair Competition Law in Germany*. In 1919, he took up a teaching post at the newly founded Hamburg University and in 1923 was awarded the prestigious title of "professor." Wassermann relished his lectures and the discussions with students just as much as he enjoyed his legal practice.

Wassermann's work as publisher and university teacher was closely aligned to the private practice that he ran with Pels. Their focus on intellectual property law was successful and the practice was growing. In 1914, they took on Walther Fischer as third partner and Kurt Bussmann followed in 1923, shortly before Pels retired.

LEFT: Martin Wassermann was one of the most distinguished IP lawyers in Germany until he was forced to emigrate in 1936.

BELOW: Wassermann combined teaching IP law at Hamburg University with his busy law practice for many years.

New instructions came largely from referrals from other firms in Hamburg and throughout Germany. Most cases involved litigation about patent, trademark, or unfair competition disputes. In one 1920s case, for example, the firm represented Engelhardt Brauerei regarding the name of its beer "Charlottenburger Pilsener." The question was whether a beer brewed in the Charlottenburg

Deutsch-Amerikanische Petroleum-Gesellschaft, a subsidiary of Standard Oil, became Wassermann's client in the mid-1920s. The litigation against imitators of Esso's red-dyed fuel was one of his most prominent cases for this client.

part of Berlin, rather than in the Czech city Pilsen, could be called "Pilsener." Wassermann argued that "Pilsener" was not a geographical denomination but a generic term. Following Wassermann's victory, the term "Pilsener" has become widely used to describe a specific type of beer. This landmark case therefore did not only have an appreciable influence on legal development—but also on German drinking habits. In another case in the early 1930s, the firm successfully represented Deutsch-Amerikanische Petroleum-Gesellschaft (DAPG), the first German company affiliated with Standard Oil. Here the central question was whether a competitor could continue to dye its motor fuel orange, thereby imitating a particular type of DAPG's Esso motor fuel that was dyed red. Standard Oil and its successor Exxon Mobil Corporation continue to use the Esso name for both subsidiary companies and their brand outside the United States. Exxon Mobil has remained a client of the Hamburg office since that time.

In 1933 Wassermann was the Senior Partner of a prosperous law firm with two highly competent partners at his side and enjoyed an exceptional reputation in his field. One would have thought him able to enjoy the fruits of his work after long years of dedication. Sadly, this was not the case.

Less than three months after the Nazis came to power, they passed the Act on Admittance to the Bar for Lawyers, which came into effect on 7 April 1933. The Act revoked the licenses of lawyers who were "not of Aryan descent." At first, Wassermann was not affected directly because Jewish lawyers who had been admitted to the bar before 1 August 1914 were exempt.

The situation changed dramatically by the summer of that same year. On 28 August 1933, Wassermann was stripped of his title as professor and his accreditation at Hamburg University was removed on the basis of the Law to Re-establish the Civil Service. In typical fashion, Nazi Germany had given a harmless name to a law with far-reaching, discriminatory intentions. Wassermann's partners Walther Fischer and Kurt Bussmann, who were not Jewish, tried to intervene on his behalf. Fischer, in a letter to the Hamburg Minister of Justice, wrote: "He [Wassermann] is the only lecturer in the field of intellectual property law who has acted as both advocate and promoter, and to whom all young attorneys active in this area owe a great part of their legal career." Fischer's intervention came to nothing and the situation escalated at an alarming rate.

On 28 September 1933, Wassermann's membership to the Hamburg Law Society was terminated on the grounds of "non-Aryan ancestry." From that point, he was barred from using all

RIGHT: In 1933 Wassermann was barred from being a member of the Hamburg Law Society due to his "non-Aryan ancestry." He was unable to attend court or use its facilities. Shown here at the Court of Appeal in Hamburg is an art installation, "Here & Now: A Monument to the Victims of National Socialist Justice in Hamburg", by Gloria Friedmann.

attorney facilities at the court, including the attorneys' room and the library.

In 1935, *Markenschutz und Wettbewerb*, co-published by Wassermann and Bussmann, came under fire. In various private and public letters, they were both called upon to cease publication. The aggression was directed not only at Wassermann, but also at Bussmann, who remained committed to co-publishing the journal. In a letter to Bussmann dated 14 December 1935, a distinguished colleague in the Hamburg legal community wrote:

Dear Bussmann,
I am deeply saddened that you of all people should be enmeshed in Jewish affairs, and that you have not found the courage to act and think as a German man. It is especially regrettable that you have allowed yourself to be exploited by Markenschutz und Wettbewerb *camouflage attempts …* Markenschutz und Wettbewerb *was from the very beginning*

LEFT: Martin Wassermann published the first edition of the highly regarded *Markenschutz und Wettbewerb* (*Trademark Protection and Competition*) in March 1906. However, with the passing of the Act on Admittance to the Bar for Lawyers in 1933, Jewish lawyers were increasingly targeted by Nazi Germany. *Markenschutz und Wettbewerb* came into the firing line and was attacked in an article (far left) "Juden als Rechtserneuerer" (Jews as Law Reformers) published in *Das Schwarze Korps* (*The Black Corps*), the SS newspaper, in which it was stated that "only Germans should be active" in the process of law reform.

Kurt Bussmann (right) and Walther Fischer (far right) were both awarded Germany's Federal Cross of Merit (Bundesverdienstkreuz) in recognition of their work.

a Jewish publication. Aryans who directly or indirectly support this journal are not acting in the interest of National Socialism. You will appreciate that I cannot judge your endeavours to preserve a Jewish enterprise within the Third Reich to be particularly meritorious.
Heil Hitler!

Similar opinions were expressed in the SS propaganda newspaper *Das Schwarze Korps* (*The Black Corps*). An article published 13 December 1935, titled "Jews as Law Reformers" describes how Jews "have wormed their way into the process of law reformation, where only Germans should be active." The journal *Markenschutz und Wettbewerb* is cited as a typical example.

On 25 December 1935, Wassermann officially resigned as co-publisher of *Markenschutz und Wettbewerb*. On 1 April 1936 the law firm Wassermann, Fischer & Bussmann was forced to split up following the Nuremberg Laws of 30 October 1935, which prohibited Aryans and Jews working together professionally. Wassermann moved his office to another floor within the building and practiced independently from Fischer & Bussmann. While Fischer and Bussmann continued to share work with Wassermann and referred cases back and forth, the spirit of a joint intellectual property practice was gone.

On 30 November 1938, the separate Wassermann firm came to an end. On this day, Jews were officially banned from practicing as lawyers in any form and Wassermann realized there was no way he could continue his profession—and possibly his life—in Germany. He left Hamburg with his wife and they began their journey into exile.

Shortly after the end of the war, Kurt Bussmann gave this update on Wassermann to a colleague:

At the end of 1938, he went first to England and in the following year emigrated to Argentina. He lives there with his wife, his eldest daughter … His other daughters are in London and New York. I have been in regular contact with him and according to all we have heard from him he seems to be doing well. He is 77 years old and still quite active.

In 1951, the German *Industrial Property Law and Copyright Journal* marked Wassermann's eightieth birthday with these words:

Chapter 1 ■ Our Founders

If Martin Wassermann was active in three areas, as attorney, editor of a legal journal and finally as an academic at Hamburg University, and any one of these tasks could have filled a man's life, we must still consider his personality as a whole, because all of these activities were aimed at the same end, namely the development of the field of intellectual property law, integrity and fairness in competition and advertising, influencing and enriching case law in this area and finally, training a new generation of attorneys who would have the necessary skills to be active in the field.

Wassermann died on 25 April 1953, in Buenos Aires.

The law firm he founded was successfully continued by his two junior partners, Walther Fischer and Kurt Bussmann. Fischer became deputy chairman of the Hamburg City Council and a key figure in rebuilding the German Bar Association after the war. Bussmann, who had completed his pioneering thesis *Name, Firm, Trademark* in 1942, had not been awarded the title of professor due to his "Jewish ties" with Wassermann. This was rectified after the war. Both Fischer and Bussmann continued to make lasting contributions to the field of intellectual property law and received the Order of Merit of the Federal Republic of Germany (Bundesverdienstkreuz)—Germany's highest official decoration—for their achievements, Fischer in 1953 and Bussmann in 1964.

One of Bussmann's and Fischer's junior partners, Helmut Droste, later became name partner of the Hamburg and then German firms Droste and Boesebeck Droste. Boesebeck Droste merged with Lovell White Durrant in 2000 to create Lovells.

The Hamburg office at Moenckebergstrasse at the beginning of the 1950s. Miraculously, the firm's offices were not damaged during the war.

41

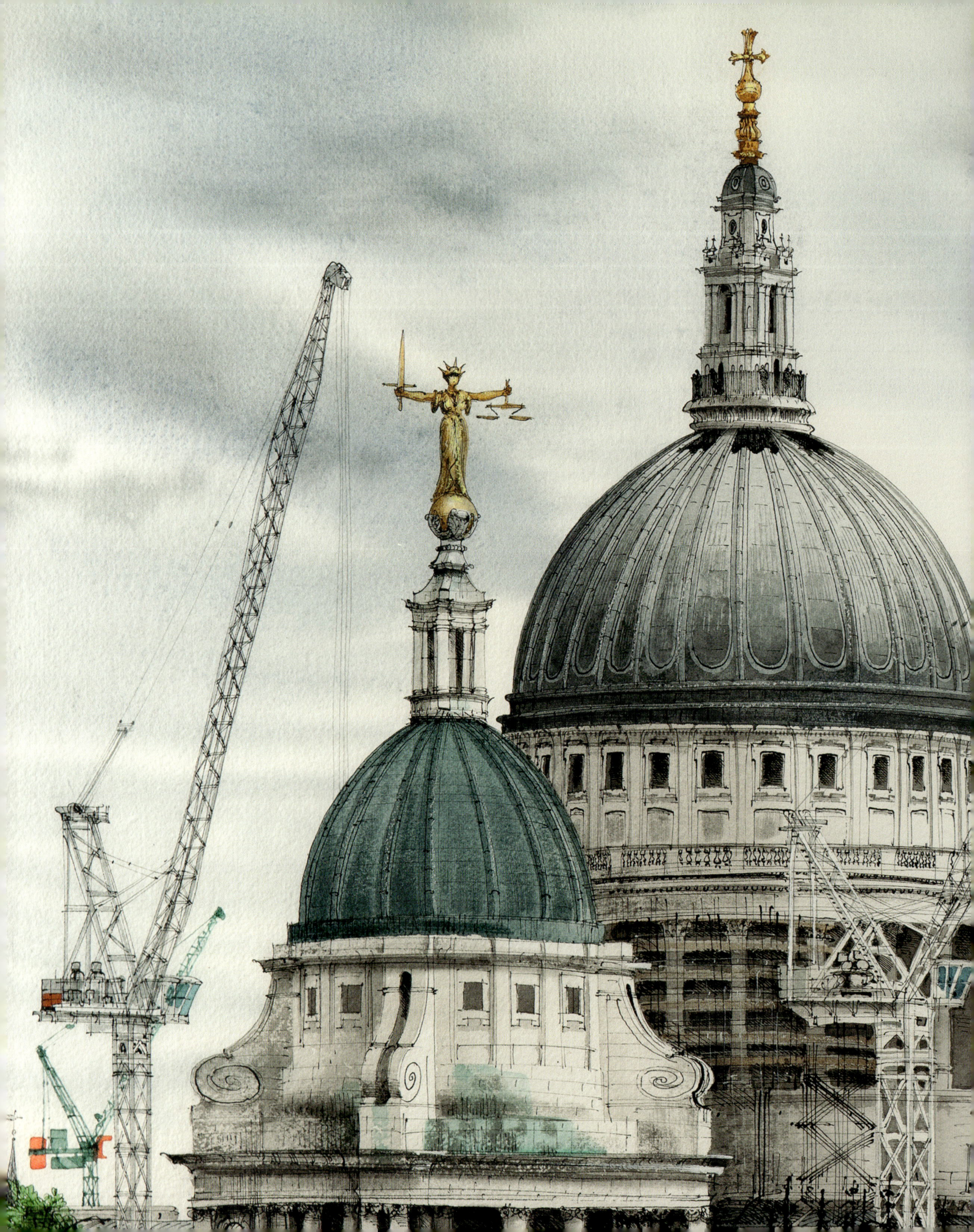

Chapter 2

Our Growth

Chapter 2
Our Growth

PREVIOUS PAGES: View of St. Paul's Cathedral from the top of Atlantic House, London, by David Gentleman.

BELOW: Geoffrey Hutchings became Senior Partner in 1935. Hutchings served as the Principal Director of Salvage and Recovery during World War II and is shown here in uniform.

LONDON

At the end of World War II, partners and staff who had been on active service gradually returned to their professional lives at Lovell, White & King, Piesse & Sons and Durrant Cooper & Hambling. Sadly, some did not return, including John Shankland of Lovell, White & King, who had been swept overboard and drowned in the North Sea. However, those returning included that firm's Senior Partner, Geoffrey Hutchings, who had been the UK's Principal Director of Salvage and Recovery and then, after D-Day, in charge of supply for Western Europe, and his brother Ben, who had fought with the Eighth Army through Africa and then in France. David Jackling had been awarded medals for bravery while with the Coldstream Guards and Oliver Huntley had served with distinction in the RAF, ending the war as a wing commander.

Some early postwar work related directly to the conflict that had just concluded. At Lovell, White & King, Oliver Huntley acted in a number of cases for the Dutch government. Some of these related to compensation for Dutch Jewish citizens whose valuables had been confiscated. The work continued well into the 1950s; in recognition of his work the Dutch government honored Huntley with the award of Officer in the Order of Orange Nassau.

Lovell White & King continued to expand after the war and there were several significant arrivals who were to play an important role in the future development of the firm. They included the Senior Partner's son, Jack Hutchings, who qualified in 1957 and then spent two years in the United States with the New York firm Hughes Hubbard & Reed. Like his father, Jack had a talent for making contacts, some of whom became clients of the firm when he returned to the UK. They included Merck, Sharp & Dohme, which at the time was expanding its operations in the UK and Europe. Jack became a partner in 1961, alongside Peter Gerrard and Geoffrey Grimes—the former would later become Senior Partner while the latter was instrumental in cementing the firm's reputation as a litigation practice.

At the same time Piesse & Sons was slowly moving away from its century-long history as a family firm. Monty died in 1953, succeeded as Senior

Partner by Jack Piesse. Cavan Taylor, who later became Senior Partner of Lovell White Durrant, was one of the new recruits at that time, joining the firm as a partner in 1966, to assist Jack with Esso's considerable continuing work.

At the end of 1963, a year in which Lovell, White & King's turnover reached just over £430,000, Geoffrey Hutchings retired as Senior Partner. He had been with the firm for over 30 years. It had been his ability, business sense, connections, and hard work that had saved the firm from the oblivion that might have been its fate following the death or retirement of, successively, White, Lovell, and King. He passed the baton to Pat Herron, but Herron was Senior Partner for only two years before he himself retired, and was succeeded by Ben Hutchings.

It was in the 1960s that changes in the three firms and their practices, reflecting those in the wider world of business, began to accelerate, followed by even more rapid change through the 1970s. These included a gradual relaxation of the formality that had formerly been the norm. Symbolic was the disappearance of the bowler hat, which had been obligatory headgear in the City of London financial district since the nineteenth century. The penultimate wearer of such a hat at Lovell, White & King was Geoffrey Grimes, who only reluctantly

ABOVE: Crowd listening to Geoffrey Hutchings addressing a salvage rally in Trafalgar Square, 1943.

LEFT: The ubiquitous bowler hat worn by so many in the City of London was seen less and less during the 1960s.

ABOVE: The firm acted for three of the Beatles and their manager, Allen Klein. Andrew White from Lovell, White & King is seen at the head of the table wih John Lennon and Yoko Ono on the left.

RIGHT: "The Beatles," from Peter Blake's Alphabet Series (1991), hangs in the firm's London office.

gave his up when the office cat gave birth to a litter of kittens in it. A while later, Frank Williamson, the last member of the firm to sport a bowler, reluctantly abandoned his.

Another event, representative in a different way of the new era, was the brief connection between Lovell, White & King and The Beatles, which arose when three of the group's members appointed Allen Klein as business manager in 1969. A year or so later, the fourth Beatle, Paul McCartney, brought an action against Klein and the other three Beatles to close down their company, Apple. Lovell, White & King acted for Klein, John Lennon, George Harrison and Ringo Starr. In the event they failed to prevent the winding-up of Apple, but the occasional appearance in the office of at least three of the Fab Four brightened the lives of younger members of the firm's staff. It is said that around the same time the Rolling Stones also arrived on the firm's doorstep but that Mac, the ex-army doorman, refused to admit them on the grounds of their unsuitable dress.

Until 1967, legislation had limited the number of partners in a legal partnership to twenty, but after the removal of this limit many London law firms grew quickly. The view was gaining ground that the future would belong to larger firms, with more resources and specialized knowledge. It was in this context that Piesse & Sons and Durrant Cooper & Hambling decided in 1972 to merge their practices as Durrant Piesse, with John Thomlinson as Senior Partner. At around the same time, Lovell, White & King was also involved in its first merger, with the firm Haslewoods, whose history stretched back to the late eighteenth century. William Haslewood, whose family gave its name to the firm, had practiced as a lawyer in the early years of the nineteenth century. His most famous client was Admiral Lord Nelson.

In the 1970s, at Lovell, White & King, Ben Hutchings saw the need to react to the changing external world with internal reform. The reshaping of the firm provided the then twenty-four partners with a structure that would allow for further growth. Similar changes took place at Durrant Piesse. The firms were beginning to resemble more closely the modern business that later gave rise to both the increased specialization of lawyers and the development of new fields of work.

It was through one of Jack Hutchings' transatlantic contacts that work following the collapse of Investors Overseas Services (IOS) began at Lovell, White & King in the 1970s. IOS had been established by Bernard Cornfeld and Edward Cowett in the 1950s as an offshore investment fund. Its success was much admired and by the end of the

Chapter 2 ■ Our Growth

"Killing" or "holding" the front page was a task faced with some trepidation by junior lawyers who had to read *The Guardian* newspaper for libel shortly before it went to print. This *Legal Business* cover is mocked up to look like the satirical magazine *Private Eye*. The magazine's editor, Ian Hislop, is shown holding a banana which alludes to his words after the magazine lost a high-profile libel case in 1989: "If that's justice I am a banana."

1960s it had nearly $2.5 billion under management. However, in 1971 it emerged that "the actual profits, after all the creaming-off by salesmen, managers and the international overheads, were almost nonexistent … and the whole structure crashed, ruining investors everywhere." As the journalists investigating the corporation's activities later wrote, IOS was "an organization steeped in financial and intellectual dishonesty, and directed so recklessly that it was absurd that it should have been entrusted with so much of other people's money, let alone praised for the brilliance with which it was managed." The official investigations began in Canada, where some of IOS's companies had been registered, and it was through his own contacts that the insolvency work on the English interests first came to Jack Hutchings. By Hutchings' own account, he did little else between 1973 and 1982, his work playing a significant role in enhancing the firm's reputation and establishing its subsequent insolvency practice.

Another new area of specialism that evolved in the 1970s was employment law. Trade union density in the UK during that decade was higher than in France, Germany, or the United States; it peaked in 1980 and thereafter declined. Industrial disputes followed a similar pattern. A combination of confusing legislation and industrial discontent meant that the area was a minefield many lawyers were reluctant to enter; those who did found themselves busy. The work benefited both Durrant Piesse and Lovell, White & King, the latter acting for the *Express* newspaper group, which was then seeking to control what it saw as the over-powerful print unions. Another long-term newspaper client was *The Guardian*. Unlike *The Express*, it was not at that time read for libel by junior lawyers, so members of Lovell, White & King's litigation department would be called to the newspaper's offices around 5.30 p.m. to check the next day's copy if it seemed likely to be contentious. "Killing the front page" was a high-profile and delicate task for the lawyer making the decision.

William Haslewood and Nelson

William Haslewood's most distinguished client was undoubtedly Admiral Lord Nelson, to whom Haslewood was both professional adviser and friend.

Haslewood looked after Nelson's affairs during his long absence at sea. Thanking Haslewood for the successful outcome of litigation concerning prize money, Nelson wrote: "You have acted not only as able lawyers but a most friendly part through the whole business." Haslewood was involved in the purchase of an estate at Merton in Surrey where Nelson lived with his mistress, Lady Emma Hamilton. In that same letter, addressed as "Private for yourself— and most secret," Nelson included a codicil to his will setting out financial provisions he wished to make for Lady Hamilton and his "adopted" daughter, as he described Horatia, his illegitimate daughter. At the end of the letter he wrote: "Burn it when read."

Following Nelson's death, Haslewood acted as executor of his estate. It was the matter of Nelson's illegitimate daughter which interested the popular press of the time: was Horatia the daughter of Lady Emma or not? Haslewood was often approached and asked, even after he retired, but he always denied that she was.

William Haslewood (1774–1849).

Admiral Lord Nelson (1758–1805).

ABOVE: The UK's entry into the European Economic Community (EEC) in 1973 brought much new work to the firm. Margaret Thatcher, leader of the Conservatives, is shown here with her predecessor, Edward Heath, urging people to vote against leaving the EEC in a referendum that was held in 1975. Thatcher became prime minister in 1979.

RIGHT: The coal-miners' strike of the early 1970s led to the government imposing a three-day week to conserve energy. Shown here are clients of a Fleet Street pub drinking by candlelight in London.

Political developments and new legislation played a part in determining the work that arrived at the practice. Until 1979, almost every transaction with any international element involved advice in relation to exchange control regulations. In that year, such work disappeared overnight when the incoming Conservative government abolished exchange control. Sterling–dollar convertible issues on which the firm acted for Ford and Texaco, were "hideously complicated" in the days of exchange control. The Eurobond market, which started in 1962, was centered in the City and continued to grow in the 1970s and early 1980s; total turnover in the market was $4.7 trillion in 1987. Lovell, White & King acted on a number of Eurobond issues in this period.

The UK's entry to the European Economic Community (EEC), now called the European Union (EU), brought the introduction of value added tax at the beginning of 1973. This resulted in an additional area of work. The firm's portfolio of U.S. clients, among them Woolworth's, Ford, Mars, Merck, Sharp & Dohme, and Texaco, continued to be the largest in London and attracted others. The Southland Corporation, based in Dallas, became a client of the firm in the 1970s after it was listed on the New York Stock Exchange and started to expand its 7-Eleven stores to other countries, including the UK.

Late in December 1973, the secondary banking crisis, described as "the biggest emergency in British banking" during the twentieth century, rocked the City's foundations. Durrant Piesse, with its strong reputation in the banking sector, found its lawyers in great demand. Secondary banks had flourished with the growth of new money markets in the City, using short-term borrowing to finance investment and lending, much of it in the property sector. When the markets began to turn in 1973, with credit restrictions and the minimum lending rate increasing to 13 percent, many companies found themselves in danger of failing. Cedar Holdings, a specialist in second mortgages, was found to be on the brink of collapse in mid-December, sparking a series of meetings at the Bank of England attended by Senior Partner Thomlinson and Kenneth (later Sir Kenneth) Cork. What the Bank feared was "a domino effect" on other secondary banks if Cedar went down and, even worse, repercussions through the banking system as a whole. In a "midnight marathon" a rescue package was "cobbled together" for Cedar, with Cork playing

Chapter 2 ■ Our Growth

an important role in persuading Cedar's directors to accept it and Barclays Bank agreeing to contribute.

At the same time a crisis in industrial relations in the coal-mining industry led to the three-day working week, which had a more immediate effect on office life. For more than a decade successive governments had attempted to contain inflation by restraining wage increases and, from mid-1973, the Conservative government led by Edward Heath had been facing a demand for a large pay increase from the miners. In pursuit of their claim they were already working to rule, thus reducing the stocks of coal available to the electricity industry. In October 1973, the Organization of the Petroleum Exporting Countries (OPEC) announced a 70 percent hike in the price of oil, putting further pressure on the coal industry. As the prospect of a miners' strike in the new year increased, the government announced that from midnight on 31 December until 8 March 1974, a scheme to ration electricity supplies—known as the three-day week—would come into effect.

Preparations for this were made in the City and at Durrant Piesse as Neil Fagan recalled:

Of course we couldn't go on the three-day week because that's not the way life works. We had camping gaslights; a blue container where you put a little light on top. We were all issued a candle and camping gas stoves. The manual typewriters came out of storage and were brought back into action again. It was an extraordinarily exciting time in a curious way.

By March, the crisis was over, the government was defeated in the February election and the strike was resolved. The electric golf ball typewriters were back on the desks.

Twelve partners had signed the Durrant Piesse merger agreement in 1972. By 1982, the firm had nineteen partners including its first female partner, Sally Riley. At Lovell White & King, Harriet Dawes had been admitted as the first female partner in 1980. The following year Lesley Belton (later MacDonagh), who had joined the firm as a qualified solicitor and worked in the planning department, became the second female partner. She would play a key role in the years ahead.

The internationalization of business was changing attitudes. Arising from the UK's entry into the EEC, now the EU, Lovell White & King opened an office in Brussels in 1972. The firm was also instrumental in establishing a "Club" of law firms practicing

Lord Byron by Richard Westall.

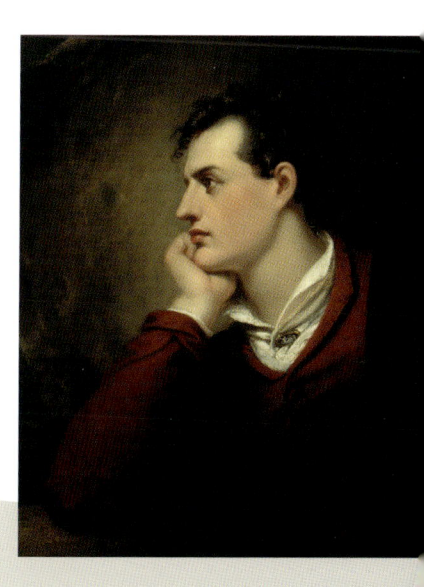

The Byron connection

Durrant Piesse's relationship with Barclays resulted in an interesting encounter in 1976. At the Pall Mall branch of the bank, a strongbox, left untouched since it was deposited in 1820, was opened. It had belonged to Scrope Davies (1782–1852) "a dandy and friend of Lord Byron." Davies was a Fellow of Kings College, Cambridge and an inveterate gambler who left the box when fleeing from his creditors. He never returned to Britain, dying in Paris.

The box contained manuscripts and letters to Byron and the original of one of the cantos of Byron's *Childe Harold's Pilgrimage*, long thought to be lost. Anthony Pugh-Thomas recalls:

It was quite a find. And we were asked to advise on what should be done. So we made enquiries and also spoke to people who asserted that they were related to Scrope because it would be worth having all these manuscripts, they had considerable value. But they hadn't quite established a claim, so eventually the box and its contents were put on deposit at the British Library.

The regulatory revolution of 1986, known as "Big Bang," brought sweeping changes to the City of London.

in Europe, representing Belgium, Denmark, France, Germany, Ireland, Italy, Luxembourg, the Netherlands, the UK, the U.S., and later Spain. The Club served the firm well for many years as an informal vehicle for the passage of referral work within Europe and the United States. However, with the Brussels operation up and running, the partners decided in July 1976 that the firm's next international venture would be to open an office in 1977 in New York, its principal purpose being to service the firm's many U.S. clients. In 1982, Lovell, White & King opened its first office in Asia: in Hong Kong with Andrew Walker, later Senior Partner of Lovell White Durrant, and Lovells.

The Creation of Lovell White Durrant

By the mid-1980s merger and acquisition (M&A) activity in the City was at an all-time high among companies across all sectors. One of the most high-profile takeover battles was that between Guinness and Argyll in 1986–1987 for control of the Distillers Company. It was won by Guinness, but soon after the battle ended, details began to emerge of the methods used to do so. Durrant Piesse acted for the City's Takeover Panel in this affair and prosecutions later followed an investigation by the Department of Trade and Industry (DTI). British and Commonwealth Holdings was another company that expanded rapidly by acquisition; its collapse in 1990 led to work for the firm's insolvency team.

M&A activity was particularly marked among financial firms, where the regulatory revolution of 1986, known as "Big Bang," brought profound changes to the City.

The urge to merge spread to professional services, with several of the large accountancy firms merging in the 1980s and it reached the legal profession. As *The Economist* noted, over the twenty-year period from 1967 to 1986, 100 law firm mergers had taken place—an average of five a year. Writing in 1989, it went on to say: "Since May 1987 there have been around three law firm mergers a week, or more than 300 in total."

By May 1987, discussions were well under way between Lovell, White & King and Durrant Piesse about a possible union. Tradition has it that the idea of merging the two was first floated by two partners, one from each firm, following their meeting at an insolvency conference. They returned to London, enthusiastically urging it on their partners; the idea caught on and within a short period of time two teams had been appointed to explore the potential merger. For Lovell, White & King the group included Andrew Walker, Michael Maunsell, Dan Mace, and Philip Collins, while for Durrant Piesse there were Cavan Taylor, Anthony Pugh-Thomas, Andrew Gamble (who would go on to become the first London Managing Partner of Hogan Lovells), and Adrian Lickorish.

Secrecy was essential and early on the Durrant Piesse partners decided to refer to Lovell, White & King as "Genesis," derived from the link of Collins' name to that of the popular rock band. In a more biblical—or cinematic—response, Lovell, White & King began using "Exodus" for Durrant Piesse. The success in keeping the merger talks under wraps is well illustrated by John Young's recollection of becoming a partner in May 1987. When meeting Peter Gerrard, Young said, "one of the things that he mentioned … confidentially, was that the firm was in negotiation with Durrant Piesse to merge. That was a complete bombshell: none of us knew anything about it, for it had been genuinely kept completely confidential." Confidentiality was maintained until the press got the story just a few days before the official announcement.

The negotiations required a venue where the presence of the partners from two firms would go unnoticed, something which proved difficult. They tried various hotels, finding their attempt to remain anonymous on one occasion being severely compromised by the hotel posting an announcement in its reception area that a meeting was taking place between the two firms. It was then decided they should meet at Michael Maunsell's house in Islington; Cavan Taylor and Anthony Pugh-Thomas went to the right number but in the wrong street, before finding their way to the right house. Dogged by these problems, they moved negotiations to the Lovell, White & King partners' apartment; Taylor and Pugh-Thomas, with Andrew Walker, took the lift. "There was a sudden jolt and the lift ascended at least six inches before shuddering to a halt. Frantic pushing of each of the buttons produced no further movement." Rescuers had to be called in but, according to Pugh-Thomas' recollection, they were locked in "just long enough to agree the order of names on the notepaper before we were released."

Initially, attention focused on the possible problems; these were financial compatibility, potential conflicts of interest between clients and the issue of Senior Partner. It was soon established that there was broad financial compatibility, enough to go ahead, and the Senior Partner issue was removed from the table when Alan Parsons said he was happy to be deputy to Peter Gerrard as Senior Partner. As far as client conflicts were concerned, Cavan Taylor recalled:

> *We then got down to the nitty-gritty of saying, "Well, what clients do you act for and are there going to be conflicts?" There was one particular one, because Lovell, White & King acted for Texaco and we acted for Exxon. I went to New York to talk to Exxon to see if there was a problem. The work that I did for them was rather different from the work that Lovell, White & King did for Texaco; so as far as Exxon was concerned—and our relationship with them was very, very good— Exxon said "No, we're very happy for you to continue and there won't be a problem."*

Agreement on the name—Lovell White Durrant—was also reached. Finding a name that would not only preserve the goodwill built up over the years but would also satisfy both firms had been a stumbling block for a number of proposed unions.

ABOVE: The former offices of Durrant Piesse on Cheapside, London, housed the banking and City practices of the newly formed Lovell White Durrant in 1988.

BELOW: Headed paper of the newly merged firm.

The negotiations were a learning process. As Pugh-Thomas explained:

While we were exchanging information about the two firms—particulars, further and better particulars, further particulars of those particulars, and voluntary particulars wended their way up and down Cheapside, between the offices—two things were certain: whatever the result of the negotiations by the time the vote was taken both firms would be far better informed as to how they ran themselves and—this was a pointer in favour of the merger—very clearly we both had made the same mistakes in how we did run ourselves ... incidentally, as the negotiations proceeded, one thing did become plain—we liked each other.

Over the summer, final arrangements were agreed to and laid out in documents. These were circulated to all the partners shortly before they met in their respective firms to come to a decision. At both meetings the vote was unanimously in favor. Telephone calls were made to announce this and partners from both firms met for a celebratory drink. The merger was publicly announced on 29 September 1987: "We decided to merge because of our complementary practices, similar approaches and compatible personalities." The new firm came into being on 1 May 1988.

Lovell White Durrant

Over the five years following the merger, the firm's turnover rose steadily, from £60 million in the first year to £102 million by 1993. Contributing to this was a rush of insolvency work, which followed during the recession sparked by the stock market crash of October 1987.

The litigation groups were also busy. The newspaper clients of Lovell, White & King continued to bring work to the new firm. One high-profile case was the libel action in 1987 brought by the politician and author Jeffrey Archer against the *Daily Star*, a paper belonging to the Express group. In 1987, the newspaper lost the case, but in 2001 Archer was tried and found guilty of perjury and perverting the course of justice at the 1987 trial; he was sentenced to four years' imprisonment.

From 1986 to 1989 Jack Hutchings was much involved in litigation on behalf of the Libyan Arab Foreign Bank which was seeking to recover funds that had been locked in New York since 1986, following a Presidential Order freezing all Libyan property in the United States or in the possession, or control, of the United States. Two U.S. banks were involved, Bankers Trust and the Manufacturers Hanover Trust Company which had, before the order, regularly transferred funds from New York to London. In Hutchings' words, "It was an important case for the City—if dollar deposits could be frozen here unilaterally by the United States, it would undermine the City's independence." The cases were complex and hard-fought but in both, eventually, the U.S. banks lost. By the end of the 1980s, Hutchings had become "a formidable expert in tracing ill-gotten assets worldwide," for example, working with Peter Horrocks to chase the money belonging to the miners' union that its leader, Arthur Scargill, had deposited in Europe. It was this reputation, along with that of the whole insolvency group of Lovell White Durrant, which led to the firm's appointment in 1991 to act for the liquidators of the Bank of Credit and Commerce International (BCCI). Hutchings retired from the partnership in 1994, continuing as a consultant until 2000. His retirement then marked the end of the Hutchings family's direct involvement with the firm, which had lasted for more than 70 years.

The BCCI work was good for the firm as reduced work in some areas reflected the downturn in the economy and recession of 1992. However, the firm also gained important new clients during the 1990s. In 1991, the commercial property group began working for one of the largest institutional investors, the Prudential. Today, Prudential (or M&G) is one of the largest clients of the London office. Granada, acquired as a client by Dan Mace, embarked on a large takeover bid in 1996. Its target was the Forte hotel and catering business built up by Sir Charles Forte, who had started with a milk bar and later developed catering businesses and acquired hotels through a merger with Trust Houses. By 1996, the company was in the hands of Sir Charles's son, Rocco. After a hard-fought battle, Granada succeeded in acquiring Forte. Granada later became part of ITV and has remained a client since then.

The privatization work of the 1980s also continued into the 1990s. In most of the transactions in which Lovell White Durrant had been involved, it had acted for private equity clients buying into privatized businesses. In the late 1990s, however, the firm found itself turning from "poacher to gamekeeper" when it won the contract to act on the privatization, through a public–private partnership, of the National Air Traffic Control Services (NATS), proposed in 1998 and completed in 2001. Following the 9/11 terrorist attack in the United States later that year, air traffic dropped dramatically and there was a financial restructuring of NATS on which the firm also acted.

Jeffrey Archer leaving the High Court in London with his wife, Mary, after winning his case against the *Daily Star* in 1987. In 2001 Archer was found guilty of perjury and sentenced to imprisonment.

LEFT: The work on the insolvency of BCCI occupied many lawyers of the firm for more than a decade. BCCI employees are seen here demonstrating outside the Bank of England.

BELOW: Jack Hutchings joined the firm in 1952 and became an expert in "chasing the money." He led the firm's work for BCCI throughout the 1990s, eventually recovering for the creditors more than 90 cents in the dollar.

BCCI

The Bank of Credit and Commerce International (BCCI) was established in 1972 and grew rapidly to become one of the ten largest banking groups in the world. Its operations and legal structure were complex and hid its involvement in money laundering, fraudulent accounting, and other criminal activities on a massive scale. The opaque structure kept regulators at bay for some time and disguised the fact that its assets were nowhere near sufficient to pay its overall liabilities, estimated in 1991 to be in the region of $20 billion.

In a coordinated action by several international regulators, including the Bank of England, the bank's key operating companies were closed down and put into various forms of insolvency in July 1991. Peter Horrocks and Jack Hutchings were on hand in Abu Dhabi to receive instructions on behalf of Lovell White Durrant; the BCCI liquidation thereafter became the largest job handled by the firm for several consecutive years, and provided continuing work for over two decades.

The international nature of BCCI's business meant that many of the firm's then international offices were involved, from New York to Tokyo. The initial work included investigating the affairs of the bank and stabilizing its assets, estimated to be sufficient to pay out only in the region of ten cents to fifteen cents in the dollar. For this purpose substantial teams were based for over a year in the former BCCI offices in Abu Dhabi, Grand Cayman, and London. In addition, as John Young recalled, "There were a number of us on call to fly off to negotiate quick sales of subsidiaries in places where they had not been tainted too much by the corruption and insolvency of BCCI itself."

As time went on, the focus of the work moved to conducting aggressive and innovative litigation toward parties who were deemed to have been at fault in causing or facilitating BCCI's activities. An attempt to sue the Bank of England concluded unsuccessfully, but the overall result was a remarkable final payment to the bank's unhappy creditors of more than 90 cents in the dollar.

As the changes that had begun in the previous decade played out in the 1990s, City law firms found themselves in a very different environment. Size alone made impossible the close-knit partnerships of the past and the expectation that partners would make a lifetime commitment to the firm (or vice versa) began to diminish. As *The Economist* noted in 1989:

Just as Big Bang brought with it an end to the clubby way of running City brokers and banks, so changes in the legal world have ended another gentlemanly way of doing things. Who would have thought, even five years ago, that legal firms would be poaching staff from each other—that lawyers would be defecting?

Competition increased with the arrival in the City of several large U.S. firms and there were more opportunities for lawyers outside firms than ever before. As in-house legal teams grew in size and status, regulatory bodies mushroomed and the pace of globalization accelerated.

Within the firms there was increasing specialization, driven both by the growing complexity of the law and by the trend for large corporations to share their work among firms, following the expertise for different areas of work. What might be seen as a cult of "experts" was fostered and encouraged by the new legal journals launched in the early 1990s. *The Lawyer, Legal Week* and *Legal Business* took a very different approach to the profession from that employed, for a century or more, by the traditional legal press, the *Law Society's Gazette*, the *Law Times*, and the *Solicitors Journal*. Details of the activities of law firms, including their involvement in individual cases and transactions, their income levels and partner moves, were publicized in a manner that would have been unthinkable, even in the 1980s. *Legal Business* published a special feature each year in the shape of its "highly recommended," identifying practitioners of excellence in every area. In 1995, seventeen partners of Lovell White Durrant were featured in it, notably for the work they had done in specializations including insolvency and civil fraud; European Community and competition; M&A; employment; patents and copyright; pensions; property litigation; securitization; structured debt finance; and VAT. The new annual directories, especially *Legal 500* and *Chambers*, fuelled this trend. Originally resented—particularly by more senior practitioners—these developments soon came to be seen as opportunities to be used for the benefit of the firm, encouraged in Lovell White Durrant, as in other firms, by its developing marketing team.

In the wider environment the economic downturn of the early- and mid-1990s affected the City badly. In an internal annual review of 1992–1993, the firm's Senior Partner, Cavan Taylor, noted:

The year under review has been the most difficult for lawyers in the City for several decades. The recession has caused a substantial fall in work levels in several areas of our practice. Our property and corporate groups have been particularly affected. We are, however, fortunate in having probably the strongest insolvency practice in the City and this, needless to say, has been very busy. Banking work, too, has been at a high level as companies in financial difficulties have sought to vary the arrangements with their banks. The other advantage we have is our strong litigation practice and, in times of recession, there tends to be an increase in this area of work.

Inevitably at a time of economic problems the partnership board also reviewed the firm's practice and as a result of this in 1995 it was decided firstly that the firm should no longer take on shipping work and secondly, in line with other City firms, that it should also cease to do private client work.

Andrew Walker stepped down as one of the Managing Partners in 1993 to be succeeded by Michael Maunsell and two years later the firm became the first in the City to elect a woman partner, Lesley MacDonagh (then head of the planning team) as Managing Partner. Cavan Taylor retired as Senior Partner in 1996 and was succeeded by Andrew Walker. It was Walker, therefore, who presided over the celebratory client dinner in November 1999, marking the century that had passed since John Spencer Lovell started his practice in London.

ABOVE LEFT: Cavan Taylor (on the right), presenting a cup "for cunning on the croquet lawn" at the Exxon Corporation Lawyers' Outing, Pelham Manor, New York 1985.

ABOVE: Lesley Belton (later MacDonagh) became the second woman partner in 1981 and Managing Partner, the first in a City of London law firm, in 1995.

Hogan Lovells ■ Our Story

Front cover of the firm's brochure from 1999, reflecting the international focus of its work.

Becoming International

When Lovell White Durrant was formed in 1988 its "foreign offices," as London law firms had called their overseas branches since the 1960s, numbered four: Lovell, White & King had offices in Brussels, Hong Kong and New York, while Durrant Piesse had a presence in the Chinese capital, Beijing. Lovell White & King's fifth office was about to open in Tokyo. Together they made an annual contribution of less than 5 percent of the firm's total turnover.

From the beginning there was a broad consensus that the firm would have to expand its international practice considerably, to meet not only the challenges posed by its competitors but also the needs of its business clients in a world in which national economies were rapidly globalizing. It was also a world in which sweeping changes between 1989 and 1991—the end of the Cold War, the dissolution of the Soviet Union, and the reunification of East and West Germany—were reshaping countries and their alliances. In the second half of the twentieth century the growth of some Asian economies— first that of Japan, then those of Hong Kong and Singapore, and later that of China—gave those countries a new significance in the world economy.

By 1996, the firm had 144 partners and ten international—as they had become known—offices. The original five had been increased by the addition of Chicago, Ho Chi Minh City, Paris, Prague, and Shanghai. The firm's well-articulated intention to expand further internationally led to changes in its management structure.

In 1997, it was agreed that the Managing Partner, Lesley MacDonagh, should have two "wing" partners, one international and one finance: Don Kelly became the finance partner and John Pheasant became the firm's international partner. Under their aegis the firm's international operations grew and were reshaped. Initially the goal was limited to the establishment of presences in a variety of jurisdictions that could serve the clients of the London office, and new offices were generally headed by a London partner on secondment. The concept of a truly international firm sourcing and serving its clients from a multitude of offices on a worldwide basis evolved from the mid-1990s.

In 1997, Pheasant assembled a team of partners who were in agreement that "we needed to do something quite dramatic in Europe." From a review of the firm's existing international offices, "the strategy that we settled on was that we wanted to expand in the major jurisdictions of Europe and we would do that if at all possible through merger, rather than establishing our own office; and the reason for that was because we wanted to be a local firm in each jurisdiction and not a foreign firm." The project was given the overall code name "Blue Sky" and represented a major step forward. The first priority was a merger with a firm in Germany, by far the dominant economy among the European jurisdictions.

The Merger with Boesebeck Droste

Until 1989, German firms were restricted to operating in only one state within Germany; in a federal country with no single dominant "commercial capital" this was a major disincentive to international relationships. The removal of this prohibition, in what has been described as the country's "legal Big Bang," resulted in a series of mergers between German firms, creating national firms out of smaller firms formerly established in different regions of the country—but this took some years.

In this flurry of merger activity three firms from Dusseldorf, Hamburg, and Munich agreed to combine forces and to operate under the single name Droste. It soon became clear that a truly national firm would not be complete without a strong office in Frankfurt, the center for corporate finance work in Germany. After an attempt to set up an independent operation in Frankfurt, Droste's partners came to the conclusion that it made more sense to merge with an established firm. Negotiations with the Frankfurt firm Boesebeck, Barz & Partner took place and the new firm of Boesebeck Droste came into being in 1997.

Each of the four Boesebeck Droste offices—in Dusseldorf, Frankfurt, Hamburg, and Munich—had their own long and distinguished history before eventually merging. They shared an enthusiasm to broaden their horizons and by 1999 they were seventh in Germany's domestic listing of law firms and looking to expand into different markets.

The merger with Lovell White Durrant was announced in late September 1999. It was, *The Lawyer* noted, the third merger announced of "a top-10 UK law firm with a German practice in as many weeks." In an interview with the magazine, Andrew Walker, Lovell White Durrant's Senior Partner, dismissed suggestions that the firm was "joining in the rush to crack the German market," adding, "We sense what other firms are doing but we are not directed by the competition. What directs us is what our clients want and they are saying we need to be in Germany." This was a union that suited both parties and to which both came with the useful experience of having been involved in previous merger activity.

At the time of the merger with Lovell White Durrant, Boesebeck Droste had six domestic German offices, in Berlin, Dresden, Dusseldorf, Frankfurt, Hamburg, and Munich as well as offices in Alicante and Warsaw, which had opened in 1991. The issue of a name for the merged firm was resolved amicably on the basis that the name of the English firm would be adopted—but it would have to be shortened. Consequently on 1 January 2000, the merged firm became Lovells, the name commonly used by many in the London market for decades.

Celebrating the merger with Boesebeck Droste in 2000: Walter Klosterfelde, Andrew Walker, Lesley MacDonagh, Oliver Felsenstein, and Michael Leistikow.

The firms that became Boesebeck Droste

Boesebeck Droste was the result of a series of mergers of German law firms in the 1990s following the opening up of the German legal market. For the first time, German firms could operate in different states and ambitious local partners looked for opportunities for expansion. The firm that became Boesebeck Droste traced its origins to four separate practices based in Hamburg, Dusseldorf, Munich (Droste), and Frankfurt (Boesebeck, Barz & Partner).

Droste's Hamburg office was founded in the late nineteenth century and survived World War II against the odds. The firm grew to include Walther Fischer, Kurt Bussmann, Helmut Droste, and Sibylle Weber, its first female partner, in 1951.

In the 1960s, the Hamburg partners, led by Hermann Sprick, began to diversify their practice beyond intellectual property law. Sprick handled the insolvency of Schlieker Wharf, which belonged to a very high-profile client, Willy Schlieker. Schlieker was the poster boy for Germany's economic boom after World War II. After building an iron and steel empire, he fulfilled a lifelong dream and launched his own shipyard in Hamburg. However, the first postwar economic downturn at the beginning of the 1960s and a chaotic corporate structure put an end to Schlieker's dream.

In the 1970s, Hamburg partners made legal history when representing the publisher of Klaus Mann's famous novel *Mephisto*. Thinly disguising the career of the German actor Gustaf Gründgens who was famous in Nazi Germany for playing the role of Mephisto, Mann implied that Gründgens cooperated with the Nazis. Gründgens' family tried to stop the novel's publication. The case ran for five years and eventually reached the German Constitutional Court, Germany's highest court. The court's 1971 decision set a groundbreaking precedent finding in favor of the family and upholding the right to privacy. However, the novel was later republished and became an Oscar-winning movie.

The Dusseldorf firm of Triebel & Weil was founded by Louis Henry Farnborough. Farnborough qualified as a lawyer in Germany in 1933 but escaped from Nazi persecution to England in 1936 where he changed his name from Ludwig Heinrich Farrenbacher to Louis Henry Farnborough. He returned to Dusseldorf in 1946 as legal adviser to the then-called British Army of the Rhine. Turning down an offer to become president of the Dusseldorf Court of Appeals he set up in private practice as Honorary Legal Adviser to the British Consulate-General in Dusseldorf. Farnborough maintained strong ties to the legal community in England and acted for individuals and funds that sought compensation or restitution for stolen and confiscated property in the years before 1945. The firm continued to develop its international profile under the leadership of partners Kurt-Gerd Weil and Volker Triebel until the merger with Droste in 1989.

Thanks to Jakob Strobl the Munich office had very strong ties to the legal community in the United States. Strobl had worked in New York for the German Ministry of Finance, on the settlement of debts owed by Germany both before and after World War II, in line with the famous London Debt Agreement.

Chapter 2 ■ Our Growth

LEFT: Willy Schlieker, owner of the Schlieker shipyards, arriving for the naming of a new ship in Hamburg.

RIGHT: Jakob Strobl established the Munich office in 1960.

BELOW: The Frankfurt office today.

He returned to Munich and opened his own practice in 1960. The astute tax lawyer's extensive network of contacts, including American lawyers and financial advisers, formed the basis for his success in Munich. In the years that followed, Strobl's junior partners became very active members of the International Fiscal Association as well as the International Bar Association.

The representation of a consortium led by Exxon in the 1990s stands out in a long list of headline cases handled by the Munich office. The arbitration concerned the exploitation of gas reserves in the Netherlands by a number of German companies. With $10 billion in dispute, the case was the biggest and commercially most significant to have been heard by the International Chamber of Commerce to that date.

The Frankfurt office was founded in 1919 by Julius Lehmann. Like Wassermann in Hamburg and Farnborough in Dusseldorf, Lehmann also left Germany in 1933 for Switzerland to escape persecution. The firm survived, led for many decades by two outstanding partners, Ernst Boesebeck and Carl Barz. Despite the difference in their approach to work, with Boesebeck being a man of detail and Barz efficient and succinct in the extreme, they complemented each other well and were an effective partnership. Legend has it that Barz maintained the firm's revenue at the same level following the outbreak of World War II—even though his three fellow partners had joined the armed forces and were not available for client work.

The most prominent instruction of Boesebeck Barz came in 1946 when they were tasked to liquidate IG Farben, then the world's largest industrial conglomerate of chemical and pharmaceutical companies. Founded in 1925, IG Farben was a major supplier of Germany's army and its affiliated companies produced the infamous nerve gas Zyklon B, which was used extensively in the Nazi extermination camps. The dismantling of this conglomerate was high on the agenda of the Allied Forces after 1945.

In the decades that followed, Frankfurt became the center for corporate finance in Germany and Boesebeck Barz became the legal advisers to many of the leading banks and corporations in the Rhine-Main area.

Hogan Lovells ■ Our Story

Further Expansion into Europe

Neither party to the merger saw it as an end in itself but more as the first step in the formation of an international firm with solid foundations in Europe. The partnership agreement of the merged firm declared the ambition to:

Become justly recognized as rapidly as possible within the legal and business communities as a European-based worldwide business law firm renowned for all-round excellence in its key markets. Achieving this goal will require the Partnership to remain or become a top quality full service firm with partners in at least France, Germany, Italy, the Netherlands, Spain, and the UK.

Within a year or so after the union with Boesebeck Droste, the new firm of Lovells carried out two more European mergers, in the Netherlands and France. In the Netherlands, negotiations led to an agreement to merge with the Amsterdam firm of Ekelmans Den Hollander and in 2001 with the Paris firm of Siméon et Associés and its Brussels office.

Ekelmans Den Hollander, founded in 1978, had developed a successful commercial practice with international corporate clients such as Merck, Sharp & Dohme, Honeywell, and Glaxo Wellcome as well as a number of financial institutions. Some of these were already clients of Lovells in the UK and the London office of Lovell, White & King had had a long-standing connection with the Dutch government in the mid-twentieth century. The founders of the Dutch firm retired in 1999 and 2002, but at the time of the merger the firm had thirteen partners and forty lawyers.

The well-regarded firm of Siméon et Associés had been established in 1974 and at the time of the merger with Lovells had twelve partners and around thirty-five other lawyers. Practice areas included corporate, EU and competition, litigation, tax, and employment, with particular strengths in the energy, telecoms, and insurance sectors with clients such as Axa, Motorola, and Total.

In Italy, it proved more problematic to find a firm that met the criteria for a merger, and Lovells decided the best option was to open its own office. In October 2000 a team of three partners from London went to Italy, two to Rome to open there, one to Milan to be joined by a partner from Germany; the core of each office was made up of lateral hires from Italian firms.

BELOW: Jan de Snaijer and Bert Oosting, from leading Amsterdam law firm Ekelmans Den Hollander, after its merger with Lovells in 2000. (Inset) Brochure marking the merger.

BOTTOM: Pierre de Montalembert, Lesley MacDonagh, John Pheasant, and Robert Follie at the time of the merger with French firm Siméon et Associés.

At a reunion of former Senior Partners in 2014: from left, Peter Gerrard, David Harris, Cavan Taylor, Andrew Walker, John Young, Nicholas Cheffings, and Alan Parsons.

In Spain, similar difficulties emerged when trying to find "a willing and suitable firm with which to establish a close relationship." In 1999, the Lovells European working party described the legal market there as "in turmoil," since foreign law firms, mostly English, as well as international firms of accountants, were looking for relationships. So, as in Italy, the firm opted for a greenfield development in Madrid. The office there opened officially in 2005, headed by José Maria Balañá who would go on to serve as a Board member of Hogan Lovells.

The decade leading up to the end of the twentieth century was one of rapid change in the business world, with globalization accelerating as well as developments in communications technology and travel which enabled international integration to take place in ways previously not possible. By 2000, globalization was particularly advanced in the City's financial services industry. This, in turn, led to the growth and internationalization of City law firms. In a relatively short time, Lovells had transformed the scale and scope of its international operations, making significant progress in Europe and Asia toward its goal of making itself an international law firm.

For any law firm, "becoming international" was a development that meant its existing management structures and ways of operating had to adapt. In 2002, the firm established a partnership council and an international executive. The Partnership Council would be wholly elected, chaired by the Senior Partner and with responsibility for matters relating to partners as owners of the firm, including the appointment, performance, and remuneration of partners. The International Executive would be chaired and appointed by the Managing Partner and would be responsible for the management of the business of the firm. Both Senior Partner and Managing Partner would be directly elected by the partners, and in due course, after strenuously contested elections, John Young succeeded Andrew Walker as Senior Partner in 2004 and David Harris succeeded Lesley MacDonagh as Managing Partner in 2005. In that year, Lovells was ranked as the fifth-largest firm in Europe.

Lovells was evolving from a traditional partnership into "an international business, reflecting the change in the market and the move to a much more business-type approach to the way the practice of law was carried on." As a result, the firm converted, in 2007, to a limited liability partnership.

Meanwhile, the partnership was also looking more seriously at another way to expand its operations in the United States—through merger. Underpinning this was the belief that "logically as you become truly international, you need an American element; no other industry would call itself international without that."

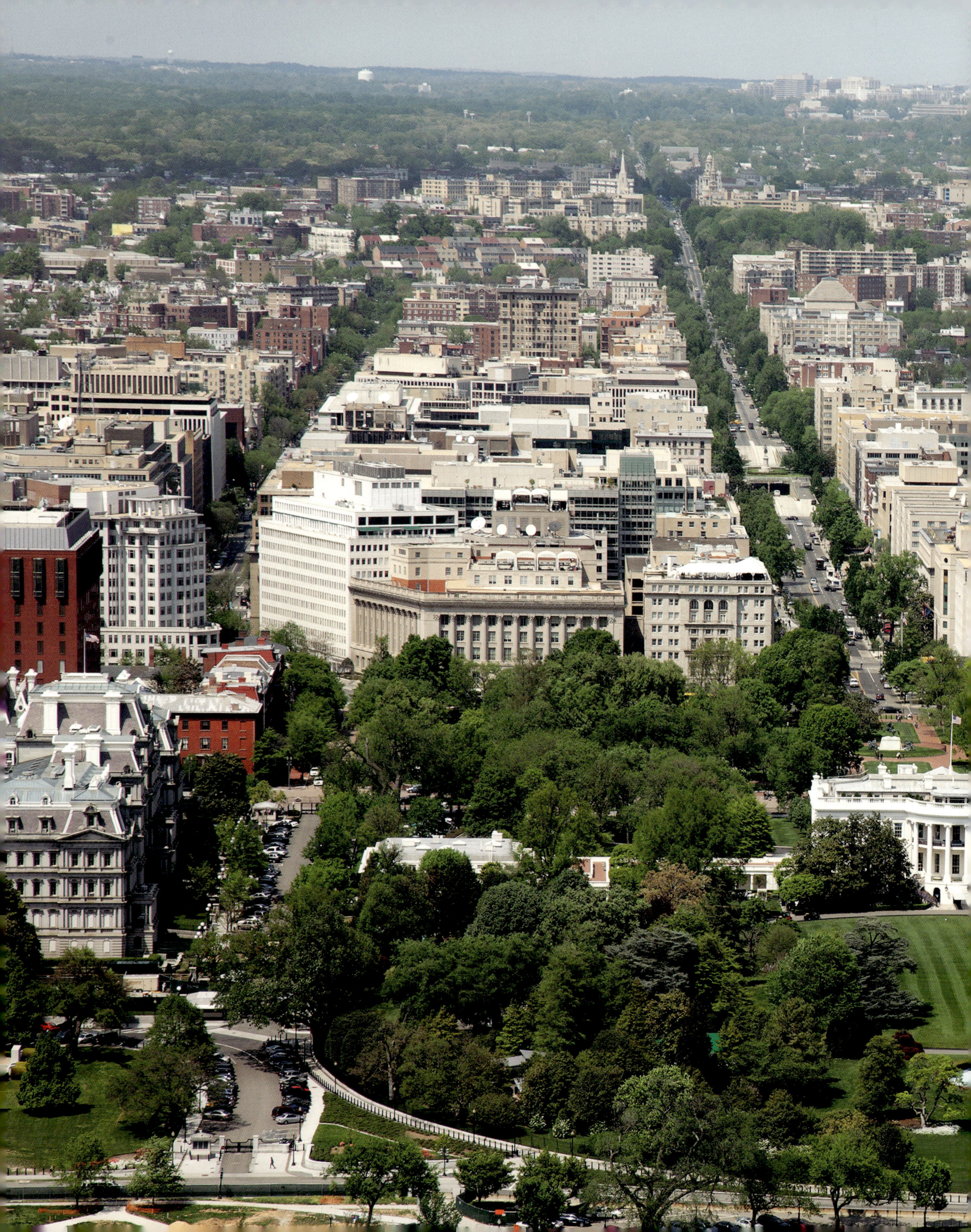

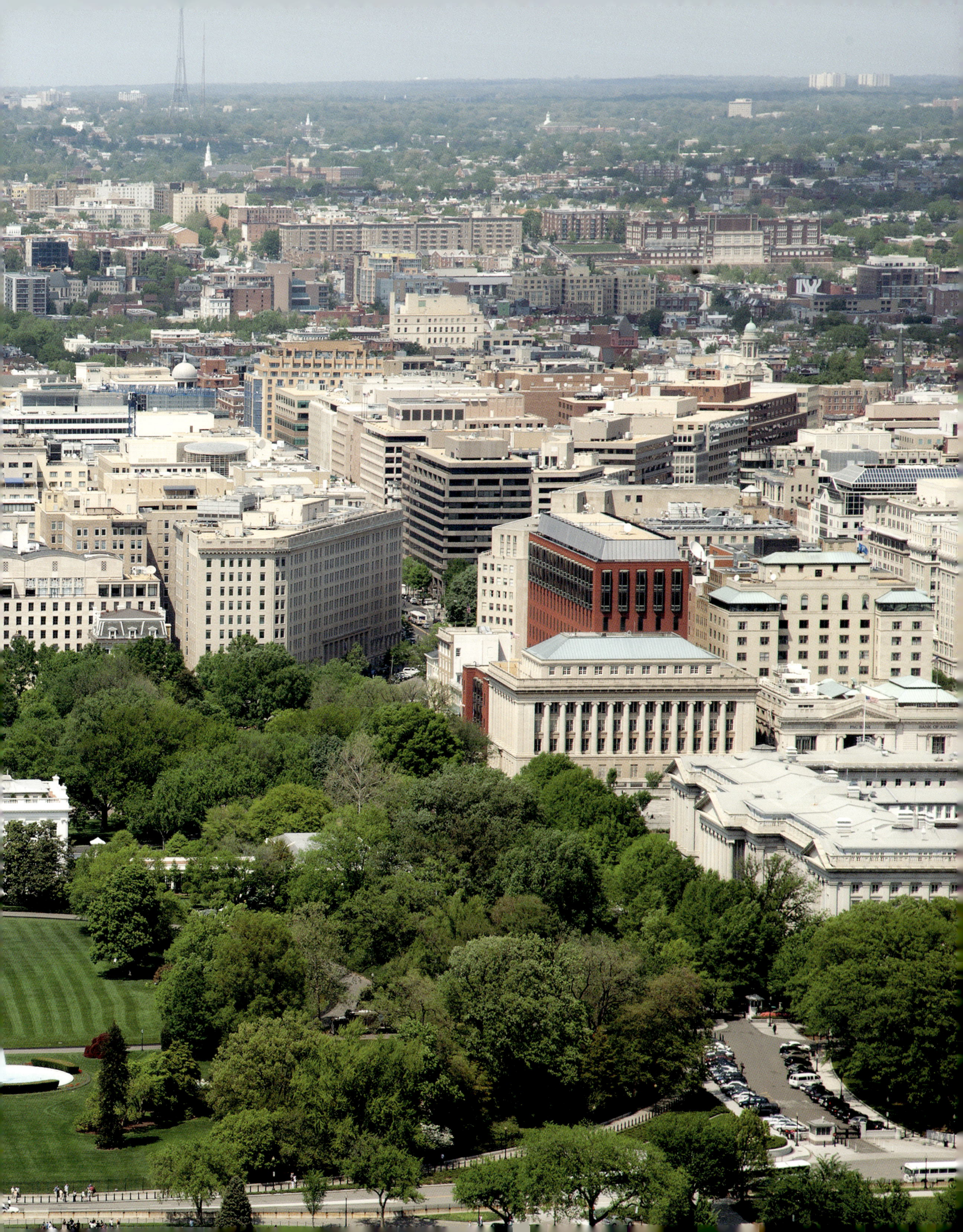

Frank Hogan was featured on the cover of *Time* in 1935. He died in 1944.

WASHINGTON, D.C.

Washington, D.C. appeared more the Southern town than the national capital when Frank Hogan entered full-time legal practice in 1904. To be sure, federal regulatory authority was expanding in this Progressive Era. But the next four decades dramatically accelerated the pace of change, transforming both the city and the practice of law. By the time Hogan died in May 1944, the federal government had become a powerful force in the daily life of the nation and, indeed, the world. Few Americans considered all of the implications of this development; instead, they had accepted it as necessary to address national crises—the Great Depression and World War II.

PREVIOUS PAGE: Aerial view of Washington, D.C.

The Postwar Years

The end of the war in the Pacific on 14 August 1945 touched off nearly as much change in the United States as had the nation's entry into the war. Demobilization upended the wartime workforce as industry shifted gears from the production of tanks and bombsights to automobiles, appliances, and other consumer goods. Nearly half of the nation's sixteen million veterans went to college or took vocational training thanks to the GI Bill that President Franklin Roosevelt signed into law on 22 June 1944. The additional assistance of 2.4 million home loans under the GI Bill helped forge a new American middle class.

Feverish growth continued in the capital city, which the war had stretched beyond its limits to house, feed, transport, and entertain the approximately 5,000 new federal employees per month who arrived after 1940. At the war's end, the federal budget had reached almost $93 billion, ten times what it had been just six years earlier. And while history usually takes note of the government's expansion, it was also true that local D.C. businesses—banks, real estate companies, newspapers, bus services, hotels, and department stores—all grew commensurate with the federal presence and provided patronage to local law firms like Hogan & Hartson.

Nelson Hartson had intended to develop the firm's tax practice when he joined in 1925, but he had been partly diverted by the fiscal depression and war. The focus on tax law sharpened in 1946, however, when the firm hired thirty-six-year-old Seymour Mintz, formerly a lawyer at the U.S. Treasury and the Internal Revenue Service. Mintz soon acquired eccentric billionaire Howard Hughes as a client. Acknowledging straightforwardly that

"The power of the purse is quite tremendous," Mintz advanced rapidly to partnership and to leadership positions on the firm's Executive Committee. Twenty years later, the contribution that Seymour Mintz made to the firm's diversity is recognized by Hogan Lovells in the Seymour Mintz Excellence Award which is presented to members of Hogan Lovells who demonstrate outstanding dedication to the firm's citizenship ideals.

Recruitment at Hogan & Hartson was happenstance in the immediate postwar years and through the early 1960s. The firm was an informal place with a decidedly anti-bureaucratic style. Partners expected that growth would continue, but felt no great pressure to plan for it. It seemed enough to work hard and, if the right person happened along at an opportune time, to hire him—it was almost always a "him" in those days.

Stanley Harris, a future judge on the District of Columbia Court of Appeals and the United States District Court for the District of Columbia, was a recent law school graduate in 1953 when he opened a letter from Hogan & Hartson. There were no openings, it said, but he was welcome to drop by anytime he was in town. Soon enough Harris wandered into the Hogan & Hartson offices in the Colorado Building on F Street, and into a job. His timing had been fortunate, for the firm had just encountered a flurry of radio and television license work.

By 1940, almost 28 million homes had radios—double the number in 1930—and in the five years after the war, the number of radio stations nearly tripled. Broadcast television also thrived in the postwar years, with the number of U.S. households owning a TV set skyrocketing from just under a million in 1949 to twenty million just four years later. As the number of stations and license applications increased, so too did disputes requiring legal representation before the Federal Communications Commission. About a quarter of Hogan & Hartson's lawyers worked full time on these regulatory matters, which often involved lengthy hearings and appeals.

After two years at the firm, Stan Harris was talking with a law school friend he thought would

ABOVE: Howard Hughes (right) with his general counsel, T. A. Slack. Hughes became a long-term client of Hogan & Hartson when Seymour Mintz was instructed to work on his tax affairs.

LEFT: President Franklin D. Roosevelt signing the GI Bill in June 1944. The Bill opened up higher education to nearly eight million war veterans.

fit in very well. However, the friend seemed uninterested. Barrett Prettyman explained he was just too busy to look for a job. In 1955 he was nearing completion of an extraordinary series of clerkships for three U.S. Supreme Court Justices—Robert Jackson, Felix Frankfurter, and John Harlan. The previous year, Prettyman had urged Justice Jackson toward a vigorous opinion in the landmark school desegregation decision, *Brown v. Board of Education* (1954), which overturned the court's 1896 "separate but equal" doctrine. A historian of the *Brown v. Board of Education* case later wrote, "It is doubtful if any of the excellent young men who have come fresh out of the law schools or soon thereafter to serve the Justices of the Supreme Court ever served more faithfully or usefully than Barrett Prettyman served Robert Jackson." Prettyman's absorption in court activities at such a historic time was understandable. But when his clerkship was over, Prettyman listened more carefully to Harris. He accepted an offer to join Hogan & Hartson.

Prettyman's first case, with partner Joseph Judson Smith, former chief counsel in charge of the Federal Trade Commission's (FTC) appellate division, was a massive, groundbreaking antitrust matter involving the Pillsbury baking company. *The Pillsbury Company v. The Federal Trade Commission* was the first case prosecuted under the Clayton Antitrust Act's Section 7, which restricted mergers. And when the FTC ruled against Pillsbury, Prettyman crafted a novel appeal that won a favorable ruling from the Fifth Circuit Court of Appeals. He argued that an exceptionally harsh congressional grilling of FTC Chairman Edward Howrey about the length of time the agency was taking to decide the Pillsbury matter had biased the agency, making it impossible for the commission to render an impartial judgment. The court agreed.

The case was subsequently cited as an example of inappropriate congressional intrusion into the decisions of administrative agencies.

One day, Nelson Hartson, impeccably dressed but looking a bit lost, presented himself at a D.C. courthouse. He had been summoned there to represent an indigent client. The city as yet had no public defender system and relied on volunteers garnered by the local bar association. When the number of volunteers dwindled, however, judges took it on themselves to call lawyers to court to help out. At this particular time, the District's judges were exasperated by the bar association's trickle of volunteers and decided to send a message by summoning some senior partners. Nelson Hartson was among those swept up.

Hartson knocked on the door of the assistant U.S. attorney who would be prosecuting the case. From his modest quarters, young John Warner looked up to see an elegant gentleman who introduced himself and stated that he wished to discuss the matter of a certain defendant. Warner invited him to come in and sit down. Hartson confided his concerns.

Future Secretary of the Navy and U.S. Senator from Virginia, John Warner, joined Hogan & Hartson in 1960. He is seen here speaking at the Republican National Convention, 1980.

He realized that the charges of first-degree murder and multiple counts of assault could result in the death penalty for his client. He would do his best but confessed that the last case he had tried had been twenty years ago, and that had been before the Board of Tax Appeals. "But," he quickly added, "I have one of the ablest assortment of partners in trial, and this individual will have $25,000 worth of partners representing him."

Hartson and his team worked with Warner to achieve a plea bargain that saved the defendant's life. Just after the sentencing was done, Warner turned to finish up some paperwork. Hartson approached him and asked if they could chat. They walked back to Warner's office. "Now Mr. Warner," said the patrician, "this has been a very unusual experience for me, and should it happen again I want to be prepared. Will you come to work for me?" And so John Warner, future Secretary of the Navy and U.S. Senator from Virginia, joined the firm, in 1960, as Hogan & Hartson's thirty-seventh lawyer.

Barrett Prettyman, too, was eventually summoned to the D.C. criminal courts to defend an indigent client, in this instance a young woman who had been arrested while flagging down cars in the early hours of the morning on a strip of 14th Street then known for its sex trade. She had been charged with vagrancy. In preparing for the trial, Prettyman learned that the statute defining "vagrancy" included criteria such as "leading a profligate life." That was interesting, he thought. During his questioning of the arresting officer he had no trouble getting the witness to agree that such things as, for example, betting on horses at the racetrack might be considered part of a profligate life. From there it was but a short step to ask the officer if, on being advised that Federal Bureau of Investigation Director J. Edgar Hoover regularly went to the racetrack and placed bets, he thought that the FBI head would be leading a profligate life? "Yes, I would," answered the officer as the courtroom erupted in laughter. A reporter from The Washington Post joined in—and took the entertaining story back to his editor.

The next day, two FBI agents showed up at Hogan & Hartson to deliver a letter to Prettyman expressing Director Hoover's anger that his name had been used for "cheap publicity." Prettyman penned an apology, pointing out in his defense that his intent had been to use the racetrack example to dismantle a vague statute rather than to illustrate any real definition of profligacy. Eventually, Prettyman secured an acquittal for his client.

A combination of local and national matters constituted the firm's work in the 1950s and 1960s. Sometimes these intertwined in interesting ways. Litigator John "Jack" Arness, who had taken up Hogan & Hartson's work for the Capital Transit company, represented The Hartford insurance company in an accident claim. A man named Kosberg had decided to earn some extra money by using his station wagon to take children to and from school. But Kosberg had failed to update his insurance with The Hartford to include this new risk. When several children were injured in an accident involving Kosberg's vehicle, The Hartford called on Hogan & Hartson to argue that there had been no applicable insurance. When Arness won a declaratory judgment and then had it sustained on appeal, the insurance

Dining at the F Street Club in the early 1960s (clockwise from front): Parker Hancock, Barrett Prettyman, John Arness, Frank Roberson, James Rogers, Nelson Hartson, Seymour Mintz, Frank Casey, and Robert Kapp.

ABOVE: The firm's national clients included Libbey-Owens-Ford Glass and Pillsbury.

BOTTOM RIGHT: Barrett Prettyman (right) talking to Fidel Castro. Prettyman, at the request of the Kennedy administration, took part in the delicate task of negotiating the release of over one thousand prisoners held in Cuba after the failed Bay of Pigs invasion in 1961.

company became a regular client. The asbestos cases that subsequently poured into the firm from The Hartford proved a mainstay of the firm's litigation team well past the end of the century.

In the mid-1960s, Hogan & Hartson was a relatively large firm with approximately forty-five lawyers. It just missed inclusion on a list of about twenty-five firms outside New York City with more than fifty lawyers. National clients included Pillsbury, The Hartford, Columbia Broadcasting, Republic Steel, and Libbey-Owens-Ford Glass. Among local clients were *The Evening Star* newspaper and Riggs National Bank. In addition to the communications practice, the tax, commercial, real estate, antitrust, securities, litigation, and corporate departments were also thriving.

Hogan & Hartson maintained high standards of client service at all hours and in all conditions. Once the chairman of Riggs Bank called John Warner at 9 p.m. with an urgent request. Could he come over to the chairman's house right away? Warner asked no questions; of course he could. He quickly donned a suit and grabbed two satchels filled with duplicates of bank-related documents that he always kept at the ready. When the chairman opened his door, he looked down at Warner's satchels and exclaimed, "What are those for?" "You said you needed to see me," Warner replied. "No, not for that," sputtered the distressed banker, his voice rising. "My cat's in the tree! Will you help me get the damn cat out of the tree?" In short order, Warner did.

Private sector clients were not the only ones who relied heavily on the firm. When John F. Kennedy was elected president in 1960, Hogan & Hartson lawyers became closely involved in the new administration. At Kennedy's request, Barrett Prettyman, who had been a law school classmate of the president's brother Robert, traveled to Cuba in December 1961 to manage the exchange of food and other goods for the release of 1,113 prisoners taken in the failed Bay of Pigs invasion. Prettyman managed to engage Fidel Castro in discussing the work of former Cuba resident Ernest Hemingway. It was a first step to getting the prisoners back to their families before Christmas.

Edward McDermott, who had served as national security adviser to the president and participated in the tense White House meetings leading up to the Soviet Union's withdrawal of missile-laden ships in October 1962—the Cuban Missile Crisis—came to the firm at the end of 1964. He brought with him highly polished diplomatic skills with which he knit relationships with clients ranging from the Japanese embassy to automobile maker Mercedez-Benz. Prettyman used to say that if he knew one or

The Colorado Building, Washington, D.C. at 14th and G Streets, N.W. (shown here), was a prestigious address when Frank Hogan opened his office there in 1907. By 1965 the area was rundown and the firm relocated to the Chanin Building at Connecticut Avenue and 17th Street, N.W, where it stayed until 1987.

two people on an elevator, McDermott knew them all. And in 1968, Lee Loevinger, former Assistant Attorney General in charge of the U.S. Department of Justice's antitrust division during the Kennedy administration, came to Hogan & Hartson after concluding his most recent public service, as Federal Communications Commissioner.

A Time for Change

If the firm was doing well in the mid-1960s, the same cannot be said for the federal city or for the nation generally. These were the years when the civil rights movement exposed anew what the Swedish economist Gunnar Myrdal had called in a 1944 Carnegie Foundation study *An American Dilemma*—the fundamental challenge to America's values imbedded in a history of slavery and in ongoing patterns of racial discrimination. Television brought into Americans' living rooms scenes of brutality against non-violent civil rights marchers and voting rights advocates in the South. It also carried images of urban rioting and rising crime rates in cities across the land. The assassination of President John F. Kennedy in 1963 shocked the nation, and while Kennedy's successor, Lyndon Johnson, used all of his political power to pass the historic Civil Rights Act of 1964 and Voting Rights Act of 1965, in 1966 the specter of Vietnam inched over the horizon to cast a deepening shadow on Johnson's presidency and the nation.

In the District of Columbia, downtown business areas were mostly deserted at night and many considered them dangerous. Hogan & Hartson relocated from the venerable Colorado Building on 14th Street to a newer building several blocks to the west and soon embarked on a different sort of renovation, one aimed at addressing the great unrest of the times by tapping an equally strong idealism in its own ranks.

Robert Kapp, who joined the firm in 1961, had found it a conservative place, comfortably at home with the local establishment. That did not mean he considered it particularly stuffy or formal. It was a place where Lester Cohen, usually attired in a sport coat and slacks, could walk into any office, sit down, throw his leg over a chair and ask, "How ya doin'?" Indeed, when Kapp asked the Executive Committee's approval to accept some pro bono cases for the American Civil Liberties Union, an organization whose aims he suspected partners like Nelson Hartson did not wholly condone, he was surprised when Hartson

The March on Washington in 1963 attracted an estimated 250,000 people for a peaceful demonstration to promote civil rights and economic equality for African Americans. The march provided dramatic moments, most memorably Rev. Martin Luther King Jr.'s "I Have a Dream" speech. The photograph shows the leaders linking arms; Martin Luther King Jr. is in the center.

offered his generous support. As the 1960s unfolded, Kapp and others at the firm felt an increased urgency to engage the decade's many challenges.

The watershed year of 1968 opened with North Vietnam's Tet Offensive, an incursion that revealed the extent to which the U.S. government had misled the American people about the war's progress and shifted public opinion against the war they now believed unwinnable. Then, in April, the assassination of civil rights leader Martin Luther King Jr. triggered rioting in Washington, D.C., and other cities. A mere two months later, another assassination—that of presidential hopeful Robert F. Kennedy in Los Angeles—left the country appalled and disillusioned. What was America coming to? Later that summer, televised coverage of the Democratic National Convention in Chicago juxtaposed the events inside with the violent protests outside, confirming to left and right—for entirely different reasons—that the country was spinning out of control.

Yet for all the turmoil, much was accomplished during the 1960s. Attention was focused as never before on the entrenched problem of poverty in America. Lyndon Johnson's Great Society bequeathed the Medicaid and Medicare programs. Enthusiasm to use government as a means to define and defend civil rights and to give disadvantaged groups a better chance in life inspired many to public service in agencies such as the Peace Corps and Volunteers in Service to America (VISTA). Additionally, young people and women adopted the strategies and tactics of the civil rights movement to mount new challenges to old restrictions. At Hogan & Hartson, a younger generation carried the momentum into the firm's offices.

Sara-Ann "Sally" Determan was a new associate at Hogan & Hartson in 1969 when she circulated a memo announcing an upcoming antiwar rally. An irate partner called her into his office and accused her of "aiding and abetting the enemy." She figured

Chapter 2 ■ Our Growth

FAR LEFT: Sara-Ann "Sally" Determan joined Hogan & Hartson in 1968 and became the firm's first female partner in 1975.

LEFT: Vincent H. Cohen joined the firm in 1969 and became the firm's first African American partner, remaining with the practice until retiring in 2001. Cohen was known for his many public service commitments and tireless efforts mentoring young African American lawyers. He died in 2015.

BELOW: Edward McDermott, Lester Cohen, Nelson Hartson, and Seymour Mintz, 1972.

that her career at the firm was over. Bob Kapp, passing Determan in the hallway, sensed something was wrong. She told him what had happened. He advised her to stay in her office while he looked into the matter. The firm's lawyers were gathering that afternoon at a nearby club for a party in honor of a departing colleague. Determan debated whether to attend. If her career was to be indeed ruined, as she feared, the party would be an embarrassing ordeal. But if it was not, and she failed to attend, that, too, could be embarrassing. She summoned her courage and headed for the club.

When she arrived, Bob Kapp and four members of the Executive Committee greeted her on the front steps. Surely they had congregrated to tell her that she would not be welcome. "Sally!" they burst out instead, "We're so glad to see you!" Later, Seymour Mintz called a meeting of the Executive Committee, which reminded Determan's scolding partner of the firm's policy—not concerning the war, but against bullying colleagues. Determan later became the firm's first female partner.

Vincent Cohen joined Hogan & Hartson in 1969 after stints with the U.S. Department of Justice and the Equal Employment Opportunity Commission. The son of West Indian immigrants, Cohen had been raised in New York City, graduated with honors from Syracuse University while earning All-American status as a basketball player, and then edited the law review at Syracuse's law school. After graduating in 1960, he had interviewed at Wall Street firms only to be told that clients would not accept an African American lawyer. Public utility and telephone companies and, later, the U.S. government, were more welcoming. Although in the early 1960s, Cohen had the jarring experience of walking across

Pennsylvania Avenue from his Justice Department office for lunch at a coffee-and-sandwich shop, only to be told matter-of-factly after taking a seat at the counter, "We don't serve Negroes here." As he left the restaurant, Cohen could see the U.S. Capitol just several blocks away. Even closer sat the National Archives building, housing the glass-encased Bill of Rights. Within a few years the Civil Rights Act made such effrontery illegal. In 1972, Hogan & Hartson made Vince Cohen its first African American partner.

The firm's practice grew apace with the national economy through the 1960s and the early 1970s. Some partners thought this sufficient, but Seymour Mintz was among those who believed that law firms had a higher responsibility. They should address not just their paying clients' matters but also the challenges posed by social injustice and unequal access to legal services. Further, they believed that Hogan & Hartson should go about this in an organized way, more effective than voluntary efforts by individual partners could ever be. In 1969, the Executive Committee formed a subcommittee, chaired by Bob Kapp, to explore various options.

LEFT: The first assignment undertaken by the newly formed Community Services Department (CSD), now called the pro bono department, was on behalf of the Black Panther Party in 1970.

ABOVE: The firm's Community Services Department (CSD) undertook defense work for the National Association for the Advancement of Colored People in the 1970s.

Realizing the objective proved to be more complicated than anyone had anticipated. In the end, the firm settled on something that had never been done before by any law firm—creating a separate pro bono department, called the Community Services Department (CSD), to be directed by a partner recruited to head it full-time. A search soon settled on John Ferren, who had established a successful community legal services clinic in Chicago and had then gone to Cambridge, Massachusetts, to organize a similar clinic for Harvard Law School.

After receiving the invitation, Ferren called Seymour Mintz to thank him—and then promptly tossed the letter in the wastebasket. "I had become very cynical about major law firms," he admitted years later. His wife, Ann, fished the letter out of the trash, curious about what he had thrown away with such flourish. She believed that he should at least look into it, so Ferren traveled to Washington, D.C. The visit surprised him. He appreciated Hogan & Hartson's relaxed style, contrasting it favorably to a Chicago firm that had once sent a lawyer home as inappropriately dressed because he wore a sport coat instead of a suit. Ferren decided to take the job.

His first assignment at the CSD turned out to be a stunner—a request to help the local chapter of the American Civil Liberties Union to sue the Metropolitan Police Department of the District of Columbia on behalf of the Black Panther Party. Ferren recalled the partners' reactions, "Eyes were raised to the breaking point." But they gave their assent and eventually the CSD achieved a successful settlement. The department's work soon included a variety of matters such as housing discrimination; challenging nuclear power generation; defense work for the National Association for the Advancement of Colored People; providing low-cost heating fuel for the poor; assuring food stamps for the elderly; defending rights of the mentally ill; ensuring fair wages for sugar cane workers in Louisiana; and pushing forward construction of the Vietnam Veterans Memorial.

In 1975, Hogan & Hartson recognized the growing specialization of legal work by formally organizing eight practice groups—antitrust and trade regulation; communications; community services; corporate and securities; general practice and administrative law; litigation; real estate and banking; and tax. Alongside energy-related projects such as the Trans-Alaska Pipeline, which involved the firm in the mid-1970s, new environmental laws also sparked a budding practice headed by Patrick Raher. Additionally, several notable appellate cases undertaken by Barrett Prettyman, along with his authorship of

Chapter 2 ■ Our Growth

LEFT: Hogan & Hartson partner, John Sirica, left the firm to become a federal district judge in 1957. He rose to national prominence while presiding over the Watergate trials.

BELOW: John Sirica, accompanied by his wife, being sworn in as a federal district judge.

TOP: Hogan & Hartson's John Warner (center, with program in his pocket) and to his left, Sandy Mayo, at the groundbreaking ceremony for the Vietnam Veterans Memorial in Washington, D.C., 1982.

ABOVE: A moment of quiet reflection at the Vietnam Veterans Memorial, Washington, D.C.

John Sirica and Watergate

Former Hogan & Hartson partner, John Sirica, had been raised in poverty and supported his studies at Georgetown University by boxing. Sirica served as an assistant U.S. attorney in the early 1930s but then, on leaving and starting his own practice, he found himself living hand to mouth during what he called "his starvation period" until he joined Hogan & Hartson in 1949. He worked actively for the Dwight D. Eisenhower presidential campaigns of 1952 and 1956, and left the firm in 1957 following his appointment to the federal bench. Sirica's courage and no-nonsense toughness earned him high praise while presiding over the Watergate trials in the 1970s. The Watergate scandal resulted from a botched break-in at the Democratic National Committee headquarters at the Watergate complex in Washington, D.C., and the Nixon administration's attempted cover-up of its involvement. Sirica had voted for President Richard Nixon in 1972, but after hearing the White House tapes, he admitted, "I felt foolish."

the award-winning book, *Death and the Supreme Court*, augured a future appellate specialty practice at the firm. In 1972, Prettyman had served as the first president of a newly established Washington, D.C. Bar. The new association, created at the same time as a thorough reorganization of the D.C. court system, aimed to unify and reform the previous voluntary bar associations in the city. It was fitting that the firm Frank Hogan had founded led the way in making the D.C. Bar responsive to changing times.

ABOVE: Hogan & Hartson partners at the F Street Club, 1980.

BELOW: U.S. Senator J. William Fulbright helped develop the firm's international trade practice.

New Challenges of Growth

By 1983, Hogan & Hartson had 160 lawyers, four times the number it had in 1963—about double the rate of increase in lawyers in the United States generally. The growth reflected the waxing importance of Washington, D.C., but there was a downside to this trend for the city's established firms: increased competition. Many outside law firms began to open offices in the nation's capital rather than rely on D.C.-based firms like Hogan & Hartson. Additionally, recent U.S. Supreme Court rulings had struck down minimum fee schedules as well as the American Bar Association's ban on lawyer advertising. And in 1984, the Supreme Court ruled that admissions to law firm partnership were subject to Title VII of the 1964 Civil Rights Act, thus making the fair consideration of women and minorities a matter of law as much as good practice. New publications such as *The American Lawyer*, *Legal Times*, and *The National Law Journal* brought heightened publicity and relentlessly ranked practitioners, thereby ratcheting up competitive pressure.

Hogan & Hartson responded by implementing more affirmative management, while still insisting on balancing informality and individual autonomy with organizational efficiency. With Bob Glen Odle at the helm of this new administrative structure, the firm embarked on a trajectory of unprecedented growth. For the first time, it opened offices beyond the District of Columbia, starting with Northern Virginia in 1985 and Baltimore in 1988. The firm continued to develop and refine its practice groups. Former U.S. Senator J. William Fulbright, for example, helped develop the international trade practice after retiring in 1975 from a distinguished career that included chairmanship of the Senate Foreign Relations Committee from 1959 to 1974—its longest serving chair in history. Fulbright also participated in informal, daily lunch chats around a table in the firm's cafeteria. There was only one rule at his table: "You're not allowed to talk about anything you know a lot about."

Chapter 2 ■ Our Growth

LEFT: In 1982 Ann Morgan Vickery (fifth from left on the U.S. Capitol steps), Earl Collier, and Paul Rogers helped the National Hospice and Palliative Care Organization win Medicare coverage for hospice services.

BELOW: Schoolchildren and members of the National Association for the Advancement of Colored People demonstrate in Washington, D.C., on 17 May 1979, the 25th anniversary of the U.S. Supreme Court's ruling in Brown v Board of Education, which ended racial segregation in American schools.

Elsewhere in the firm, partner David Tatel returned from two years' service as Director of the Office for Civil Rights at the Department of Health, Education, and Welfare and started the firm's education practice in 1979. In 1994, he was appointed to the U.S. Court of Appeals for the District of Columbia Circuit. Also in 1979, former U.S. Representative Paul G. Rogers joined Hogan & Hartson after twenty-four years in Congress, where he had become the foremost leader in promoting medical research and healthcare. Now Rogers worked for those same causes at Hogan & Hartson. Known as "Mr. Health," he was universally esteemed, and in December 2000 the National Institutes of Health dedicated its main plaza in his name.

If the growth of federal regulation had expanded law practice through most of the century, deregulation efforts by the Reagan administration in the 1980s might have been expected to reduce it. In some areas, such as antitrust law, that proved to be the case. But elsewhere the opposite happened. Hogan & Hartson lawyers were closely involved in developing new cable television businesses, for instance, while Warren Gorrell, after only three years at the firm, helped oversee the sale of a major international oil company. Others such as George Beall, Ty Cobb, and Stephen Immelt became nationally known as specialists in "white collar crime," while Howard Flack and Charles Allen found ample opportunity to apply their intimate knowledge of the savings and loan industry. Even in antitrust, Jan McDavid, chair of the ABA's section of Antitrust Law in 1999–2000, remained fully engaged with defense-related clients whose unique needs required specialized knowledge of the field.

The Community Services Department achieved a major success in the 1980s when it helped desegregate schools in Prince George's County, Maryland. And in 1987, Pat Brannan made her debut, pro bono, before the U.S. Supreme Court by arguing successfully that spray-painting swastikas on a synagogue in suburban Maryland should have been prosecuted as a hate crime rather than mere vandalism. Brannan came to the court well prepared. She had completed a clerkship with John Ferren, who had been appointed to the D.C. Court of Appeals in 1977, and had the strong support of Barrett Prettyman as she prepared for her first Supreme Court argument. Prettyman continued to draw superior appellate talent to the firm, including former U.S. Supreme Court clerks Allen Snyder and John G. Roberts Jr. Brannan would go on to become U.S. general counsel for Hogan Lovells and Roberts, the Chief Justice of the United States.

ABOVE: President George Bush attended a signing ceremony in 1991 to mark a major piece of pro bono work undertaken by Hogan & Hartson to reduce air pollution in the Grand Canyon.

BELOW RIGHT: Hogan & Hartson's first overseas office was opened in London in 1990.

The CSD also won a major case for the Grand Canyon Trust, the National Wildlife Federation, and two other organizations trying to stop hydroelectric power operations in the Grand Canyon, pending completion of environmental impact studies. It was Patrick Raher's involvement in that matter that spurred him to develop the firm's environmental law practice.

During a vacation to the Grand Canyon, Raher and his family noticed a dense fog filling up the canyon and learned that it was not fog, but pollution from a power plant. Back in Washington, Raher discovered that one of his partners, Paul Rogers, had chaired committee hearings prior to the passage of the Clean Air Act Amendments of 1977 and was a leading authority on that issue. Raher and Rogers got the wheels turning in Washington—all on a pro bono basis—and when they stopped, an agreement was in place with power companies that would soon reduce pollution in the Grand Canyon by 30 percent and, over time, virtually eliminate it. It was the first regulatory action ever taken by the federal government to improve visibility in a national park, and it drew President George H. W. Bush to the Grand Canyon for a signing ceremony on 18 September 1991 to mark the milestone achievement.

In June 1989, *The American Lawyer*'s Steven Brill had written a widely influential article, "The Law Business in the Year 2000," in which he projected a "shakeout" as a result of ongoing competition among law firms. Brill foretold that hard work at large firms would increase, not diminish. Computers and client demands would combine to tie earnings more closely to billings, which would be tracked ever more carefully. There would be more lateral recruiting, and large firms would become even bigger to provide the kind of "one-stop shopping" that international clients increasingly demanded. These developments were no surprise to Bob Odle. He had foreseen it all and agreed with Brill's analysis. In late 1989, the firm, which had doubled in size during the previous decade, organized a major planning effort among its now seventeen practice groups. Hogan & Hartson was going global.

A Global Perspective

December 1990 brought Hogan & Hartson's first overseas office in London. The following year came offices in Brussels, Warsaw, and Paris. The fall of the Iron Curtain in 1989 helped open opportunities in Europe, but the major impetus to growth was the

Chapter 2 ■ Our Growth

LEFT: In the 1990s Hogan & Hartson opened a number of offices. Shown here are the office buildings in Tokyo (far left), and New York.

BELOW: Warren Gorrell (left) took over leadership of the firm from Bob Odle in 2001. They are seen here under the watchful eye of the firm's founder, Frank Hogan.

sheer momentum of economic expansion around the world, with markets exploding due to trade agreements, digital communications, financial innovation, and container ship transport.

Working out of the firm's Washington, D.C. and Miami offices, Claudette Christian led a team representing the Brazilian energy company Petrobras in the construction of a $2 billion, 3,100km pipeline to import gas from Bolivia. Other representations included a wireless communications project in Bolivia and a 28,000km undersea fiber-optic cable running from Britain to Japan with landing points in Europe, the Middle East, Africa, and Asia. This was global practice at its leading edge. (Christian would go on to become Co-Chair of Hogan Lovells and later relocated to Brazil to open the firm's new office in Rio de Janeiro.)

In June 2000, *Legal Times* pronounced Hogan & Hartson's growth "staggering," with new practices in intellectual property and private equity, new offices in Denver (1993), Colorado Springs (1994), Los Angeles (1996), New York (1998), Miami, and Tokyo (2000), and 700 lawyers—more than double the number just a decade earlier. After twenty-one years of bringing all this to fruition while sustaining the deep-dyed Hogan & Hartson style of informality and teamwork, Bob Odle was ready to transfer its leadership into new hands.

Warren Gorrell put Hogan & Hartson in the forefront of corporate finance practice with pioneering work in real estate investment trusts. He was named "Deal Maker of the Year" in 1998 by *The American Lawyer*. In January 2001, Gorrell became the firm's first Chairman, with the Executive Committee establishing a Senior Management Group to assist him with his responsibilities. Gorrell's

ABOVE AND RIGHT: Hogan & Hartson's 100th anniversary celebrations in 2004 coincided with the opening of the Shanghai office.

BELOW: Howard Squadron, 1926–2001, founded the firm of Squadron Ellenoff in 1970. The firm merged with Hogan & Hartson in 2002. Squadron (right) is shown here with Senator Joseph Lieberman.

understanding of the firm's legacy was clear: "Look at yourself in the mirror," he advised anyone seeking to join. "If you can't honestly say that you're a team player, self-select; don't come here, because you won't do well." When the New York firms Davis, Weber & Edwards and Squadron, Ellenoff, Plesent & Sheinfeld merged with Hogan & Hartson in 2000 and 2002, respectively, Howard Flack led Hogan & Hartson's effort to make the new partners feel at home. "The worst attribute of a law firm," said Flack, "is when lawyers in the firm feel disconnected. Nobody's telling them that they're valuable, and I don't mean paying them money. I mean making them feel like they're valuable persons. That's not just management's job; it's every lawyer's job to do that with their fellow lawyers."

Hogan & Hartson held firm to this principle through more office openings in Berlin (2001); Beijing (2002); Munich (2003); Shanghai (2004); Geneva, Caracas, and Hong Kong (2005); and Houston (2006), Philadelphia, Abu Dhabi, Silicon Valley, and San Francisco (2008).

The firm's Community Services Department also increased its efforts, commensurate with the enhanced energies and resources of new lawyers and new ideas.

During its centennial in 2004, Hogan & Hartson appointed Pat Brannan the firm's ninth partner in charge of the Community Services Department with a mandate to broaden the base of participating lawyers. Litigators had always seemed a natural fit but, as Brannan noted, "There are lots of ways that corporate, finance, tax, and other lawyers can

BELOW: Loretta Lynch became a partner at Hogan & Hartson in 2001 and left in 2010 to serve for the second time as U.S. Attorney for the Eastern District of New York. In 2015 she became the first African American woman to become Attorney General of the United States.

BOTTOM: John G. Roberts Jr. started at Hogan & Hartson as an associate and later headed up the firm's appellate practice. He was appointed Chief Justice of the United States in 2005 and is shown shaking hands with President Barack Obama after his inauguration ceremony in Washington, D.C., 2009.

contribute." It was her job—and it was Hogan & Hartson's collective job—to find creative ways to serve. Warren Gorrell led by example, asking lawyers in the firm to volunteer a minimum of twenty hours each to CSD every year. In 2005, they responded with almost 90,000 hours. "It's an essential part of who we are and what we are as a law firm," said Gorrell.

That spirit extended across the globe as partner Loretta Lynch accepted an appointment as special counsel to the International Criminal Tribunal for Rwanda (ICTR) to investigate charges of false evidence and witness tampering in genocide trials that had been conducted in 2004. Lynch, a former U.S. Attorney for the Eastern District of New York, made several trips to Rwanda in 2005–2006 and submitted her findings to the ICTR, which handed down indictments in 2006. Lynch would continue to serve the public in 2010, when she left the firm to return to the U.S. Attorney post in New York at the request of President Barack Obama, and again in 2015, to become the first African American woman Attorney General of the United States.

Hogan & Hartson alumnus John G. Roberts Jr. also carried forward the firm's service tradition when he was appointed judge on the U.S. Court of Appeals for the District of Columbia Circuit in 2003 and, just two years later, became Chief Justice of the United States. During his career, including fourteen years at the firm, Roberts had argued thirty-nine cases before the U.S. Supreme Court, including a double-jeopardy case on behalf of an indigent client.

Models at the launch of Jaguar and Land Rover in Mumbai, India, 2009. The firm represented the Ford Motor Company in its sale of Jaguar Land Rover to the India-based Tata Motors in 2008.

The firm's growing global perspective was manifest in its burgeoning Latin America practice. Through the cultivation of relationships with local lawyers in several countries a network of alliances was established, strengthening Hogan & Hartson's capabilities across the entire region, including a preeminent, award-winning project finance practice. In 2005, the firm opened an office in Caracas, Venezuela, centering on state-owned petroleum and petrochemical companies. Similar work ensued in Mexico, Ecuador, Colombia, and other Central American countries. In addition, over this same period Daniel González, Richard Lorenzo, and others built one of the leading international arbitration practices in Latin America.

These matters soon involved finance and communications partners in the New York and Washington, D.C. offices, while the firm's record of working comfortably with diverse cultures helped win the confidence of the Chinese and Japanese entities that were providing financing, construction, and other services to projects in Latin America. One result was an agreement in 2010 between Ecuador and China to build a $2 billion "clean energy" hydroelectric project in Ecuador, "the largest construction project in the history of that country," Miguel Zaldivar observed. Elsewhere in the world, the firm represented Ford Motor Company in its 2008 sale of Jaguar/Land Rover to India-based conglomerate Tata, and in Ford's sale of Volvo to a Chinese holding company two years later.

Crisis and Renewal

The end of 2007 brought the beginning of the Great Recession and Global Financial Crisis, an economic crisis larger than any since the Great Depression of the 1930s. It lasted, officially, until June 2009. As Prentiss Feagles reflected, "Major institutions were collapsing, and it was really unclear whether the government could prop up the ones that needed to function and indeed whether the system could continue to function." Feagles had been in London with Warren Gorrell and Steve Immelt in September 2008 when Lehman Brothers declared bankruptcy. Immelt also remembered their musings as they watched television reports of events unfolding across the Atlantic. "We wondered what the world was going to end up looking like."

Chapter 2 ■ Our Growth

The firm's diverse practice helped it weather the crisis, though Prentiss Feagles later observed that the fundamental paradigm of practice changed for all large law firms. "Clients were under intense cost-cutting pressures, and they have not forgotten the lessons they learned." Pressure increased on law firms to provide multiple services efficiently and expertly, at lower cost, wherever clients needed them. Clients were looking for new markets, particularly in a recession when the U.S. and European markets were contracting.

The new paradigm favored a traditional attribute of the firm—creativity—as the Denver office demonstrated when the Great Recession undermined conventional bond financing for renovation of the city's Union Station area. The firm found new potential funding sources in two federal programs intended for railroads but never before used for railroad stations. Hogan & Hartson argued that Union Station's renovation would include bus and light rail capabilities and residential-retail development that

The collapse of the investment bank Lehman Brothers, in 2008, was an early indicator of the global financial crisis.

81

Hogan Lovells ■ Our Story

Hogan & Hartson was involved in obtaining federal financing for Denver Union Station. The project reinvigorated downtown Denver and many businesses have relocated to the area.

would save energy and reduce pollution. The federal government accepted that reasoning and offered a $300 million loan to the firm's client consortium, the Denver Union Station Project Authority (DUSPA). Said Cole Finegan, then Office Managing Partner of the Denver office: "It absolutely transformed downtown Denver. In fact, we're moving our offices down there to be a part of it."

Foresight accompanied creativity. For example, when partners realized that privacy issues were becoming increasingly relevant in many sectors of the internet economy, the firm formed a privacy and information management practice group that rapidly became a preeminent practice of international stature. In keeping with the firm's tradition, these new resources were available for public service as well as commercial practice, as when in 2009 several partners left to take senior positions in the executive branch of the newly elected Obama administration.

In 2009, the firm welcomed back John Warner, then 82 and recently retired after five consecutive terms as a U.S. senator from Virginia—the second-longest term ever for a senator from Virginia. Senator Warner had served as an enlisted sailor in World War II; a lieutenant in the Marines Corps in Korea; Secretary of the Navy for more than five years during the difficult closing years of the Vietnam War; and Administrator for the American Revolution Bicentennial Administration before his election to the U.S. Senate in 1978. He had agreed to speak with

Hogan & Hartson retreat in San Diego, 2008.

Warren Gorrell before considering the numerous options available to him upon leaving the Senate. Gorrell was "very persuasive—and still is," Warner recalled. The firm's solid record of ethical practice proved equally compelling and Warner returned to serve as senior adviser to the firm on matters pertaining mainly to the executive branch of the federal government.

Law practice had changed greatly since Warner first joined Hogan & Hartson in 1960. The senator could remember the days when Washington, D.C.'s legal, real estate, and banking "barons," as he called them, were "a close-knit community" that dominated local affairs from their offices in a small area just east of the White House. "They used to line up along 15th Street, almost in single file," he chuckled, "heading for the Metropolitan Club or the University Club for lunch." By contrast, the firm he rejoined in 2009 employed more than 1,100 lawyers in twenty-seven offices worldwide. Much had changed, to be sure; but as the senator's return affirmed, Frank Hogan's well-laid foundation remained squarely in place.

Hogan Lovells

Chapter 3

Our Combination

Chapter 3
Our Combination

The idea of a combination with a U.S. law firm had long been in the minds of many Lovells partners. The rationale and strategy for such a combination were set out in a memorandum as early as April 1998, recommending further expansion into Europe in service of "the long term strategic objective ... to become a worldwide business law firm." The memorandum also stated that the firm should be "prepared to consider at any time the possibility of a merger with a New York firm; the two objectives are not mutually exclusive."

The idea to create a strong European firm, with a limited U.S. presence, which would be attractive to the right U.S. combination partner in due course, led Lovells to complete mergers in Germany, France, and the Netherlands, and to set up strong offices in Italy and Spain, before the focus was turned back to the United States. The Lovells International Executive, supported by a U.S. working party, engaged in a thorough and lengthy process to identify the most appropriate potential partner. David Harris and Patrick Sherrington led the process, beginning with a review of all AmLaw 100 firms and progressing to more detailed analysis and short-listing. The U.S. working party built on its internal research and analysis through its work with many U.S. firms and by seeking insights from consultants specializing in the U.S. legal market.

Lovells had established clear criteria for the evaluation of merger candidates: the nature and quality of their business—their footprint and capabilities; their client base, which had to include a substantial number of major U.S. companies with strong international needs; and commonality of both vision and culture. These criteria were intended to ensure that a merger would result in a stronger firm, with a significantly enhanced market positioning, which would be an attractive place to work for partners and staff.

In the course of this analysis, it became clear to Lovells that merging with a leading New York M&A or finance firm was not a desirable option: they did not align with the firm's breadth of practice, and their profitability and cultures were very different. But one firm—Hogan & Hartson—aligned well in all respects. It came to the top of the shortlist.

Hogan & Hartson followed a different path to the combination. Beginning in the early 1990s, the firm began to expand outside the United States, opening offices in London, Brussels, and elsewhere in Europe. As it had in the U.S., the firm relied on both "greenfield" projects—starting new offices from the ground up—and acquisitions. By 2007, Hogan & Hartson had fourteen offices outside the United States, in both Europe and Asia, which accounted for about 20 percent of the firm's lawyers and just under 20 percent of the firm's revenues.

It was becoming increasingly clear, however, that merely having a network of international offices would not be enough to ensure success. As clients required more cross-border and international services, they were rightly focusing on firms that could offer the critical mass, depth, and quality of service across multiple jurisdictions. For Hogan & Hartson to achieve that through lateral recruitment of individual lawyers and small groups, market by market, would not only have been extraordinarily expensive and time consuming—it realistically could not have been done successfully.

Warren Gorrell had said at the beginning of his tenure in 2001 that he would not lead the firm into a big, transformational merger. But by 2008, he recognized that the global legal market was evolving dramatically and the firm needed to be open to major change to succeed. Accordingly, Hogan & Hartson began to explore the options for a step change, focusing particularly on firms with a significant presence in London but not only in London. Gorrell led the effort with support from Steve Immelt, who was at that time Hogan & Hartson's partner responsible for its international offices. As that process progressed, one firm kept popping up in terms of geographic and practice fit: Lovells.

The Washington, D.C. office of Hogan & Hartson moved to Columbia Square, in the Pennyslvania Avenue area just east of the White House, in 1987.

Hogan Lovells ■ Our Story

Talks about Talks

Sherrington knew a number of U.S. firms well, not least through Lovells' membership in the Pacific Rim Advisory Council, of which Hogan & Hartson was also a member. In June 2008, while visiting Los Angeles, Sherrington met with Gorrell; the two had met many times before, and had become friends. That meeting, in the Century City Plaza Hotel, was the first time the prospect of combining the two firms was raised.

In mid-July, Gorrell and Prentiss Feagles travelled to London to meet with Sherrington and David Harris for a day. The consensus after the meeting was that the idea was worth exploring in greater detail, with the first focus being on gaining a better understanding of the two firms' respective practices and the likely opportunities to expand those practices.

It is in the nature of such discussions that they need to be kept highly confidential and restricted to a very small number of partners. In mid-August, Harris, Sherrington, the Lovells practice stream leaders and several corporate partners flew to Washington, D.C. to spend a day with Gorrell, Feagles, Immelt, and other members of Hogan & Hartson's Executive Committee. Those early discussions naturally focused on business and clients, to ensure that the strategic rationale for a combination made sense, and the firm's initial due diligence tested the rationale for a merger and key challenges to pulling it off. All of the information and the work at that point were kept to a small number of the firms' leaders.

It was clear following that meeting in Washington, D.C. that there was increasing mutual interest on the part of each firm to learn more about the other. In late September, Gorrell, Immelt, and Feagles flew to London to meet with Harris and Sherrington and to have dinner with some of the Lovells International Executive. Between the meeting in Washington in August and the meeting in London in September, however, the world financial system had reached the brink of collapse—Lehman Brothers had failed,

The combination talks took place against the backdrop of the world financial crisis in 2008.

Chapter 3 ■ Our Combination

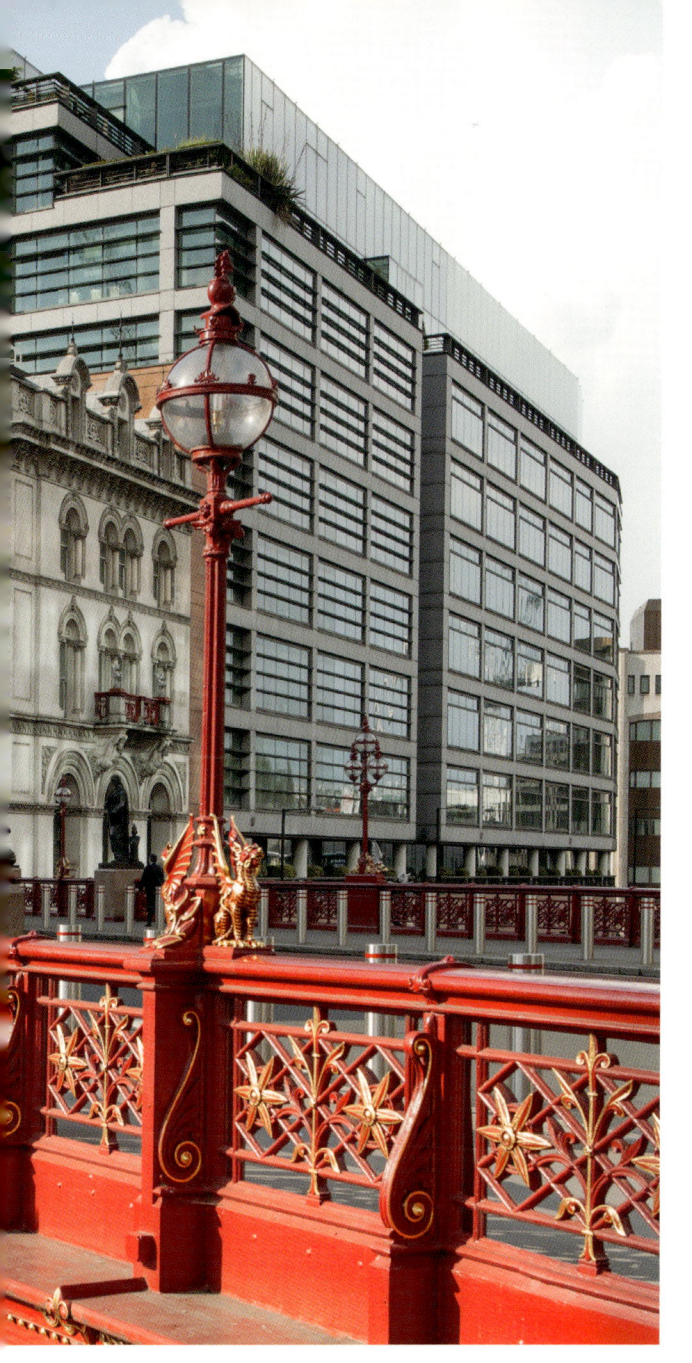

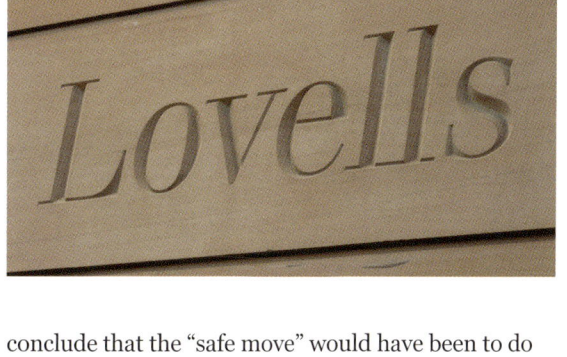

In 2002 Lovells moved to new premises in Atlantic House on Holborn Viaduct, a stone's throw from its first office in Snow Hill, which was established in 1899.

AIG had been effectively taken over by the U.S. government, and the UK and European banking authorities were struggling to deal with a number of financial institutions on the brink of failure. Thus, the September discussions took place in an atmosphere infused with the sense that the world in general—and the legal market in particular—was changing in ways that would be both profound and unpredictable.

In that September 2008 meeting, and throughout the discussions that ensued, the thought was voiced more than once that the massive changes in the world financial markets meant that maintaining the status quo might be as—or even more—risky than taking a bold step toward a combination. At the same time, it would have been easy for the leaders of both firms to conclude that the "safe move" would have been to do nothing. To their credit, however, Harris and Gorrell each saw that the "safe step" was not necessarily the best for their partners in the long term, and thus they agreed, with the support of the small teams involved in the discussions at the time, that it would be desirable to continue the discussion in the coming months.

Strategic Rationale

The rationale for combining the two firms was the simple equation of pairing strength with strength. Hogan & Hartson's revenue in 2008 was $916 million; Lovells' revenue for 2008–2009 was $881 million. The firms had similar levels of profitability. The combined firms would rank among the top ten globally by revenue, with a profile and standing commensurate with the scale of the practice. More importantly, if achieved, it would be the first merger of its kind, bringing together two high-quality firms of equal standing with real strength in all major markets. The proposition would also be distinctive: the combined firm would be a clear leader in the field of regulation and strongly placed in many regulated industry sectors; and it would have a market leading litigation practice, a strong global intellectual property practice and a global corporate and finance practice.

A merger would provide not only an enhanced scale but also a breadth and depth of capability in all of the key markets, repositioning the combined firm among the market leaders. With enhanced market standing and reputation, the firm would have a much stronger foundation for further development in key areas and access to a larger client base with international needs, creating significant cross-selling opportunities across the international practice.

To assist in assessing all of the prospective combination's complex strategic considerations, Lovells retained Peter Zeughauser of the Zeughauser

ABOVE: The upper floors of Atlantic House afford splendid views over the City of London.

Group and Hogan & Hartson retained Tony Williams of Jomati Consultants. Both firms were asked to assess the position of the other firm in its markets and the impact of combining the firms.

The consultants' analysis confirmed the firms' assessments: this was a strong match. Both management teams concluded after their analysis that this was something worth pursuing further. The team was expanded and meetings of practice heads from each firm began. Project Oak was born, with Lovells known as "Redwood" and Hogan & Hartson as "Cherry" throughout.

The Difficult Bits

The two firms now began serious discussions. Warren Gorrell and Prentiss Feagles led the Hogan & Hartson team and David Harris, John Young, and Patrick Sherrington headed up the team from Lovells. The talks were briefly suspended, however, while Harris fought and won a contested election for his role as Managing Partner of Lovells. On resumption, the teams completed detailed due diligence on each other's practices, clients, and finances. Potential client conflicts were identified, both with respect to legal conflicts and client business sensitivities about the firm acting for industry competitors. Given the firms' tens of thousands of clients, a number of potential conflicts were to be expected; the actual number was fewer than might have been anticipated. Nonetheless, at the appropriate time, some delicate discussions would be required with a number of clients and some clients and matters would have to be given up. There were no conflict issues, however, that were significant enough to derail the potential merger.

The firms' due diligence led into negotiations on key points. The necessity to reflect the "one firm" approach desired by both parties and the need to be "fair to everyone" were considered as prerequisites for the financial arrangements relating to the proposed merger. The firms worked closely to develop a compensation system that would work globally from the two quite different systems used by Hogan & Hartson and Lovells, as well as to overcome the complicated tax and associated cash issues arising from the change of accounting basis that make a true transatlantic merger of firms of comparable size difficult to achieve.

The teams looked at profitability trends over the previous five years. An important aspect, as with virtually all U.S. firms, was that Hogan & Hartson accounted on a cash basis with a calendar year-end, while Lovells, typical of UK-headquartered firms, accounted on an accruals basis with an April year-end. Hogan & Hartson aligned its accounts to be on the same accrual basis as those of Lovells; Lovells aligned its accounts to the calendar year, and the U.S. dollar was adopted as the common currency. The adjusted accounts enabled the teams to consider the relative performance of the two firms and would form the basis for a deal.

Simultaneously, the teams worked on how the firms could be integrated financially. This involved creating a tax-efficient but practical structure, as well as developing a means of bringing the compensation systems together and addressing other differences arising from issues such as pension liabilities.

On compensation, the two firms' systems were quite different; Lovells had a "modified lockstep" system denominated in sterling and Hogan & Hartson had a contribution-based system denominated in U.S. dollars. Although a change for Lovells partners, Hogan & Hartson's system was far more closely aligned to Lovells than the system operated by many other U.S. firms, due to both firms' similar philosophies and approach. For Lovells, it was also the further evolution of a compensation system that had already commenced changing in order to give greater flexibility in rewarding strong contributors and recruit key lateral hires; Harris and the Lovells leaders were clear that the compensation system would continue to evolve even without a combination with Hogan & Hartson. Based upon a wide range of factors, including historical profitability trends and expected business production, the parties agreed to a merger coefficient by which Lovells "points" and Hogan & Hartson "shares" would be converted into Hogan Lovells "units," thereby creating a common global distribution mechanism for all equity partners. The firms developed a graduated approach to ease the transition and build confidence among the Lovells partners, with the goal being to complete that transition over a period of several years.

A currency coefficient was designed to mitigate the effect of currency movements on partner earnings to the greatest possible extent. This recognized that some 45 percent of the equity partners in the combined firm would be U.S. dollar-based, with the remainder almost equally split between euros and British pounds.

Next was the critical question of governance; much effort was put into structuring the leadership and management of the combined firm. It was agreed early on that responsibility for the management of the firm would rest with a CEO and an International Management Committee (IMC) to lead and drive the new combined firm forward. Warren Gorrell and David Harris were selected to serve as the initial Co-CEOs; the initial IMC comprised Harris and Gorrell, as well as the eight leaders of the combined firm's five practice groups, its five Regional Managing Partners and its co-heads of finance.

It also was agreed that a Board, elected by the partners, would have a supervisory oversight role on behalf of the partners with respect to both the Co-CEOs and the IMC. John Young and Claudette Christian would become the initial Co-Chairs of the firm. Unlike with Lovells, however, future Board Chairs and CEOs would not be elected by the partners it being felt that, in some cases, such elections could be divisive. Instead, the Board, after an extensive consultation process with the partners, would designate a proposed Board Chair or CEO and the partners would be asked to vote to ratify that designation. In the end, the overall governance structure was drawn from the quite different governance structures that Lovells and Hogan & Hartson had, in effect creating a "new Hogan Lovells" governance structure taken from the better elements of each firm.

ABOVE: David Harris (left) and Warren Gorrell.

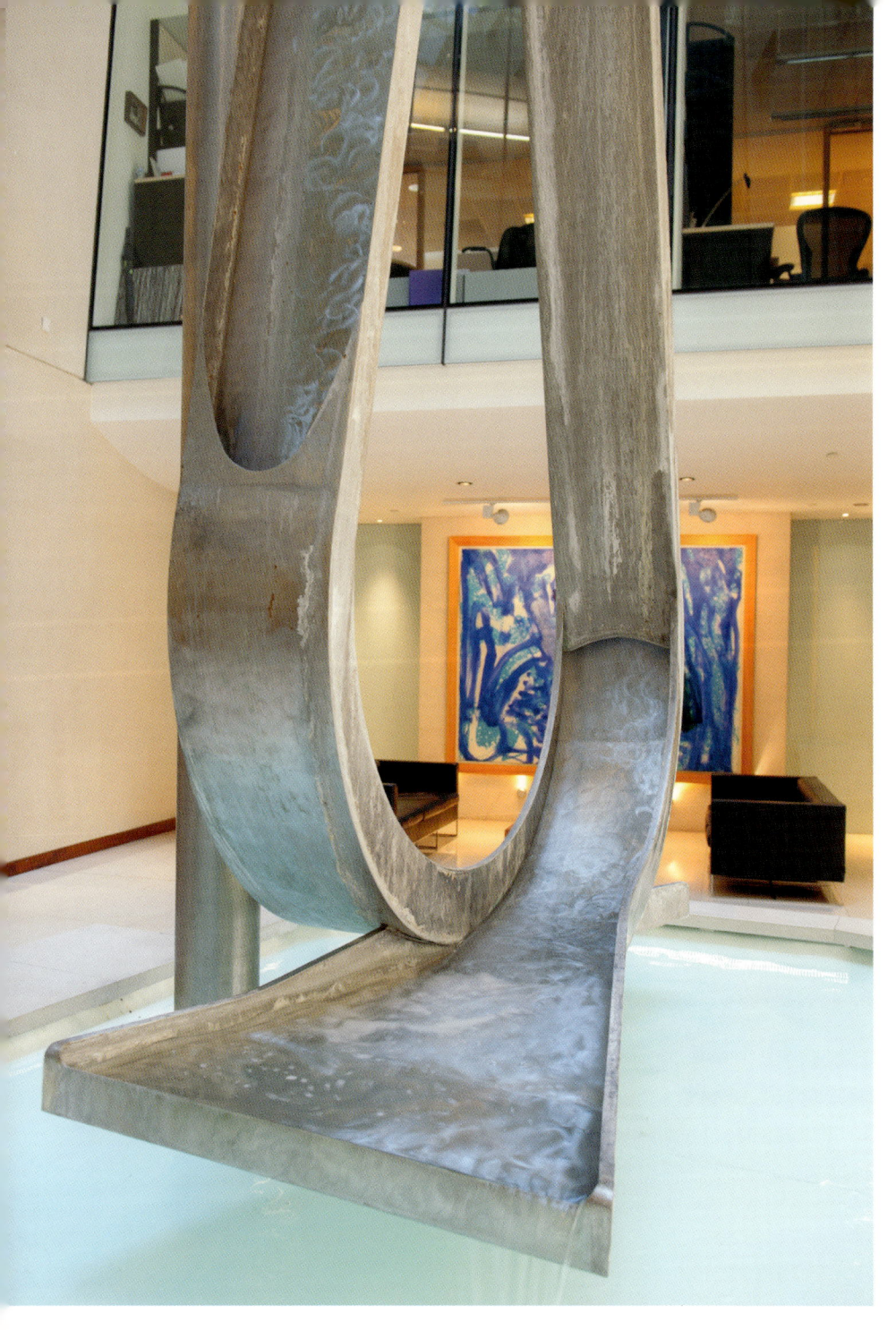

LEFT: The main reception at Atlantic House with the water sculpture, "Libra", by Angela O'Connor. Prentiss Feagles and Warren Gorrell of Hogan & Hartson signed in at reception under the aliases of "Mr. Marks" and "Mr. Spencer" during the combination negotiations in 2008.

BELOW: The distinctive "lime green" box of Lovells was adopted by the combined firm of Hogan Lovells for brand identification.

markets. The discussions were at a stalemate until Gorrell became intrigued by the unique Lovells "lime green box," which led him to propose putting the Hogan name first and adopting "the box" for brand identification. The agreed approach was that the new firm should be called Hogan Lovells, with the visual identity and brand style reflecting that used by Lovells—an approach that was received well by partners in both firms as well as the market.

As with any major transaction, the terms of the deal required formal agreements. This also involved the preparation of new partnership documents and a "deal report" for distribution to all of the partners to explain the deal and its rationale. Jim Rosenhauer, Todd Miller, and Don Kelly, working with the principals on each side, carried the primary burden of drafting documents to implement the transaction, a task made particularly challenging by the knowledge that their work product would be scrutinized by hundreds of legal experts.

The management team recognized that there were a number of potential risks in relation to any proposal of this type, including the potential failure to persuade the partnerships to vote for a merger, the potential loss of clients or partners, and the potential inability to

The name and branding of the combined firm naturally occupied a prominent place in the discussions. Both firms enjoyed strong name recognition and associated reputational strength in their major markets, and there was considerable attachment internally within both firms to their names. So, should Hogan or Lovells come first? Recognizing this attachment and the natural desire by both firms to feature prominently in the branding of the merged firm, both parties were clear that the decision must be guided by what was best for the new firm from a business perspective across its different deliver on the strategic objectives, and the insufficient integration of the firms once combined. Much time was spent identifying and mitigating these key risks before the proposal was put to the partnerships. Confidentiality remained a key consideration during this entire delicate process, both inside the two firms and externally. When visiting London, Gorrell and Feagles were asked by Lovells to use aliases when signing into Atlantic House. (Feagles was "Mr. Marks" and Gorrell was "Mr. Spencer.") And once when visiting Washington, D.C., the Lovells team had to hide in Dulles International Airport to avoid being spotted by clients who were, coincidentally, on the same flight. Amazingly, despite these close calls, the deal was kept confidential until the time was right.

The Partnerships Decide

Whatever the firms' managements thought of the potential merger, it was ultimately for the two partnerships to decide—and both partnerships would require substantial majorities to vote for the combination for the deal to proceed.

After a long period of well-maintained confidentiality, the potential combination was made known to all partners, numbering some 800, in October 2009. Growing speculation and questions from the press made it necessary to finally brief the press.

Lovells was to hold its annual partnership conference in Lisbon in November 2009. The presentation to the partners would be critical in obtaining strong support for the combination, particularly one that entailed such a substantial change to the firm's compensation system.

Presentations to the Lovells partnership were made by the core deal team and Lovells' independent market advisor, Peter Zeughauser. Hogan & Hartson's management was invited to present at the conference; Gorrell, Feagles, Steve Immelt, Jeanne Archibald, Claudette Christian, Stuart Stein, and Dennis Tracey joined the conference in Lisbon. On arrival at the airport—and after all the discussions about the name and branding—the Lovells lime green logo shone out like a beacon for the Hogan & Hartson team as they searched for their taxi.

The presentations went well. The Hogan & Hartson team also realized that the Lovells partners knew how to party; Harris and Gorrell will go down in history for their striking karaoke duet of "Maggie May." When the Hogan & Hartson team left for the airport at 5 a.m., the karaoke was still going strong.

Hogan & Hartson, for its part, held partner meetings in each of its offices to discuss the rationale for and features of the proposed combination. Harris and Young, David Hudd, Andrew Skipper, Andreas von Falck, Susan Bright, and Marc Gottridge, along with Tony Williams of Jomati, travelled to the U.S. for question and answer sessions to give reassurance on critical points.

Both firms provided online deal packs, including a confidential information memorandum, for their partners before proceeding with the voting. By large majorities, both partnerships approved the combination of the two firms to form Hogan Lovells on 1 May 2010.

Lawyers from Lovells were briefed on the proposed combination with Hogan & Hartson at their partnership conference in Lisbon in 2009.

What's in a name?

Answer—a lot. The name and branding of the new firm was of crucial importance, both to the external market, where both firms enjoyed strong brand recognition, and internally where there was considerable attachment and history surrounding the names of Lovells and Hogan & Hartson. Long before the final choice of name was settled the firms' lawyers embarked on the huge task of protecting the trademarks and domains associated with potential names for the new firm.

Meanwhile, in the UK legal market *The Lawyer* had swiftly coined "Love Harts" as its preferred name for the firm following the announcement of the combination in 2009, running several articles about the new firm under this name and highlighting the potential risks if the trademark lawyers got it wrong in this "spoof" article published on April Fools' Day in 2010!

THE LAWYER

Hogan Lovells to rethink name over trademark issues

1 April 2010 | By Gavriel Hollander

The merger between Hogan & Hartson and Lovells has hit another snag after it emerged that the Hogan Lovells name has already been trademarked by a road haulage company in Nebraska.

The soon-to-be-merged firm could now face a costly litigation battle unless the name is changed.

It is understood that senior management at both firms are considering a number of alternative monikers including Love Harts, Love Hog and HoLo.

Hogan Lovells Haulage confirmed that it has instructed counsel to stop the transatlantic firm from using

Implementation and Integration

Nick Cray and Rob Johnston were working on a detailed plan that comprised thousands of tasks even before the vote took place so that the plan could be brought into action right after the vote was completed. The key objectives were that from 1 May 2010, the combined firm must appear as one new "firm" to clients, with the ability to provide continuation of client service being paramount. Members of the new firm in the same geographic region had to be able to collaborate easily on client work and projects and the degree of change introduced needed to be kept under control. In other words: not much of a challenge.

The implementation plan set up new management structures for the combined firm and created a special implementation committee. The plan defined key management structures and the membership of the main bodies. Practice groups and areas, industry sectors and regional practice teams were settled and client development and work generation initiatives progressed. The implementation plan also put in place the initial structure and management of the combined business services teams.

There were many necessary legal steps required to enable the firm to operate as Hogan Lovells in all jurisdictions from 1 May 2010. These included clearances from competition authorities and regulators, name changes, registrations with regulators and transfers of business, employment contracts, leases, software licences, operational supply contracts, and new signage, stationery, and business cards. A competition clearance was even required in Cyprus—where neither firm had ever actually had an office.

The finance team had to determine structures for each jurisdiction and complete tax-efficient business transfers; set a harmonized approach to pricing; and amend systems for time recording, billing, routine accounting transactions, and management reports. Banking and insurance arrangements also had to be amended to reflect the new combined firm. The finance, legal, and tax teams never underestimated the complexity of setting up and implementing the new structures.

With the help of Andreas Renck and David Taylor, the firms took steps to protect the trademarks and domains for a variety of potential names for the combined firm even while a number of name combinations were still under consideration. Ultimately, this led to hundreds of domain name registrations to protect the Hogan Lovells name.

As for technology, the ideal objective would have been to have everything combined into single-system platforms by 1 May—but that was clearly an impossible feat to accomplish in five months. However, some thirty-five work streams were established with the result that all systems were linked together in a way that everyone could produce documents and e-mails and have access to their historic documents and e-mails, even if they were moving between offices, legal entities, or technology networks. It was a prerequisite that all lawyers were able to record and bill their time easily. In addition, all new hoganlovells.com e-mail addresses were operational (with e-mails sent to historic addresses appropriately rerouted) and all externally facing systems had Hogan Lovells branding. Where two physical offices remained in the same city, high-quality technology links were set up and telephone systems in single cities were combined into a single switchboard.

Both firms had their own intranets and portals to obtain access to legal practice knowledge and general information. It was not possible to migrate to a single intranet, but both InterLovells and Channel H were made open to both organizations while the team built HLGlobal, the single global intranet introduced a year later.

Legal conflicts and material commercial conflicts were identified and resolved to the maximum extent possible prior to 1 May and a conflicts identification process was set up for the combined firm. The former task was a massive undertaking. Each firm had approximately 10,000 live clients, approximately 40,000 live matter files, and hundreds of thousands of closed files. Bill Ball and his team worked tirelessly with Sandy Mayo, Michael Seymour, and John Trotter to clarify the applicable rules, obtain necessary waivers, and facilitate some tough decisions.

In a stroke of unplanned but welcome serendipity, 1 May 2010 fell on a Saturday. Most of the detailed preparations for the big day had taken place already, during the frenetic activity of those five previous months. However, pen and ink still had their place: members of the senior management teams of both firms were up until after midnight on Friday 30 April signing and dating the copious documentation that would give the venture legal effect.

The London Research Team in front of the countdown clock in the reception of Atlantic House hours before Lovells and Hogan & Hartson combined on 1 May 2010.

Hogan Lovells ■ Our Story

ABOVE AND RIGHT: The combination took place on a Friday night and over the following weekend Hogan Lovells signage was installed around the world.

BELOW RIGHT: While the majority of the firm's signage reflects the combination, the firm's London roots can still be seen engraved on this manhole cover outside the office.

There were ten cities where both firms had offices; for those cities a joint premises team determined the best option for each location. Moves took place for the launch date in eight cities—Brussels, Hong Kong, London, Moscow, Munich, New York, Paris, and Tokyo. Hogan Lovells signage was put in place on all buildings globally over the weekend, involving over a thousand replacement signs. In a number of locations, the old signs were auctioned for charity. Signs were found in the most unexpected places—outside and inside buildings and adjacent to lift buttons in cities from Tokyo to Los Angeles. One or two proved resistant to change. For one thing, the Lovells name is engraved indelibly on a British Telecom manhole cover in the street outside Atlantic House in London. The most visible impact on the day of the combination itself was achieved due to the tireless activities of individuals worldwide armed with hammers, screwdrivers, and glue. On that day, the thousands of Lovells and Hogan & Hartson signs were replaced in over forty offices in more than twenty countries worldwide.

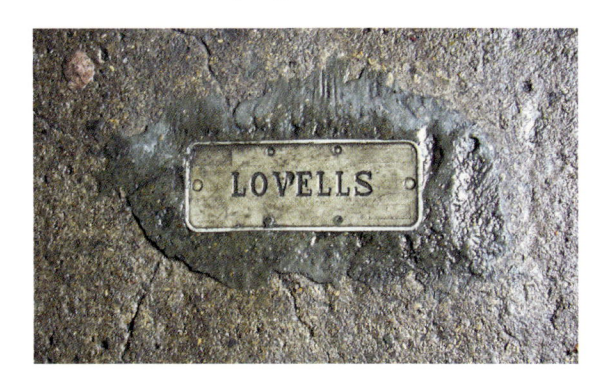

On Monday 3 May, the former members of Lovells and Hogan & Hartson entered their rebranded offices to visibly find that they had become members of one of the largest legal practices in the world. The implementation project had been a great exercise in teamwork across the business services teams, dependent on many people and many areas. The changes were very significant and complex and the results of the immense implementation effort showcased the quality and commitment of the business services teams and played a significant part in the successful birth of Hogan Lovells.

Chapter 3 ■ Our Combination

BELOW: Shortly after Lovells moved into Atlantic House, London, in 2002, a team of yellow plastic ducklings appeared in the water feature in the atrium. They are thought to have been introduced by a trainee lawyer. Since that time, new species of ducks have arrived overnight to coincide with major events in the life of the firm: the green duck to mark the combination of Hogan & Hartson and Lovells; red, white, and blue to celebrate the London Paralympics; and the "wooden" duck (shown here) for the five-year anniversary of Hogan Lovells. The tradition has spread to other offices, with a German duck sporting traditional legal wear of a hat, wig, and waistcoat, and in 2015, the Johannesburg office saw the arrival of the rare yellow beaded duck. The ducks have become collectors' items and can now be spotted in Hogan Lovells offices around the world.

The Combined Firm

The combination that formed Hogan Lovells created a unique proposition in the legal market: the first true transatlantic law firm merger based on a combination of equals, creating a truly high-quality, high-end global law firm. With turnover of around $1.7 billion, this catapulted the firm into becoming one of the world's top ten firms. The combined firm had over 2,500 lawyers with forty offices: seventeen in Europe, fourteen in the United States, six in Asia, two in the Middle East, and one in Latin America; 38 percent of its lawyers were in the Americas, 32 percent in Continental Europe, 21 percent in London, and 8 percent in Asia or the Middle East.

The firm had a high-quality client base, with a good balance across industries, including a strong presence in aerospace and defense; energy and utilities; finance; food and beverage; industrials; life sciences; media; professional services; real estate; transport; technology and electronic equipment; telecoms; and transport industries. And just as importantly, the combined firm had a common ethos that placed emphasis on clients, with excellence, commitment, teamwork, collegiality, and good citizenship as core values.

Hogan Lovells ■ Our Story

ABOVE: Keynote Speaker President Bill Clinton at the partnership conference in Toronto, 2014.

BELOW: Celebrating the firm's fifth anniversary in Hong Kong, June 2015. Patrick Sherrington (below right), Regional Managing Partner.

Looking Back

The creation of Hogan Lovells was a groundbreaking transaction; it influenced the reshaping of the market for legal services around the world. And in the five years following the combination, the firm continues to break new ground. Hogan Lovells now has a top ten global brand for legal services and has risen in the M&A rankings, has won significant new clients and deepened relationships with existing ones, and handled a range of cutting-edge work across all practices and offices—increasing profitability even during a time of market uncertainty.

And Hogan Lovells has not stood still. In just five years since the merger, the firm has opened in Ulaanbaatar, Mongolia; Rio de Janeiro; Luxembourg; São Paulo; Minneapolis; and Sydney and Perth in Australia. Hogan Lovells also completed further significant combinations with leading firms in two other countries; Barrera, Siqueiros y Torres Landa in Mexico City and Monterrey, Mexico, and Routledge Modise in Johannesburg, South Africa. In 2014, the firm also opened both a Global Business Services Centre in Johannesburg and a Legal Services Centre in Birmingham, England.

Chapter 3 ■ Our Combination

ABOVE: Nicholas Cheffings, Chair of Hogan Lovells, speaking at the partnership conference 2014.

LEFT: Steve Immelt, CEO, and David Hudd, Deputy CEO.

RIGHT: The Hogan Lovells big "5" decorated with photos sent in by members of the firm from around the world.

99

Hogan Lovells ■ Our Story

Mexico

Mexico, Latin America's second-largest economy, boasts an ever-growing industrial sector. Mexico's sweeping structural reforms in 2013, and increased client demand for expertise in Mexico, prompted Hogan Lovells to consider establishing a physical presence in the country. The firm had already developed a market-leading Latin America practice. In 2014, it looked for new opportunities to support its global clientele of multinational companies and financial institutions doing business in Mexico, as well as Mexican multinationals doing business in the U.S. and around the world. It found that opportunity with a leading Mexican firm, Barrera, Siqueiros y Torres Landa (BSTL).

BSTL opened in 1948 under the name Hidalgo, Barrera y Siqueiros, during one of the most significant periods of modernization in Mexico. Its founding partners were Eduardo Hidalgo, Jorge Barrera Graf and José Luis Siqueiros, all three of whom were dedicated to excellence in legal services focusing primarily on corporate law, as well as advising on foreign investment, technology transfer and labor relations.

Eduardo Hidalgo brought experience gained from his professional practice in the United States, his home country; indeed, after his retirement from the firm Hidalgo served as Secretary of the Navy during the Carter administration. Jorge Barrera Graf was at the time of the firm's formation already an established lawyer specializing in business law; within a short time he earned a strong reputation both professionally and in the academic field, becoming one of the most prominent legal scholars in Mexico. And José Luis Siqueiros, who completed his graduate work at Harvard, was a specialist in international law. He held key posts in the Mexican government, serving as the state secretary and later lieutenant governor for the state of Chihuahua. Siqueiros also actively represented Mexico at multinational forums on private international law.

After some years with the firm, at the beginning of the 1970s, Juan José Torres Landa was admitted as a new partner, bringing

The founding partners of BSTL Eduardo Hidalgo, Jorge Barrera Graf, and José Luis Siqueiros, were joined by Juan José Torres Landa.

enthusiasm and energy to face the new economic challenges in Mexico. He also continued to instil the firm's core values: professional and academic excellence, commitment to clients, and above all, moral and ethical principles in the practice of the legal profession. With this addition, the firm changed its name to Barrera, Siqueiros y Torres Landa, S.C., consolidating its reputation and sustained growth.

Over the years, the firm has consistently contributed to the development of Mexico through its participation in various aspects of legal development, including international trade, foreign investment, and regulation of multinationals and joint ventures. The firm's members have also participated in training generations of new lawyers. In July 2004, the firm opened its first office outside of Mexico City: in Monterrey, Nuevo León. In doing so, the firm recognized the need for services to be offered locally in the second most important economic hub in the country, ensuring the satisfaction of both current and future clients with operations in that part of Mexico.

In August 2014, Hogan Lovells combined with BSTL, becoming the first global legal practice to merge with a large, full-service firm in Mexico. Today, as Hogan Lovells BSTL, a large team of lawyers in Mexico City and Monterrey offers a full range of legal services to clients regardless of where they are operating in the country.

TOP LEFT: The ceremony to mark Hogan Lovells combining with Barrera, Siqueiros y Torres Landa (BSTL) in 2014.

TOP RIGHT: Hogan Lovells BSTL lawyers in the Mexico City office.

ABOVE: Hogan Lovells BSTL has offices in Mexico City (shown here) and Monterrey.

South Africa

Hogan Lovells had been active in Africa for some thirty years before associating with leading South African law firm Routledge Modise in December 2013. With this association, it now has a well-established office in Johannesburg, sub-Saharan Africa's most developed economic hub and the gateway into Africa for many international companies.

The firm that became Routledge Modise was founded in 1892 by William Frost, then a twenty-nine-year-old lawyer. Born in 1863, he commenced legal practice in 1887 in Pietermaritzburg, and in 1892 came to Johannesburg, only a couple of years after gold was first discovered in the Witwatersrand. William Routledge, a qualified Scottish solicitor, came to Johannesburg in 1897 and worked for Frost while qualifying himself as a Transvaal lawyer. In 1902, he became the third partner in the firm, after the conclusion of the second Anglo-Boer War. The firm's main areas of business at that time were registration and protection of mining claims, registration of titles to land, formation of businesses, partnerships, and new companies.

Routledge Modise's early partners witnessed the Jameson Raid, the First and Second Boer Wars, the introduction of English law to the Transvaal and the return of Roman Dutch law with the Union in 1910. By the turn of the last century its work had expanded to the flotation of public companies, stock exchange work, banking, and complex commercial agreements.

Just prior to World War II, Routledge was joined in the practice by his son, William Quentin Durward Routledge. When war broke out, and others joined up, Routledge Junior remained behind to run the firm.

Lavery Modise, a well-respected employment lawyer, joined the firm in 1998 and in 1999, Routledges, as it was then known, changed its name to Routledge Modise before going on to complete a series of small mergers in the early part of the twenty-first century. The firm joined Hogan Lovells in December 2013, completing its rebranding as Hogan Lovells (South Africa) in February 2014.

While the Johannesburg office still advises the mining sector today, Africa's transformation into one of the world's key emerging markets means that the team now provides the full services of a global legal practice, advising on cross-border and local matters on the ground in Africa.

The Johannesburg office is also home to the firm's Global Business Services Centre, which opened in the summer of 2014. This includes teams that carry out conflicts clearances, client due diligence, research, and billing; and teams that provide technology support to the firm and support the finance, people, and other business services functions.

LEFT: Lavery Modise (far left), with practice leaders and senior managers in the Johannesburg office of Hogan Lovells.

Chapter 3 ■ Our Combination

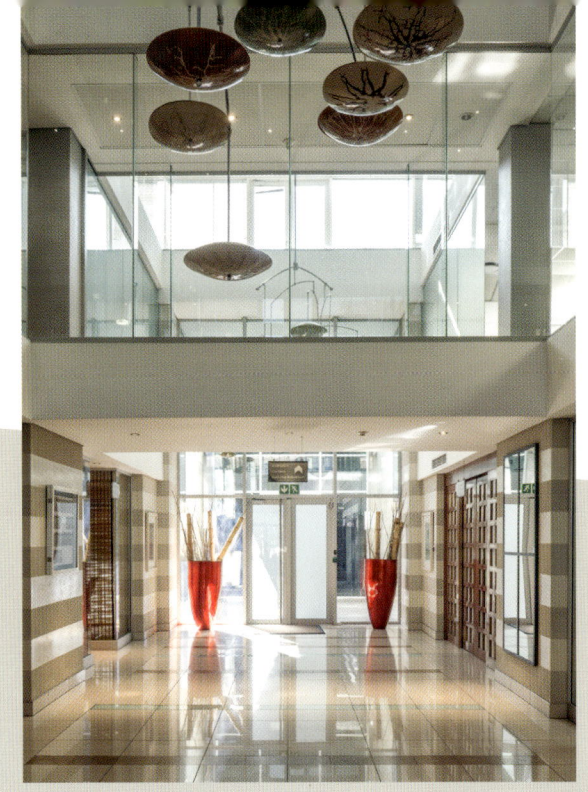

FAR LEFT: Members of the Global Business Services Centre Team.

LEFT AND BELOW: Interior and exterior of the Johannesburg office.

103

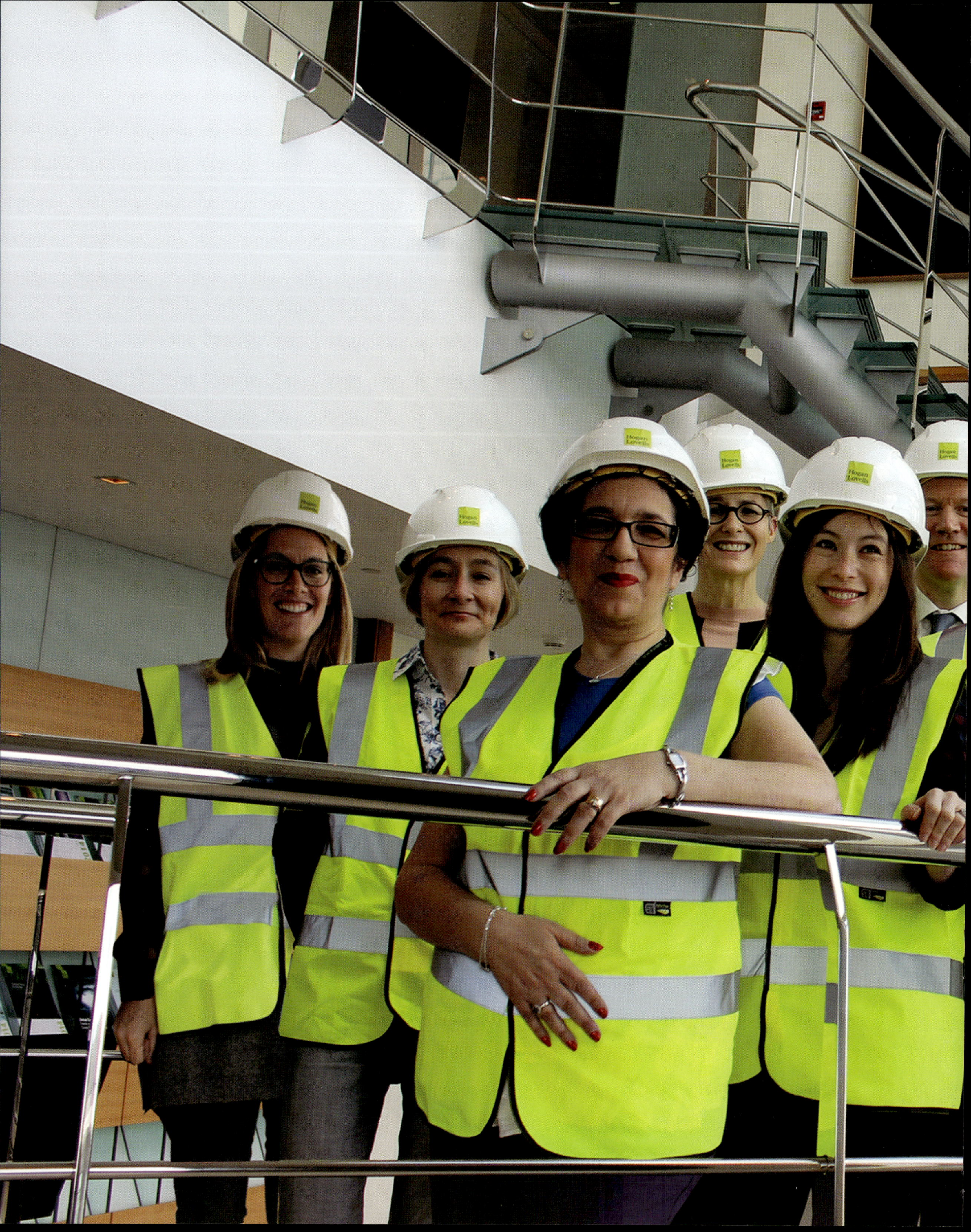
Hogan Lovells

Chapter 4

Our Business

Chapter 4
Our Business

PREVIOUS PAGES: The London Construction and Engineering team.

Over a century ago, Lovell & Broad opened its doors in London and Frank Hogan represented his first client in Washington, D.C.'s criminal court. Today more than 3,000 partners and other qualified lawyers, and approximately 500 trainees, specialists, paralegals, and other fee-earners support the Hogan Lovells five broad practice groups: corporate; finance; government regulatory; intellectual property, media and technology; and litigation, arbitration and employment (LAE). Practice areas within each of these groups have lawyers with specialized interests and experience. Almost 3,000 personal assistants and business services professionals support the firm's lawyers and other fee-earners.

The firm's lawyers are further organized into industry sector groups representing a span of industries: aerospace, defense, and government services; automotive; consumer; education; energy and natural resources; financial institutions; infrastructure; insurance; life sciences; real estate; sports and recreational facilities; and technology, media, and telecommunications. The sector groups connect lawyers across practice groups and offices to more efficiently and effectively serve clients in these industries.

Hogan Lovells has undertaken thousands of client representations. This book cannot cover them all. The handful of examples below show how lawyers in each of the five broad practice groups have embraced Hogan Lovells "one team" approach, to their clients' great benefit.

CORPORATE

The Hogan Lovells corporate practice group includes more than 800 lawyers across the globe—more than 250 are partners. The majority work on mergers and acquisitions, joint ventures, and equity capital markets. Others specialize in commercial law—counseling clients about contractual and regulatory issues, as well as complex outsourcing, partnership, strategic alliance, and other structures. Some work primarily in the real estate industry, supporting cross-border real estate transactions and real estate financing transactions, with significant focus on real estate investment trusts, and on the hotel and leisure industry. In addition to providing stand-alone tax advice, the group's tax lawyers team with other corporate lawyers to help plan and structure transactions and provide transactional tax advice. Their work also often extends well beyond the corporate group to project finance, employment, and litigation matters with tax implications.

By their nature, mergers and acquisitions are interdisciplinary endeavors; every takeover or asset disposal has regulatory, employment, antitrust, and/or tax implications. The Hogan Lovells M&A team therefore relies on the regulatory experience of colleagues to facilitate transactions in the highly regulated financial, energy, natural resources, technology, media, and telecommunications industries. The firm's lawyers provide regulatory advice alongside their colleagues in the corporate practice with regards to making investment decisions, and in relation to post-investment portfolio company management, growth strategies, and exit strategies.

In the past four years, the Hogan Lovells corporate team has advised on more than a thousand transactions globally with an aggregate value nearing $600 billion. Here are a few:

Dell

Late one Friday afternoon in August 2012, corporate partner Richard Parrino received an urgent phone call from the Austin, Texas, headquarters of Dell Inc., one of the world's largest computer companies. Dell's general counsel informed Parrino that Michael Dell, the company's iconic founder, largest stockholder, and chairman, had decided to try to "take the company private" by purchasing all company shares owned by public stockholders. The general counsel asked Hogan Lovells, the company's U.S. securities and corporate counsel since 2009, to advise the company's board of directors on the process it should follow in responding to Dell's proposal.

That call inaugurated a project that eventually involved more than a hundred Hogan Lovells lawyers and would culminate more than a year later with the completion of Dell's $24.9 billion "going-private" transaction in October 2013. Dell was the largest company—as measured by revenue—ever to have completed the transition from public to private ownership in a leveraged buyout.

The journey from that first call to the closing was filled with dramatic events that frequently generated press headlines. Protracted negotiations over the buyout terms were followed by acrimonious opposition to the announced transaction led by noted investor activist Carl Icahn that succeeded in thwarting stockholder approval of the original terms. Stockholders approved the transaction only after the buyout share price was increased and Chancellor Leo E. Strine Jr. of the Delaware Court of Chancery, in a memorable oral judgment rendered from the bench, permitted the revised transaction to proceed

Hogan Lovells acted for Michael Dell on Dell's transition from public to private ownership in 2013.

Katie Banks, relationship partner for Kodak Pension Plan, collecting the *Financial Times'* Most Innovative Law Firm in Corporate and Commercial Law award in 2014.

to a stockholder vote. Controversy did not cease with completion of the buyout: Stockholders dissatisfied with the final share price approved by the majority filed the largest judicial appraisal action in Delaware history. (The litigation is ongoing at the time of writing.)

From the small group of lawyers first tapped to work on the transaction, the Hogan Lovells team supporting Dell expanded across offices and practices over a period of fifteen months. Corporate and SEC lawyers in the Washington, D.C. and Northern Virginia offices advised Dell on the buyout negotiation process and documentation; Dell's public disclosures; a threatened proxy fight and other stockholder challenges to the announced transaction; Dell's $1.5 billion offering of notes to finance a portion of the buyout price; and an SEC-registered global tender offer for Dell employee securities. Members of the finance practice in New York and Hong Kong counseled Dell on credit and asset securitization arrangements negotiated as part of the $12 billion debt-financing package. Teams in Brussels and Beijing supported Dell in obtaining expedited antitrust clearance of the transaction in a number of European Community countries and China. Labor lawyers in Paris and banking specialists in Rome solved intricate regulatory problems raised by the transaction. Lawyers working in employee benefits, IP, government contracts, and other specialties in the firm's U.S. and international offices provided timely, tireless, and expert assistance.

Kodak Pension Plan

In another matter involving hundreds of Hogan Lovells lawyers, the pension group represented the trustees of the Kodak Pension Plan (KPP) when the KPP found itself amid a funding crisis.

Hogan Lovells had advised KPP for several decades. In 2004, KPP secured a guarantee from Eastman Kodak Company that it would be fully funded on an ongoing basis by 2015 and that all members would receive their pension benefits on time. Three years later, however, in the face of a growing funding deficit, KPP agreed to extend the timeline for full funding until 2022. Even with this extension, the promised payments were put in jeopardy in January 2012 when Eastman Kodak filed for bankruptcy.

Led by partner Katie Banks, a London-based pensions partner and relationship partner for KPP, and Chris Donoho, a New York-based business restructuring lawyer responsible for dealing with Eastman Kodak's bankruptcy, the effort to assert claims on behalf of KPP that arose from the Eastman Kodak guarantee eventually involved more than 300 lawyers from over twenty Hogan Lovells offices. KPP filed a claim for $2.8 billion, representing the cost of an insurance policy that would guarantee full payment to members, and became Eastman Kodak's biggest unsecured creditor by a factor of two.

Lawyers from the business restructuring and insolvency team then developed a strategy to position KPP's claim as structurally superior to those of other unsecured creditors. But Eastman Kodak's attempts to liquidate its assets, including its digital imaging and personalized imaging businesses, to satisfy its creditors delivered disappointing results. The Hogan Lovells team knew that if Eastman Kodak could not raise sufficient cash, the unsecured creditors would recover only a small percentage of their claims. They further recognized that KPP's likely recovery would not be enough to prevent the plan from being taken over by the UK Pension Protection Fund—an unattractive option that would have reduced some members' pensions significantly.

At this point, KPP trustees began wondering about the true value of Eastman Kodak's digital imaging and personalized imaging businesses. This in turn led to the formulation of a proposal that KPP acquire those two business units through a mixture of release of claims and $325 million in cash, on the theory that over time, those businesses could generate income sufficient to finance members' pension benefits.

KPP called on the advice of Hogan Lovells lawyers from multiple disciplines to formulate and execute this unusual proposal. Corporate lawyers advised KPP on the valuation of and due diligence on the business units to be purchased. They drafted complex agreements to separate the two business units—which operated in ninety jurisdictions—from Eastman Kodak. That effort proved particularly challenging because KPP had no corporate structure in which to host the two business units. Therefore, a global corporate holding company had to be established, complete with board members and all other corporate necessities.

In parallel with these efforts, the pensions team was negotiating with the UK pensions regulator and the Pension Protection Fund to convince them that the purchased business units would provide cash flows sufficient to deliver member benefits. Even with the business acquisition, however, KPP's ability to meet its full obligations was in doubt.

Hogan Lovells lawyers thus designed an innovative way to reduce the expected cost of benefits by more than £300 million. They did this by creating a new pension plan. Hogan Lovells lawyers aimed to ensure that the new plan was more attractive to members than benefits provided by the Pension Protection Fund, and also had to convince the Fund to take on the old plan, which would continue to serve any members who did not opt to join the new plan. They also needed to persuade a sufficient number of plan members to move to the new plan. Once the Hogan Lovells team accomplished the first two goals, the team toured Great Britain with their client, explaining the new plan to over 2,500 members in dozens of hours of presentations. The communication program proved convincing; more than 96 percent of KPP's members approved the new benefits.

The novel solution the Hogan Lovells team developed and implemented was significant for several reasons. First, by offering an attractive alternative to the reductions in benefits that otherwise would have occurred under the Pension Protection Fund, the Hogan Lovells team managed to reduce accrued pension rights in bulk—an industry first. Second, the KPP team was able to develop a proposal

A Kodak pensioner outside the company's U.S. headquarters in Rochester, New York. Hogan Lovells advised the trustees of the Kodak Pension Plan on settlement of their $2.8 billion claim against Eastman Kodak. The settlement involved the acquisition of two global businesses and the agreement of the majority of members to revised benefits.

that both benefited the pensioners, and delivered value to other constituencies in the bankruptcy case. Third, the extracted businesses, now called Kodak Alaris, have commenced profitable trading. And the transaction allowed Eastman Kodak to emerge from bankruptcy and restart successful trading.

General Electric

In April of 2015, Hogan Lovells advised General Electric (GE) in connection with its agreement to sell its global real estate equity and debt portfolio business to Blackstone Group and Wells Fargo & Company. The portfolio constituted approximately $27 billion worth of investments in commercial mortgage debt, office buildings, joint ventures, and other commercial property worldwide. The transaction was the largest in the real estate industry since Blackstone acquired Equity Office Properties Trust for $39 billion in 2007, and the second largest ever.

General Electric is one of the firm's largest clients.

This transaction was the critical first step in GE's plan to dispose of most of its financial services business to focus on its leading industrial businesses. GE expects that by 2018 more than 90 percent of its earnings will be generated by its high-return industrial businesses, up from 58 percent in 2014.

The transaction was enormously complex, involving more than 500 properties, seventy-five joint ventures and over $17 billion of commercial mortgage loans in the United States, United Kingdom, Germany, France, Spain, Italy, Poland, Canada, Mexico, and Australia. It had far and away more geographic diversity than any other M&A deal in the real estate industry and showcased the firm's leading high-end global practice in this area. Even more impressively, it was put together and negotiated in three weeks, which is unprecedented for a transaction as large and complex as this one.

Warren Gorrell, who led the team of more than seventy-five Hogan Lovells lawyers, was at the forefront of negotiations with Blackstone and its counsel, working closely with GE's in-house counsel and business leaders and a core team of Hogan Lovells partners (primarily Bruce Gilchrist and Prentiss Feagles) to solve the myriad issues that arose in the course of getting the deal done. GE set a firm deadline of 9 April in order for the deal's announcement to coincide with GE's announcement of its GE Capital disposition plan, and the Hogan Lovells team literally worked around the clock for days to deliver on time.

The closings occurred from May 2015 through the end of the calendar year. Special pricing mechanics were needed to address the different closing times and different asset types. Special arrangements also had to be negotiated to address French labor considerations and to afford GE the opportunity to sell the German assets and European joint venture

LEFT: The Hôtel George V in Paris is one of the many hotels owned by Kingdom Holding Company.

BELOW: HRH Prince Alwaleed Bin Talal hosted a dinner for HRH The Prince of Wales during his state visit to Riyadh in 2015. Mark Mazo from Hogan Lovells (left) is shown here with the two princes.

interests separately. Different arrangements had to be devised for the assets being acquired by Blackstone and those being acquired by Wells Fargo. And finally, various remedies were negotiated to address the consequences of a default by any party, including a $1.5 billion termination fee payable by Blackstone if it failed to meet the closing deadline.

Hogan Lovells has advised GE on M&A work for almost 15 years. Gorrell is one of a team of partners responsible for the firm's relationship with GE and has been responsible for earning GE's trust to work across all five practice groups and around the world. Mark Landis, GE's executive counsel for M&A, who quarterbacked the transaction from GE's legal side, is a former partner of Hogan Lovells who helped Gorrell start the New York office in 1998 when he was still an associate. Today GE is one of the firm's largest clients.

The Prince

The corporate team, along with finance and LAE partners, has a long history of working with HRH Prince Alwaleed Bin Talal Bin Abdulaziz Alsaud, a member of the Saudi Arabian royal family. Prince Alwaleed is a prominent international investor, along with his 95 percent-owned company, Kingdom Holding Company (KHC), which is listed on Tadawul, the Saudi Stock Exchange. Prince Alwaleed and KHC have extensive holdings in finance, media, hotels, and real estate.

Prince Alwaleed is a nephew of Saudi King Salman, a grandson of Abdulaziz Alsaud, the founder of modern Saudi Arabia, and a grandson of Riad Al Solh, Lebanon's first prime minister. Prince Alwaleed is ranked 14th on the Bloomberg listing of the world's richest people.

The Hogan Lovells team, led by relationship partners Mark Mazo and Jim Rosenhauer, with extensive involvement by many others in the firm such as Bruce Gilchrist, Nancy O'Neil, Todd Miller, and Bruce Parmley, has provided corporate, finance, and private-equity counsel relating to numerous of Prince Alwaleed's investments since the early 1990s. The firm's first major transaction for Prince Alwaleed was a $590 million investment in Citicorp

Hogan Lovells ■ Our Story

(later Citigroup), making him the bank's largest shareholder and catapulting him into the global spotlight. Subsequent investments led by the Hogan & Hartson team included his 1994 investment in Disneyland Paris (EuroDisney)—KHC is the second largest shareholder in EuroDisney behind The Walt Disney Company. Extensive investments in the hotel industry include the Hôtel George V in Paris; the Plaza Hotel in New York; the Savoy in London; and interests in the Four Seasons Hotel Management Company (jointly owned by Bill Gates' Cascade investment vehicle).

The Hogan Lovells combination and the enhanced global capabilities that followed have enabled Hogan Lovells to support KHC even more. In 2011, for example, a team of transactional lawyers based in Washington, D.C. and London represented KHC in its $300 million investment in Twitter. Two years later, a team of lawyers from Beijing, London, and Washington, D.C. helped Prince Alwaleed, KHC, and a consortium of investors acquire a $400 million interest in JD.com, one of the largest online retailers in China. More recently, a corporate team in Madrid represented an African investment fund managed by KHC in the sale of a company with extensive investments in Africa.

Prince Alwaleed and the KHC team also rely on Hogan Lovells lawyers in Paris, where Prince Alwaleed spends significant time and holds considerable investments. A Paris, Dubai, and Washington team recently advised Prince Alwaleed in connection with a $150 million investment in KHC by the French state and seven major French corporations, the first significant foreign investment in a publicly traded Saudi company. The global client team regularly takes advantage of the firm's worldwide capabilities by moving documents across time zones to drive deals forward and deliver revised documents by sunup wherever the deal is being negotiated.

FINANCE

Over 300 Hogan Lovells lawyers around the world primarily advise financial institutions, funds, and large corporate clients on complex banking and finance transactions. This practice includes work on project finance, international banking, business restructuring and insolvency (BRI), and international debt capital markets matters. And, as exemplified by the Hogan Lovells representation of the Kodak Pension Plan and Kingdom Holding Company, finance lawyers regularly work alongside corporate lawyers and litigators to guide clients through complex deals and disputes.

Shah Deniz

The firm's project finance practice is particularly known for its work in the infrastructure, energy, and natural resources sectors, including oil and gas, liquefied natural gas, nuclear, renewable energy, and conventional power projects. It is also one of the largest project finance practices in the European market—as exemplified by its representation of the Shah Deniz consortium (BP SOCAR, Statoil, Total, Lukoil, NICO, and TPAO) on projects involving a total investment of $45 billion. The Hogan Lovells team was able to build on existing relationships with both BP and Statoil to win this highly sought-after engagement in 2010.

The vast Shah Deniz project will result in more than 3,500km of pipelines opening a new southern gas corridor between Europe and one of the world's largest gas fields in the Caspian Sea off the coast of Azerbaijan. Several pipeline joint ventures will triple the transportation capacity of the Southern Caucasus

Hogan Lovells has acted for the Shah Deniz consortium since 2010, building on previous relationships with BP and Statoil. Representatives of the consortium sign an agreement in Baku, Azerbaijan, December 2013.

Pipeline, which currently transports gas from the Shah Deniz gas field to Turkey; construct the Trans-Anatolian Pipeline (TANAP) across Turkey; and construct the Trans-Adriatic Pipeline, which will connect to TANAP and extend across Greece and Albania and into Italy.

The Final Investment Decision—a public declaration that the project would go forward— also committed the Shah Deniz consortium of gas producers to significantly expand upstream production and to enter into long-term gas sales contracts with Turkey's state-owned oil and gas company, BOTAS, and nine other European gas buyers. In order to facilitate this expanded production, the consortium committed to the construction of two additional bridge-linked offshore gas platforms and undersea wells and to expand a gas processing plant near Baku, the capital of Azerbaijan.

The Hogan Lovells team led by Richard Tyler in London—with significant assistance from David Moss, Ben Sulaiman, Elisabeth Blunsdon, Matteo Matteucci, Janet Duff, and specialists in Brussels, Hamburg, and Rome—coordinated four interrelated projects across seven jurisdictions. Their work included negotiating long-term gas sales contracts with Turkish and EU buyers and the long-term gas transportation contracts that underpin the Shah Deniz gas value chain. The corporate team also advised the consortium on the structure and governance arrangements for the pipeline and gas marketing joint venture vehicles. Meanwhile, regulatory lawyers advised the consortium on third party access exemption issues, competition issues, compliance with EU and Italian regulations, and issues relating to Iran sanctions due to the participation of NICO, a Swiss-based Iranian oil company.

The team's work culminated with the signing of the Final Investment Decision in December 2013, which involved more than 1,600 signatures. Ilham Aliyev, President of the Republic of Azerbaijan, attended the signing ceremony, joined by leaders from Turkey, Italy, Greece, Bulgaria, the UK, and the U.S. ambassador to Azerbaijan. Following execution of the Final Investment Decision, implementation work continues. The Hogan Lovells team is now drafting the operations agreements necessary to make the gas value chain work at a detailed level. Gas is due to begin flowing to Turkey in the fourth quarter of 2018 and to the European Union in the first quarter of 2020.

The Shah Deniz project is of great significance to both Azerbaijan and the European Union. For Azerbaijan, the project provides a way to monetize the country's gas reserves for decades to come, spurring wider economic development. For the EU, the project opens a new gas supply region and will reduce Europe's dependence on Russian and Algerian gas imports.

Many have noted the complexity of the deal including President Ilham Aliyev, who described the Final Investment Decision as "the contract of the twenty-first century." BP's CEO, Bob Dudley, commented that the two pipeline projects "together represent one of the largest and most complex endeavours yet undertaken by the global oil and gas industry." The firm's work on this matter has also been recognized by the legal community: Among other laurels, Hogan Lovells was named "Law Firm of the Year" at the European Gas Awards in January 2015 and was named as "Energy and Infrastructure Law Firm of the Year" at the *Legal Business* Awards in March 2015.

A team from Hogan Lovells has worked on the financing of the Coca Codo Sinclair hydroelectric project in Ecuador. Pictured here is Ecuadorian Vice President Jorge Glas (center), with Coca Codo employees in April 2015.

Ecuador

Across the globe, another Hogan Lovells team led by Miguel Zaldivar has acted for the Ministry of Finance of the Republic of Ecuador in securing a series of credit agreements from the Export-Import Bank of China, the China Development Bank, and the Bank of China (BOC). These agreements have secured approximately $10 billion since 2010 for Ecuador's infrastructure projects.

The Hogan Lovells team first secured an initial credit agreement in June 2010 from the Export-Import Bank of China for the development of the Coca Codo Sinclair 1,500 MW hydroelectric generation facility—the largest infrastructure project in the history of Ecuador. At an earlier point in the negotiations, however, the nations appeared to be unable to close this financing, and serious diplomatic tensions arose between the People's Republic of China and Ecuador. The impasse was resolved, and the transaction closed, after a Hogan Lovells team developed an innovative credit loan structure that both complied with Ecuador's complex legislation and constitutional restrictions and met the equally complex borrowing requirements of the Chinese sovereign lender.

Currently under construction, the Coca Codo Sinclair project is expected to supply over 40 percent of Ecuador's electricity needs. And, perhaps even more significantly, Coca Codo marked the beginning of economic relations between the People's Republic of China and Ecuador, which has led to billions of dollars in financings and investments. These transactions are a central piece of Ecuador's plan to become more energy independent and move from fossil fuels to renewable hydroelectric energy.

The innovative lending structure that bridged the gap between Ecuador and China also facilitated numerous subsequent credit agreements between the Republic of Ecuador and Chinese financial institutions, including a 2011 loan for approximately $2 billion that Ecuador has used to develop its oil exploration and production capabilities. Additional loans have followed as well: a $509 million facility agreement for the construction of transmission lines to connect to the Coca Coda Sinclair hydroelectric plant; two agreements, one for $313 million and another for $571 million, for the construction of two additional hydroelectric generation facilities in Ecuador; and a $85 million concessional loan agreement to finance the extension of the Simon Bolivar Highway connecting Ecuador's capital city of Quito to the newly opened Mariscal Sucre International Airport.

The Hogan Lovells team, which is led from Miami and relies on significant contributions from lawyers in Beijing and Washington, D.C., has also advised on engineering, procurement, and construction contracts for some of these projects. And as a result of the extensive work on China-Ecuador transactions, Chinese financial institutions and investors have included Hogan Lovells as a panel firm for complex cross-border financing transactions. The long list of complex China-Ecuador transactions has also enabled Hogan Lovells to secure similar engagements in other jurisdictions throughout the Americas, including Costa Rica, Honduras, and Venezuela.

GOVERNMENT REGULATORY

The firm's government regulatory practice group consists of over 300 lawyers, more than 130 of them partners. Lawyers in the regulatory practice have developed deep experience and knowledge in seventeen different areas: antitrust, competition and economic regulation (ACER); aviation; communications; education; energy; environmental; U.S. Food and Drug Administration (FDA)/food and agriculture; FDA/medical devices; FDA/pharmaceuticals and biotechnology; global policy advocacy; government contracts; health; immigration; international trade and investment; legislation and political law compliance; privacy information and management; UK and EU public law and policy.

These lawyers, many based in Washington, D.C., maintain relationships with agencies that regulate these business sectors and closely monitor regulatory developments on behalf of their clients. They also advise clients who must respond to inquiries from government regulators. The vast majority of their work is confidential and thus cannot be discussed in detail here. However, the firm's quiet representation of clients in need of regulatory compliance advice significantly shapes the firm's client base. For example, the firm's expansive regulatory practice in the life sciences supports and fosters numerous litigation and corporate matters representing clients in the life sciences industry.

IBM Chairman, President and CEO, Ginni Rometty, February 2015.

IBM

The ACER group is one of the largest antitrust practices in the world. More than 130 ACER attorneys in fifteen countries represent clients in investigations relating to alleged cartels, abuse of dominance, and restrictive practices. The group represents clients in investigations conducted by the European Commission, U.S. federal and state agencies, and other national antitrust or competition authorities. The ACER group also routinely assists clients in developing and implementing strategies for clearing (or challenging) multijurisdictional and domestic acquisitions, disposals, and joint ventures.

The ACER group has handled numerous matters for IBM over the years. In the late 1990s, for example, it represented IBM in the *United States v. Microsoft Corporation* antitrust case, and subsequently helped IBM secure a $850 million

Hogan Lovells ◼ Our Story

Hogan Lovells represented IBM in the *United States v. Microsoft Corporation* antitrust case. Shown here are people collecting copies of the ruling against Microsoft in Washington, D.C., 3 April 2000.

settlement from Microsoft. Jan McDavid assumed the role of relationship partner for IBM in 2007. The Hogan Lovells combination deepened the relationship between the firm and IBM, with Hogan Lovells advising IBM in offices across the U.S., Europe, Latin America, Asia, and Africa.

IBM recently called on the Hogan Lovells ACER team to secure a multijurisdictional antitrust clearance for a $2.3 billion transaction conveying IBM's x86 server business to Lenovo, a Chinese technology firm. This required securing antitrust approvals in fifteen jurisdictions: the United States, the European Union, South Africa, China, Brazil, Canada, India, Israel, Japan, Korea, Mexico, Colombia, Taiwan, Argentina, and Turkey.

Hogan Lovells lawyers in Washington, D.C. and New York took the lead providing strategic advice about the antitrust risks in several potential deals. Once IBM decided to sell to Lenovo, ACER lawyers across the globe coordinated multiple merger filings. The U.S. team worked on the U.S. merger approvals and with the Brussels team handled the filings with the European Commission and coordinated filings in all jurisdictions. A Beijing-based team orchestrated the filing with China's Ministry of Commerce. Finally, lawyers in the Hogan Lovells Johannesburg office coordinated all necessary filings in Africa, a region of strategic importance to IBM.

The deal, announced in January 2014 and closed in October 2014, was the largest technology deal ever in China and involved the largest and fastest-growing server architecture in the industry.

The relationship between Hogan Lovells and IBM extends beyond ACER's work. Hogan Lovells lawyers advise IBM on government investigations, government contracts, and commercial litigation. The two firms have also partnered on pro bono matters, including work for Pro Bono Partnership, which provides business and transactional legal services to nonprofit organizations. The two legal teams have also joined forces to provide pro bono assistance to Shelter Box U.S.A., which provides emergency shelter and vital supplies to support communities around the world overwhelmed by disaster and humanitarian crises.

Emirates

A Hogan Lovells team led by the international trade and investment and the aviation practice areas, as well as several additional lawyers covering discrete

Chapter 4 ■ Our Business

LEFT: Hogan Lovells and IBM legal teams work jointly to provide pro bono support for Shelter Box U.S.A. The charity sends emergency shelter and vital supplies to communities around the world overwhelmed by disaster and humanitarian crises.

BELOW: Hogan Lovells acts for Emirates, one of the fastest-growing airlines in the world, serving 144 cities in eighty-one countries from its hub in Dubai. Sir Tim Clark, President of Emirates is shown here at a press conference in 2015.

issues, has been engaged to represent the Emirates airline in the largest subsidy and aviation rules dispute of 2015. The Big Three U.S. airlines—Delta, American, and United ("legacy carriers")—alleged in a public white paper that Emirates received several billion dollars in government subsidies that enabled the airline to compete unfairly against the legacy carriers. The three U.S. airlines have made additional allegations against two other Middle Eastern airlines: Etihad and Qatar Airways. The legacy carriers are urging the U.S. government to break its treaty commitments, withdraw the U.S. promise of Open Skies with the UAE and Qatar, unilaterally restrict the Gulf carriers' landing rights in the U.S., and renegotiate aviation agreements that have led to better service and more options for airline customers over the last two decades.

Emirates retained Hogan Lovells to address several legal, economic, and political issues raised by the dispute, with Emirates President Tim Clark, asking Hogan Lovells to work with the Emirates internal team to produce a "sledgehammer" public response to the legacy carriers' allegations. The Hogan Lovells team was asked to demonstrate that the subsidy allegations against Emirates were false, and that the effect of following the course urged by the legacy carriers would be bad for U.S. consumers, U.S. jobs, and the U.S. economy. Hogan Lovells is also assisting Emirates in calling attention to the fact that the rapid growth of Emirates, which now carries more international passengers than any other airline in the world, is due to its thriving business model and superb world-class customer service.

This effort relied on contributions from Hogan Lovells lawyers in the international trade and investment, aviation, legislation, global policy advocacy, media litigation, and antitrust practice groups. The Hogan Lovells team is led by Deen Kaplan, with Robert Cohn guiding the aviation law aspects of the representation.

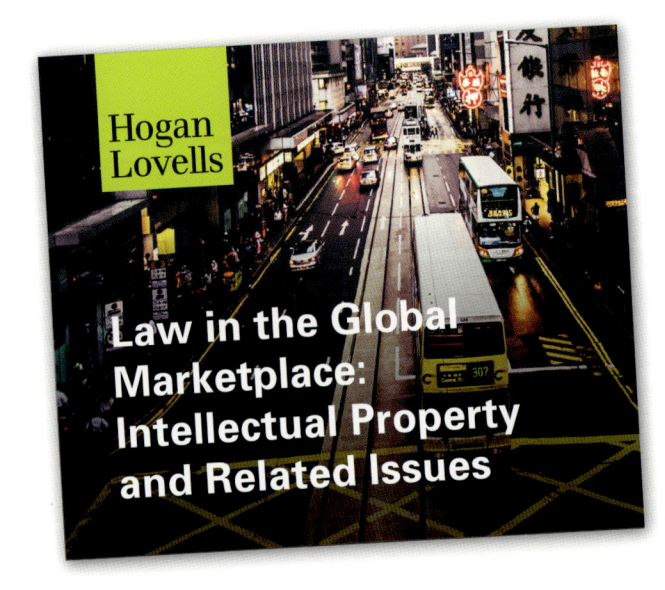

INTELLECTUAL PROPERTY, MEDIA AND TECHNOLOGY

With approximately 300 lawyers across the Americas, Europe, and Asia, the Hogan Lovells intellectual property (IP) group is known for handling complex cross-border patent and trademark disputes—primarily within the life sciences and the technology, media, and telecommunications sectors on the patent side, and in a range of industries including life sciences and technology; media and telecommunications; consumer goods; and financial services on the trademark side. Global brand owners like LEGO and Adidas turn to Hogan Lovells to help manage their global or regional trademark portfolios. The broad geographic reach of the Hogan Lovells IP team is also essential in assisting clients in protecting their trade secrets around the world.

Hogan Lovells lawyers celebrate winning the IP Global Firm of the Year award in 2012. The firm was recognized for its work in all areas of intellectual property.

HTC

The Hogan Lovells IP team recently worked throughout Europe and Japan to successfully handle one of the largest patent litigation matters on record. Mobile and smartphone company HTC engaged a team led by Martin Chakraborty in Dusseldorf to handle a series of related patent suits brought against HTC by a competitor, Nokia. Nokia alleged that several HTC phones infringed Nokia patents protecting certain of its antenna-design and mobile-payment technologies.

Nokia launched patent infringement actions against HTC in Germany, the U.S., and at the International Trade Commission, and followed these up with patent infringement actions against HTC in Italy, France, the Netherlands, and Japan. Asserting that HTC phones infringed over forty patents, Nokia sought to ban sales of HTC devices including HTC's flagship smartphone, the HTC One.

Led by Paul Brown and Stephen Bennett, HTC's London-based Hogan Lovells team—lawyers specializing in patent law as well as the non-patent issues involved in the case such as licensing, competition, and arbitration—handled all of the actions against HTC in Europe and Japan. The team also challenged Nokia's patent portfolio in the English High Court and the German Federal Patent Court, in the largest series of infringement and validity actions ever filed in the German courts and the English Patents Court diary.

The team developed a multi-part global strategy in response to the Nokia actions that comprised of: identifying ways to use jurisdictional differences to HTC's advantage; developing a licensing defence; asserting certain competition-law defences; challenging the courts' jurisdiction based on the fact that the same issues were concurrently being

LEFT: Hogan Lovells acted for HTC in a series of complex cases brought by Nokia. Nokia sought to ban sales of HTC's flagship smartphone, the HTC One. In the year of its launch, 2013, the HTC One sold over 6.4 million units.

BELOW: Hogan Lovells lawyers worked with Eli Lilly to protect Zyprexa®, its medication to treat schizophrenia, against generic versions.

addressed through arbitration; challenging the appropriateness of injunctive relief; and using third-party disclosures available under the U.S. Federal Rules of Civil Procedure to obtain otherwise unavailable documents and other evidence from opponents. The HTC team also developed a system to communicate across multiple jurisdictions to leverage findings from courts in other countries.

Success in Europe was crucial to HTC for two reasons. First, if Nokia had been successful in establishing patent infringement, HTC would have been prevented from selling any product in its crucial European markets. And second, similar cases against HTC were also pending in the U.S., meaning the outcome of the European litigation had implications for that litigation as well.

The team's work culminated in spending more than fifty days in various courts throughout Europe. The upshot: Nokia did not win a single useful injunction. During the course of the litigation, the German courts dismissed almost all of Nokia's patent infringement claims; in the few cases where an injunction was granted, it was toothless and has not caused any disruption to the client's business. The English High Court, for their part, initially found Nokia's microchip patent infringed by third-party microchips in some HTC phones. But the Hogan Lovells team successfully appealed the injunction.

The Hogan Lovells team ultimately advised HTC in settlement discussions to resolve the litigation. And in a collegial ending to a hard-fought series of cases, the Nokia litigation team attended a large Hogan Lovells reception following the settlement.

Eli Lilly

The relationship between Hogan Lovells and Eli Lilly has developed on the back of the olanzapine case—a case that has made legal history.

Olanzapine is a chemical substance used in antipsychotic medication for the treatment of schizophrenia. It was developed by Lilly and sold as Zyprexa® with several billion dollars in global sales to patients. In the mid-2000s, generic pharmaceutical companies started proceedings to invalidate Lilly's patents for olanzapine in order to sell their own generic versions of Zyprexa®. The argument against the olanzapine patent was that very similar compounds had been suggested by scientists in the past for the treatment of schizophrenia.

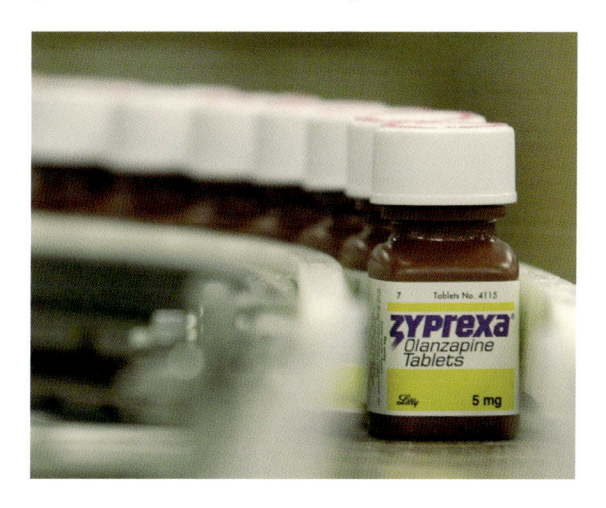

Hogan Lovells ■ Our Story

Lilly had previously used different counsel in Germany, but as the trial of the German patent revocation action came closer, it hired a team of Hogan Lovells lawyers led by Andreas von Falck to act as opposing counsel in a mock trial. After the "trial," the mock judge, a retired Federal Patent Court judge, recommended that Lilly change its legal counsel to Hogan Lovells.

When the revocation hearing began, the presiding judge appeared inclined to rule against Lilly's patent. However, there were so many arguments against this position that the hearing went on for over twelve hours, most unusual for a German case, until the judge called for an adjournment. During a second hearing a few months later, the Federal Patent Court took the unprecedented step of appointing witnesses to give live testimony on the benefits of the drug and the underlying invention. Despite their powerful testimonies, however, the patent was revoked.

Lilly appealed immediately—but the market was already swamped with generic olanzapine, reducing the price levels for Zyprexa® to 20 percent of Lilly's original price.

Hogan Lovells recommended that Lilly seek a preliminary injunction against one of the generic olanzapine companies, based on the argument that the earlier ruling and revocation of the olanzapine patent was "evidently" wrong and that the patent was therefore still valid. After long deliberation, the preliminary injunction was refused. The court maintained that it should not reverse the revocation of a patent as decided by the Federal Patent Court. Again, Lilly appealed. This time, the Court of Appeal in Dusseldorf ruled in Lilly's favor and banned the generic company from selling its cheaper version in Germany.

The injunction rocked the market for generic olanzapine. As soon as the injunction was granted, other generic companies approached Lilly for a settlement, and Lilly reclaimed its market share within a few weeks. Later that same year, the Federal Supreme Court reversed the Federal Patent Court decision and reinstated the patent. The decision redefines the standards for patentability in the area of chemical inventions. Following this, Hogan Lovells collected close to €100 million in damages for Lilly from German generic companies alone.

Hogan Lovells continues to represent Eli Lilly in patent matters in Germany and the representation has expanded to France, Italy, the UK, the Netherlands, Japan, and the United States.

Merck & Co., Inc.

In 1668, Friedrich Jacob Merck set up a pharmacy in Darmstadt, Germany, the foundation of what would evolve, many centuries later, into two of the world's

Chapter 4 ■ Our Business

FAR LEFT: The Merck family association with the pharmaceutical business goes back to the seventeenth century, when they set up the Angel Pharmacy in Germany.

George Merck was the president of Merck & Co. from 1925 to 1950. Shown below is a telegram from his New York office after the World War I which led the way to Merck buying back the firm's shares from the U.S. government.

most prestigious pharmaceutical companies: the American Merck & Co., Inc. and the German Merck KGaA. The American Merck company separated from the Merck family company in 1917, during World War I, when all family-held shares had to be transferred to the U.S. government under the Alien Property Custodian scheme. After the war, George Merck, an American member of the Merck family, bought back the shares from the U.S. government and ran the company separately from the German Merck business. Despite their separation, both Merck companies lived in friendly coexistence for most of the twentieth century, entering into various joint agreements regarding the use of the Merck company name and trademark.

That peaceful coexistence ended, however, with the arrival of social media and other internet services. Probably initiated by the application for the Facebook account "Merck," a conflict erupted that is currently one of the largest and most comprehensive pieces of trademark litigation in the world. With further conflicts looming in other countries, there are currently active court proceedings in the UK, France, and Germany. In order to safeguard Merck & Co.'s rights in these conflicts, a Hogan Lovells team led by Andreas Bothe and Yvonne Draheim devised a defense strategy based on specific arguments for each jurisdiction. Given the long corporate history of both companies, Hogan Lovells lawyers have been required to efficiently review and share a huge number of historical documents with colleagues throughout Europe and the U.S. At the same time, the team of lawyers engaged in the Merck matters have had to develop a deep understanding of the governing procedural requirements—and their differences in the various countries. At the time of writing, the outcomes of the various proceedings are still open.

Hogan Lovells ■ Our Story

LITIGATION, ARBITRATION AND EMPLOYMENT

The Hogan Lovells litigation, arbitration and employment (LAE) practice group has more than 600 lawyers, 200 of them partners, with deep knowledge in several disciplines: traditional litigators with a broad range of substantive knowledge and experience, as well as employment lawyers, international arbitration lawyers, and a global investigations team.

The firm's employment lawyers advise clients on a full spectrum of employment matters, including counseling clients about workplace policies and practices and advocating on their behalf in litigation and arbitration. International arbitration lawyers handle complex, high-value international business disputes through commercial or investment treaty arbitration. They rely on multilingual and multicultural lawyers operating from offices all over the world, including Caracas, Dubai, Frankfurt, Hong Kong, London, Madrid, Miami, Milan, Moscow, Munich, New York, Paris, Singapore, and Washington, D.C. to represent clients before important tribunals and institutions worldwide.

The Hogan Lovells investigations, white collar, and fraud group draws on the talents of more than fifty partners and many more associates who conduct investigations related to fraud, corruption, and white-collar crime. The group routinely provides compliance advice and has specific experience in industries where bribery and corruption issues are prevalent, including construction; pharmaceutical; energy, oil, and gas; aerospace and defense; manufacturing; and IT and financial services. The geographically diverse group works together to represent clients under investigation in almost every corner of the globe.

The firm's traditional litigators regularly appear before courts, arbitral panels, and other global tribunals in appellate, class action, environmental, financial services, insurance, product liability litigation, and securities matters. They often draw on the firm's global resources to handle complex matters that reach across multiple jurisdictions.

BTA Bank

Between 2009 and 2015, a team of 155 lawyers led by Chris Hardman in London represented BTA Bank in eleven claims against Mukhtar Ablyazov and others relating to allegations that Ablyazov, the former BTA chairman, had embezzled over $6 billion from the company. The litigation effort was coordinated from the London office and relied heavily on contributions from lawyers in the Moscow office to coordinate extensive litigation in the British Virgin Islands, Cyprus, Russia, Ukraine, the Netherlands, Germany, Switzerland, Kazakhstan, the Seychelles, and the Channel Islands. The Hogan Lovells team had a heightened responsibility to develop and execute the litigation strategy in this matter because a court order prevented the firm from sharing certain key information with BTA. This order was issued in light of Ablyazov's disputed allegations that the Kazakhstan government—which had an interest in BTA—would use information about his assets improperly.

Hogan Lovells lawyers secured judgments holding Ablyazov guilty of contempt of court for disposing of, moving, and misleading the court about his interest in valuable assets. For this, he was sentenced to three concurrent sentences of twenty-two months in prison. But Ablyazov then fled England, in further breach of court orders. In his absence, the team won a landmark ruling, upheld by the English Court of Appeal, that prohibited Ablyazov

Chapter 4 ■ Our Business

The firm represented BTA Bank against Mukhtar Ablyazov, the former chairman of the bank, and others, between 2009 and 2015.

from defending the fraud claims due to his continued non-cooperation with the English court system. The Hogan Lovells team subsequently secured judgments against him totaling more than $4 billion.

The Ablyazov litigation was one of the biggest fraud cases to come before the English courts. It generated more than 200 hearings, including several hearings before the Court of Appeal and applications to the Supreme Court, and resulted in more than fifty reported decisions, many of which set precedents for future fraud and commercial cases. These precedent-setting decisions included an unlimited asset-freezing order covering all of Ablyazov's overseas assets; an order requiring the disclosure of all of Ablyazov's assets; third-party disclosure orders requiring disclosure of assets held by intentionally opaque and complex offshore structures; the most extensive prejudgment receivership order ever made by an English court requiring that all of Albyazov's property worldwide be placed in the control of an independent receiver; and an order granting unprecedented access to e-mails without informing the parties to whom those e-mail accounts belonged.

BTA has recovered hundreds of millions of dollars, and despite Ablyazov's ongoing attempts to frustrate the process, significant further recoveries are expected. In the meantime, Ablyazov—located by investigators and arrested while hiding in the south of France—is facing extradition to Russia to stand trial for his fraud.

The work of the Hogan Lovells litigation team on the BTA matter earned the team several high-profile awards, including being named Litigation Team of the Year at *The Lawyer* Awards 2013; earning the Global Dispute Grand Prize from *American Lawyer*; and being "highly commended" in the *Financial Times'* Most Innovative Law Firms in Dispute Resolution category.

The Hogan Lovells team celebrate winning the Litigation Team of the Year for its work for BTA at *The Lawyer* Awards, 2013.

KPMG

Hogan Lovells can trace its longstanding relationship with KPMG, one of the world's largest audit, tax, and advisory firms, to both legacy firms. Hogan & Hartson began working for KPMG's predecessor Peat Marwick Mitchell & Co. in the early 1980s by winning trial verdicts in professional liability trials throughout the United States. The Lovells Business Restructuring and Insolvency (BRI) group represented KPMG in its role as administrator of Drexel Burnham Lambert, a prominent investment banking firm that was forced into bankruptcy in 1990 by its involvement in illegal activities in the junk bond market. Prior to that, Lovells represented accounting firms Peat Marwick and Thomson McLintock, both of which joined KPMG through mergers.

In recent years, Hogan Lovells has handled several pieces of major litigation for KPMG's U.S. firm and individual partners, several of which have been tried through to verdict. KPMG has also called on the Hogan Lovells team to represent twenty different KPMG member firms in the KPMG international network outside the U.S.

In one such matter, the Hogan Lovells litigation team, led by George Salter in New York, successfully defended KPMG (Cayman) against claims arising from Bernard Madoff's Ponzi scheme. Investors in hedge funds, that had in turn invested in Madoff's scheme, asserted securities fraud, common law fraud, and negligence claims against the hedge funds' outside auditors, including KPMG (Cayman), KPMG LLP, and Ernst & Young.

The Hogan Lovells team secured a dismissal in the district court and then protected this win on appeal. The team successfully argued that the fraud took place at Bernard L. Madoff Investment Securities LLC, not in the hedge funds, which the accounting firms were responsible for auditing. Following Ira Feinberg's argument before the Second Circuit, the panel affirmed dismissal of KPMG (Cayman) from the suit, holding that the hedge fund investors failed to adequately allege securities fraud, common law fraud, and negligence claims against the hedge funds' outside auditor. The Second Circuit panel noted that the allegations against the accounting firms that audited the hedge funds were "an archetypical example of impermissible 'allegations of fraud by hindsight'" and further held that the plaintiffs had not alleged the requisite relationship between the auditors and the hedge fund investors, as required to sustain a negligence claim under New York law.

The Hogan Lovells team also won dismissal of four other Madoff-related lawsuits filed against a different KPMG member firm.

TÜV Rheinland AG

Hogan Lovells also has a leading product liability practice covering all aspects of product safety as well as civil and criminal liability. This group represents clients with respect to a wide range of products including food, pharmaceuticals, medical devices, cars, tobacco, mobile phones, cosmetics, electrical and electronic products, consumer goods, toys, and children's products. The work of these lawyers addresses risk prevention and risk management, compliance with product safety regulations, labeling, product recalls, and complex supply chain disputes, as well as defense of unitary, cross-border, and multiparty personal injury claims.

A product liability team, led by Ina Brock in Munich, is currently handling the global defense of TÜV Rheinland AG and affiliated companies against liability claims resulting from allegedly inappropriate certification of French breast implant manufacturer Poly Implant Prothèse (PIP). The now insolvent manufacturer had fraudulently used non-declared silicone gel in some of its implants which, according to media reports, were sold to an estimated 500,000 women worldwide.

The notified body TÜV Rheinland LGA Products GmbH (the successor company of TÜV Rheinland Product Safety GmbH) is among several dozen entities in the European Union designated as a "Notified Body" for medical devices, meaning they are accredited to perform tasks under the EU Medical Devices Directive in relation to medical products. In 1997, PIP commissioned TÜV Rheinland Product Safety GmbH to conduct an assessment of its quality assurance system in accordance with the EU Medical Devices Directive.

Numerous lawsuits were filed against PIP alleging that the undeclared silicone gel filling presented health risks. The PIP litigation includes the largest product liability case currently pending in France, as well as cases and investigations in Argentina, Brazil, Colombia, Germany, Italy, Ireland, the Netherlands, Poland, Spain, and the UK. Many of these cases also assert claims against TÜV Rheinland LGA Products GmbH arising from its certification of PIP's quality assurance system.

The Hogan Lovells team in Munich is coordinating a global litigation strategy to manage the mass of individual claims. Hogan Lovells lawyers secured favorable decisions in the German courts and also in France. Cases and appeals are still pending. The German Federal Supreme Court requested the Court of Justice of the European Union to answer questions submitted in connection with one of the German cases.

The Hogan Lovells team includes lawyers in the Amsterdam, London, Madrid, Milan, Munich, Paris, and Warsaw offices. The decisions issued in the course of the PIP litigation are expected to shape the future regulatory framework for medical devices in Europe.

A product liability team from Hogan Lovells is handling the global defense of TÜV Rheinland AG against liability claims arising from faulty silicone breast impants supplied by Poly Implant Prothèse (PIP).

Hogan Lovells ■ Our Story

RIGHT: The London technology team.

BELOW RIGHT: The U.S. conflicts team in Washington, D.C., 2015.

BUSINESS SERVICES TEAMS

In addition to Hogan Lovells lawyers hundreds of other professionals support the work of the firm. Many, such as personal assistants and marketing and business development professionals, are directly engaged with the firm's clients and potential clients, while others make sure that the firm runs smoothly.

Marketing and Business Development

All key industry sector teams, strategic client teams, and practice groups have dedicated personnel supporting their efforts to develop new business and respond to opportunities to pitch for new work. The marketing and business development team maintains extensive infrastructure such as best practice tools, an experience tracker, and standardized materials that facilitate the work of its own team members and lawyers alike. All of this work is shaped by a firm-wide marketing and business development plan but is implemented locally through the daily work of its team members and partners.

The marketing and business development team also provides market research and analysis to support the firm's strategic planning. In 2011–2012, the department undertook one of the largest global client research projects ever conducted by a law firm. By speaking to 300 key client contacts around the world, the firm gained invaluable insights large and small that have since shaped its global marketing and business development strategies. Finer points gleaned from these client conversations have also impacted marketing and business development efforts for specific practices, regions, and even individual clients.

The team also helps lawyers become more effective business developers. It provides guidance and advice to partners throughout the organization on best practices, supports many of the firm's people development programs, and runs or organizes training in areas such as effective pitching, networking skills, client development, and using social media.

Finally, the marketing and business development team is also responsible for outward facing work, including managing the firm's profile and reputation through branding, media relations, and corporate communications strategies. This work includes the now ubiquitous Hogan Lovells lime green. At the time of the fifth anniversary, the visual presentation of the firm received an overhaul to keep it current and fresh, but the distinctive lime green remains sacrosanct.

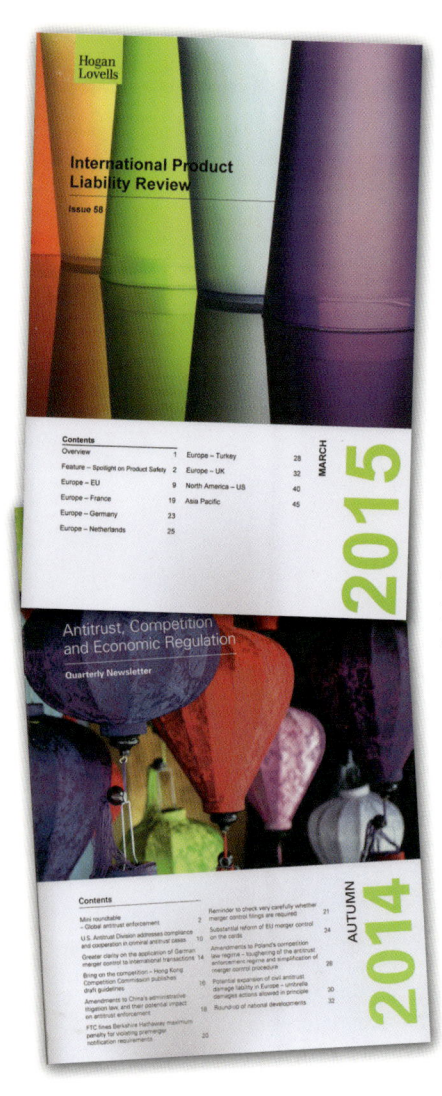

Chapter 4 ■ Our Business

ABOVE: The U.S. and London litigation support team, led by Jon Talotta, in New York for the Legal Technology conference in 2015.

LEFT: The GBSC compliance team based in Johannesburg.

Technology

Hogan Lovells relies heavily on technology infrastructure to serve its clients: the firm's global footprint and client demands mean 24/7 technology operations and support—with virtually zero downtime. The technology team operates and maintains this crucial infrastructure efficiently, partnering with the firm's practice groups and other global business units to analyze technology needs and develop applications and other appropriate solutions to meet them.

The 2010 combination itself underscored the importance of this work. The combination required the migration of numerous systems, data, and people. The technology team worked to move 450 people in twelve locations to a new systems platform. In many instances people were also moved to a new physical office along with millions of their documents and terabytes of their e-mail files. The department changed thousands of computer addresses and implemented a temporary network while simultaneously designing and implementing solutions that enabled individuals to carry on using legacy systems. Much of this happened unseen and without any disruption to users. But the department's work was not all behind the scenes. It also offered hundreds of hours of training to those who had changed systems platforms and rebranded many systems, web pages, and URLs to reflect the combined firm's marketing strategy.

When the dust settled, the technology function was one of the first functions to combine its resources and form a global organization with an endorsed global strategy. That strategy has paved the way to provide consistent technology services to all Hogan Lovells employees, wherever they may be. Some of these services, such as the recently launched collaboration tool called Lync, directly facilitate lawyers working as "one team" to provide integrated client service.

Professional Standards, Risk and Compliance

The firm's lifeblood is its steady and expanding flow of new clients and new matters. Two teams of dedicated professionals work to protect the firm and its clients from legal and financial risks inherent in this ever-growing client base. Each year, the new business conflicts team, the compliance team and members of the firm's Legal Ethics Committee review and clear the representation of over 5,000 new clients and support the opening of approximately 40,000 new matters. They also address possible conflicts of interest prior to lateral partners, associates, and other legal profession candidates joining the firm.

127

ABOVE: Working in the Penson Library, Atlantic House, London. The library is named after John Penson, a highly respected banking partner, who died at the age of 44 in 2000.

RIGHT: The German Knowledge and Research intranet site showing links to local resources.

More than seventy non-lawyer professionals work in the new business conflicts team in Denver, Johannesburg, London, San Francisco, and Washington, D.C. They work a weekend and holiday rotation system to provide global support across all time zones. The team are kept very busy as a result of this round-the-clock service and the urgency of their work is reflected in the fact that almost half of the daily new business intake and lateral new hire conflicts clearance requests are marked "urgent".

A separate team facilitates the clearance of conflicts of interest associated with new hires: still others support responses to audit letters and ensure the timely filing of lobbying reports required by the United States Congress. The conflicts team also works in tandem with the compliance team to ensure compliance with respect to sanctions restrictions. This work has become more significant in recent years as the firm has expanded and involves reviewing the ownership and control of each client, as well as the nature of each matter, to identify any potential material links to sanctioned jurisdictions. Compliance professionals based in London, Dusseldorf, and Johannesburg also perform due diligence on every new client (and new matters for existing clients), verifying ownership and control of all new clients and assessing any risk presented by anti-money laundering guidelines. The compliance team has an expert knowledge of company structures, regulatory regimes, and anti-money-laundering rules.

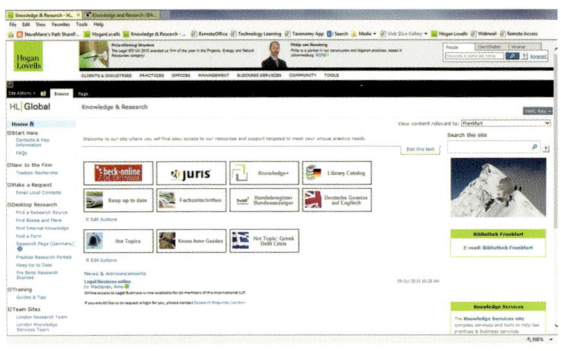

Knowledge and Research

The firm's knowledge and research department works to ensure that Hogan Lovells lawyers are the best informed lawyers in the marketplace. In addition to maintaining the firm's print and online information resources, the knowledge and research team provides research and library services to support billable client work as well as business development; practice updates that keep lawyers abreast of developments in their practice area; and solutions that facilitate collaboration and knowledge sharing to deliver cost effective services to clients.

The research services provided by the knowledge and research team are as varied as the firm's practice areas. They deal with both real-time information—a current share price or a judgment handed down today—as well as the historical, such as exchange rates from the 1950s, maps from the 1920s, and legislative debates from the 1800s, to give a few examples. The team's geographic reach mirrors that of the firm; it works hard to ensure that research requests are fulfilled by the best-placed people given access to specialized sources across the different offices, language capabilities, and particular substantive and jurisdictional knowledge.

Research services often play a significant role in high-profile matters. In the BTA Bank matter, for example, the research team conducted company searches in Cyprus, Belize, the Netherlands Antilles, and the Seychelles; tracked press reports relating to particular individuals and other aspects of the case; conducted land registry searches; and assisted with research into enforcement of judgments and debarring orders. For the HTC patent matter, researchers sourced old conference papers and articles, identified public sources for key dates, researched biographical and publication information for various experts, located old operational manuals for various products, and provided corporate structure and market research information to the litigation team.

Working closely with other business services teams such as technology and business development and marketing, the knowledge team also develops and supports tools and techniques that enhance practice efficiency. Its core initiatives include the firm's HL Global intranet; West KM and Knowledge+, which help harvest the firm's best insights; EagleEye for document review; digital drafting tools; wikis, blogs, and collaboration spaces to facilitate knowledge sharing; workflow solutions, and new tools such as the new people directory to help share the "know-who" as well as the "know-how."

Finance

As part of a major international business, the firm's financial management team has to cope with multiple currencies, both in accounting and treasury terms, producing sophisticated management information and dealing with tax and other authorities in the many jurisdictions in which the firm operates.

No business can operate successfully without funds flowing properly through its accounts. The Hogan Lovells finance team ensures that the finances of the firm remain healthy. The team ensure that lawyers' time is properly recorded, billed, and collected; and that suppliers to the firm, partners, employees, and taxes all get paid on time, with millions of transactions flowing through the firm's systems each year.

The GBSC finance team based in Johannesburg.

Hogan Lovells ■ Our Story

People

As the foregoing pages amply illustrate, Hogan Lovells draws on the talents of a large and diverse group of people across all aspects of its work. The people team's primary purpose is to help recruit, develop and retain the best people and to work with partners and senior business services leaders to create an inclusive culture in which all the firm's people, and thus the firm, can succeed. In a business where the firm's most important assets ride down the elevator every night, this is a critical activity.

Since the creation of Hogan Lovells, the people team has worked to create a new recruitment brand to sell the new firm to the next generation of lawyers, lateral hires, and business services professionals. This brand, characterized by the phrase, "The Best of All Worlds," strives to capture the global interconnectivity, the distinctive offering of high-end client work, and the ability to give back through citizenship initiatives that are available at Hogan Lovells.

The people team has also worked with the firm's leadership to construct a new shared culture that also retains local individuality and identity. The Icelandic ash cloud of 2010 played a surprising role in this effort. When it stranded a number of senior U.S. partners in Europe, John Young and Claudette Christian—the soon to be first Co-Chairs of the combined firm—took advantage of a literally captive audience to design a number of key global processes that are still in place today.

Client hosts at work on the 11th floor of Atlantic House, London.

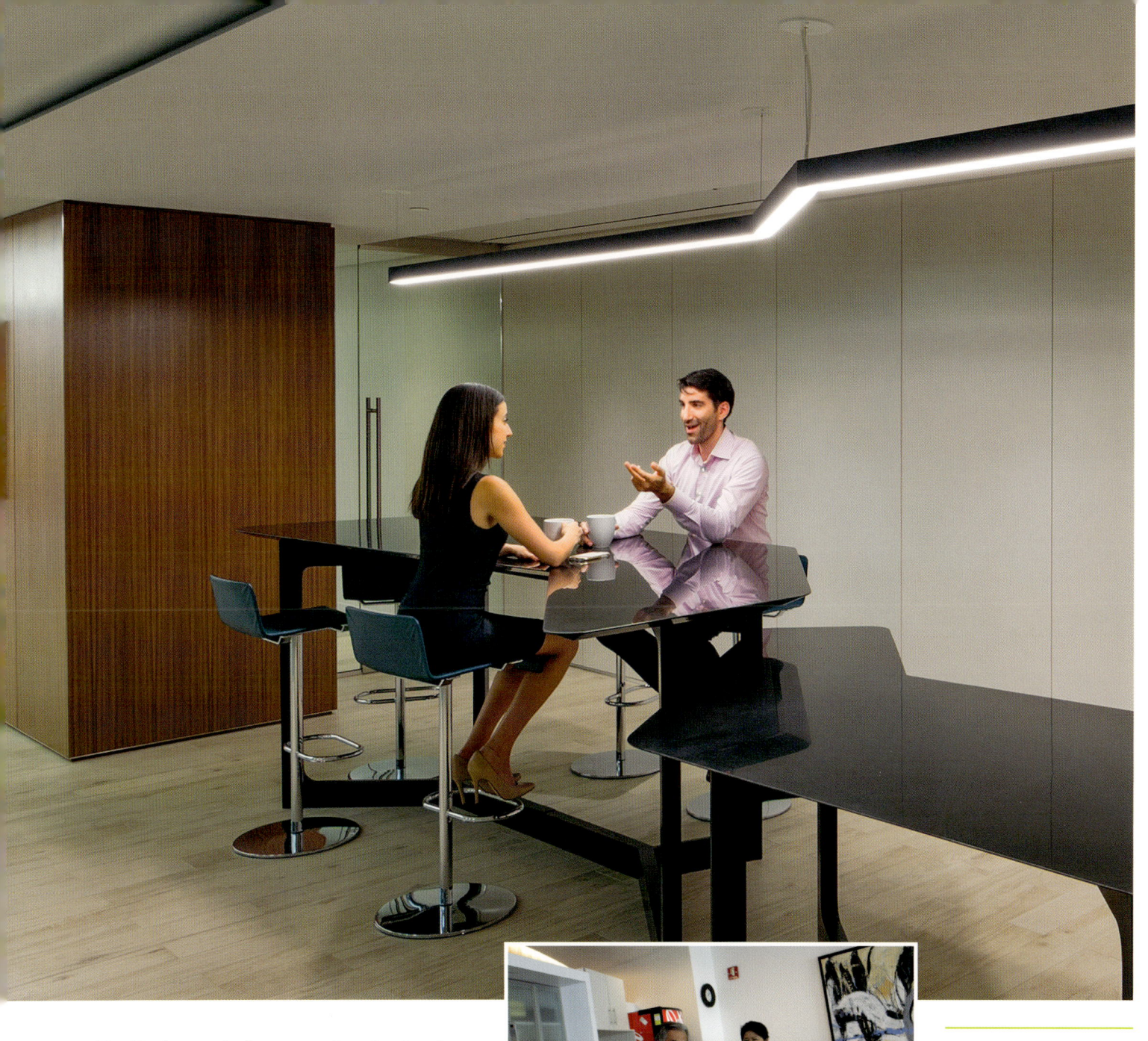

Finally, the people department has developed a truly global people development curriculum that includes programs such as Momentum, a development event for high-potential lawyers; Transform and The Leading Edge, for partners in their early years of partnership; and, most recently, Redefining Leadership, a program run in conjunction with the Oxford Saïd Business School. One participant recently described the opportunities these programs provide by explaining, "I had done a lot of thinking already about what would make me a better lawyer; this program gave me an extraordinary opportunity to turn this into a game plan. The global networking opportunity really opened my eyes to the breadth of the firm."

ABOVE: A floor in the Washington, D.C. office remodelled as part of the REvision process.

LEFT: Driver and maintenance assistant in the Mexico City office.

BOTTOM LEFT: Preparing for a client lunch at Atlantic House.

The renovation program of the Columbia Square office aimed to create a connective, welcoming, active environment that reflected the integrity of the firm. The first step was to gut part of the building (far right) and then create a pilot floor (top and above) featuring modern, multi-use areas.

Facilities and Office Services

From the right chair to on-site amenities such as a cafeteria, backup child care center, or an on-site gym, good facilities improve the life of Hogan Lovells lawyers and by extension, their service to clients. The facilities and office services teams work to maintain the physical operation of the firm so the lawyers can practice law effectively.

This work includes ensuring that the firm's physical space is well maintained and comfortable, and that supplies are available and public spaces and conference rooms are maintained and equipped. Some of this work is discrete, impacting only one lawyer at a time—for example, supplying an ergonomically correct chair to an office. Other projects change the face of the firm by shaping its physical space. The office services team also ensures that copying, mail, travel, and messenger services have the staff and equipment needed to effectively support the firm's work. This routine work is dotted with sporadic crises—the occasional search through trash for erroneously discarded files, or in one particular case a pair of shoes; investigating air quality related to paper dust; and responding to a flood or fire in Hogan Lovells office spaces to name a few. The expansion to new offices, significant renovations such as the REvision program in the United States, and building expansions keep the team extremely busy planning and overseeing construction projects.

Chapter 4 ■ Our Business

Personal Assistants

The firm's personal assistants often provide an important "personal touch" to the client/lawyer relationship. They rely on their deep knowledge of the lawyers' work to provide document editing, proofing, and formatting. They also maintain crucial files and ensure time is entered so bills are sent and paid on a timely basis. But above all, they allow the lawyers they support to focus on their clients and their legal work.

In a number of offices, the firm's assistants work in teams to ensure support is available to their internal and external clients. Some assistants have extended their team beyond their home office by volunteering to travel to new Hogan Lovells offices to support lawyers new to the firm and facilitate their smooth onboarding. Others facilitate collaboration across offices by supporting visiting lawyers.

The globalization of the firm has required staff at all levels to develop new administrative skills. In one instance, for example, the D.C. and London offices were planning retreats and considering a variety of possible locations for numerous practice groups. One assistant developed a spreadsheet to compare average hotel and flight costs in all the cities being considered in Europe and the United States. This matrix, which adjusts to reflect how many people would be flying to the various locations and converts relevant currencies, is still used today to guide firm-wide travel planning.

Assistants are also very active in the firm's citizenship initiatives and fundraising events, for example, supporting career days organized by outside organizations in offices including Denver, Los Angeles, and New York. Their contributions are also essential to firm-wide priorities such as the implementation of fire safety and disaster recovery plans, as well as the REvision process that dramatically redesigned a number of offices.

TOP AND ABOVE: Personal assistants in Hong Kong and Mexico City.

133

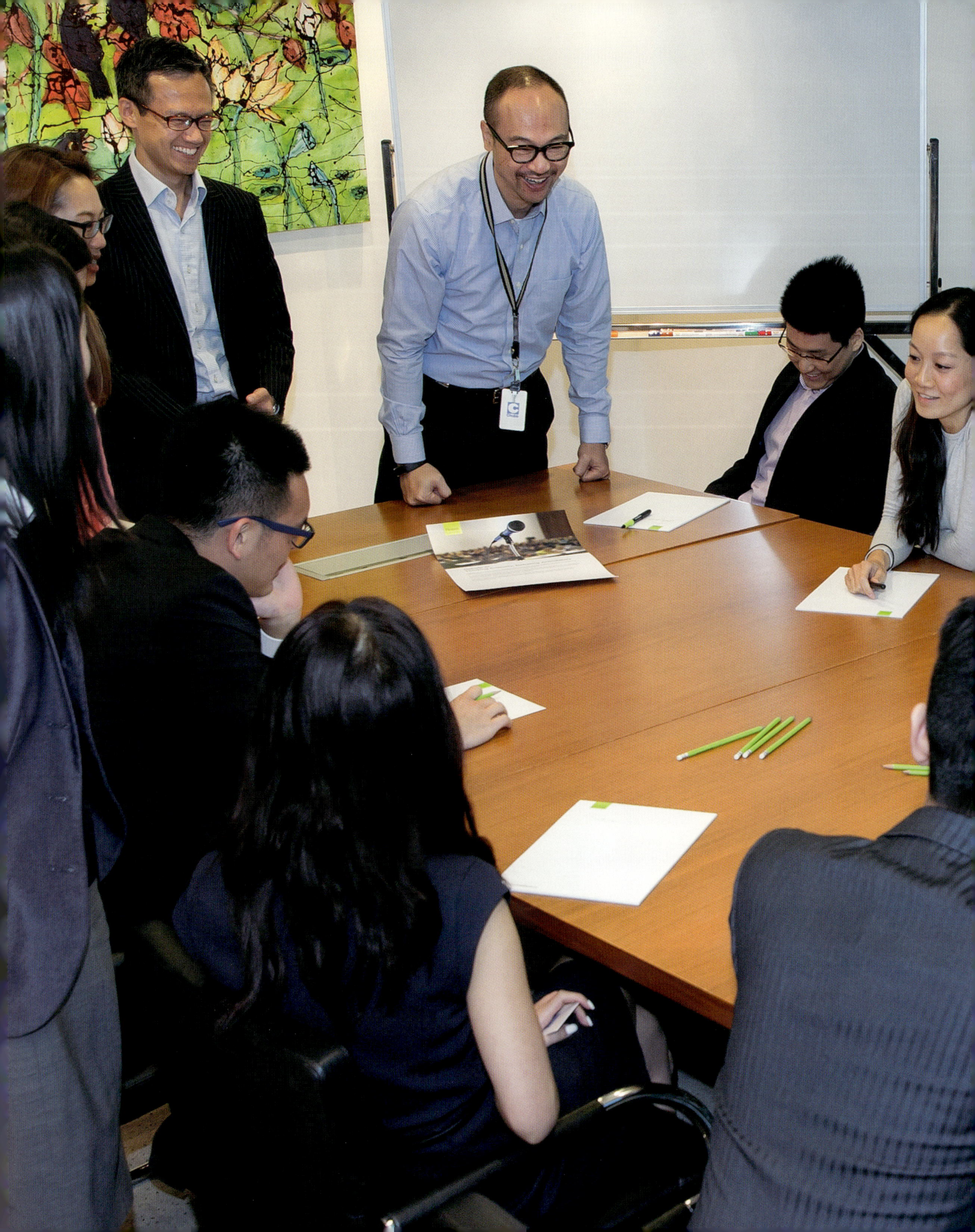

Chapter 5
Our Citizenship

Chapter 5
Our Citizenship

PREVIOUS PAGES: Participants in the firm's flagship Community Investment program Debate It! in the Hong Kong office. School children around the world are given the opportunity to develop their critical thinking and presentation skills and deepen their knowledge of current affairs.

RIGHT: Kizzie White, arrested and sent to prison in the Tulia drug raid, greets a relative on her release in 2003. Hogan & Hartson devoted more than 5,000 hours of pro bono legal services to the Tulia case.

Good citizenship is one of the core values of Hogan Lovells. The firm recognizes its responsibilities to provide pro bono legal assistance to those who need it, promote a diverse workforce, practice environmental sustainability, and work with local and global communities to effect positive change. This concept was not a new design: Hogan & Hartson and Lovells for decades had demonstrated their deep commitment to good citizenship long before the firms combined. After the combination, those efforts continued—and Hogan Lovells also marshalled its pooled resources and experiences to advance new, groundbreaking global citizenship efforts.

Hogan Lovells Pro Bono History

In the late 1960s, Hogan & Hartson's Executive Committee formed a community relations study committee to consider formalizing the firm's longstanding informal pro bono commitments. The committee's ultimate recommendation began by quoting the words of an eloquent associate: "It is abundantly clear ... that no longer can persons or groups pursue their own career or interests unmindful of the needs in the rest of the community."

The committee accordingly recommended that the Washington, D.C. office develop and conduct "a community service ... practice in precisely the same manner that it develops and conducts its paying practice." The firm adopted that proposal, forming the Community Services Department (CSD) in 1970 as the first stand-alone community services department of any major local law firm. Opening with two full-time associates, the department later expanded to one full-time partner, a dedicated senior associate, and a cadre of rotating junior associates.

In the decades since its formation, the CSD (now called the Pro Bono Department) has guided the firm's pro bono efforts, and firm lawyers have waged and won countless victories for pro bono clients and communities across the globe. As an example, firm lawyers won a substantial civil rights settlement for African Americans wrongfully arrested and convicted in a racist and corrupt sting operation in Tulia, Texas. Other lawyers have provided individual representation for wrongfully convicted individuals, including successful habeas corpus and clemency petitions on behalf of Derek Tice, a member of the "Norfolk 4" who, along with his co-defendants, was falsely convicted of a 1997 rape and murder. Outside the courtroom, the firm's health practice dedicated thousands of hours to researching and drafting *HIV/AIDS in the Nation's Capital*, a comprehensive report highlighting the Washington, D.C. government's inadequate response to the local epidemic. In recognition of these and other pro bono accomplishments, the firm received the American Bar Association's Pro Bono Publico Award in 1991 and has been a three-time recipient of the District of Columbia Bar Association's Pro Bono Law Firm of the Year award.

Lovells, too, occupied the forefront of the global movement to advance social justice and the rule of law, commencing with its work for prisoners on death row in the Caribbean and expanding to grassroots issues across its offices. In 1997, identifying a need for lawyers to offer their skills and experience to help those without access to justice, Lovells became the first European law firm to institutionalize its pro bono commitment by hiring a full-time lawyer to manage the firm's pro bono practice. That lawyer, Yasmin Waljee, would later be honored by Queen Elizabeth II with the award of an OBE (Order of the British Empire) for her pro bono service and services to the Muslim community.

Lovells' formalized pro bono commitment produced significant victories for a range of clients lacking access to legal services. For instance, volunteer lawyers provided extensive

The firm celebrated the first five years of its corporate responsibility program in Asia by firing the Noon Day Gun in Hong Kong in 2008. From left to right: Henry Wheare, Crispin Rapinet, a piper from the Hong Kong Police Band, and Allan Leung. The tradition began in the 1860s when Jardine Matheson's custom of firing a gun salute whenever the head of the company arrived by sea was frowned upon by the British Royal Navy. In penance, Jardine Matheson was ordered to fire a gun every day at noon and the practice still continues today.

Hogan Lovells ■ Our Story

ABOVE: Yasmin Waljee OBE, the firm's International Pro Bono Director seen here in her role as Vice Chairman of Mosaic, a charity founded by HRH The Prince of Wales to create opportunities for young people of all backgrounds growing up in the most deprived communities in the UK.

ABOVE RIGHT: HRH The Prince of Wales, founder of Mosaic, with HRH Princess Badiya bint El Hassan of Jordan, founding Chairman of Mosaic, and David Harris of Hogan Lovells, in the London office in 2012.

compensation claim assistance for victims of the 2005 London bombings, securing over £2.1 million in compensation. The firm also secured a new national compensation scheme for victims of terrorist incidents occurring abroad. These efforts were complemented by a successful campaign to secure the first compensation awards for human trafficking victims, a population severely underserved by local legal aid organizations. And the firm established the first social enterprise and social finance practice, which harnesses commercial clients' skills and expertise in business and finance, and uses these relationships to provide a diverse range of legal advice and support to social entrepreneurs, from drafting agreements to providing advice on employment issues. The new practice earned a *Financial Times* Innovative Lawyer Award, which commended the firm's commitment "to a forward and sophisticated approach to pro bono emphasizing sustainable solutions."

PRO BONO
Advocating for Civil, Political, and Human Rights

Hogan Lovells pro bono engagements have combatted an array of injustices, including inadequate protections for criminal defendants, unjust restrictions on voting rights, widespread discrimination against the gay and lesbian community, systematic denials of housing rights, illegal restrictions of lawful business practices, and corruption involving sexual exploitation.

The firm continues its decades-long efforts to target injustices in the U.S. criminal justice system, including racial discrimination, wrongful convictions, and unjust punishments. Miami-based lawyers represented the Public Defender of the Eleventh Judicial Circuit of Florida in a challenge to the state's inadequate funding and staffing of that office, which severely prejudiced criminal defendants' constitutional right to effective assistance of counsel. In a 2013 landmark ruling, the Supreme Court of Florida agreed with Hogan Lovells, concluding that the public defenders' excessive caseloads violate a defendant's right to counsel.

Hogan Lovells lawyers also have represented several individuals sentenced to death. One such

Chapter 5 ■ Our Citizenship

ABOVE RIGHT: The firm's lawyers provided pro bono help for victims of the London bombings of 7 July 2005. Nader Mozakka, whose wife was killed in the attacks, commented, "Unlike what we experienced on July 7 the world is full of fantastic people. Lovells lawyers are the best examples of committed professionals who were very sensitive to our feelings and pain—I am grateful for your support."

ABOVE: The firm's work for the victims of the London bombings led to Hogan Lovells providing pro bono legal support for London's Air Ambulance.

representation stands out. In 1987, the firm began representing John Ferguson, a Florida death-row inmate who suffered from paranoid schizophrenia. Over the firm's twenty-six-year representation of Ferguson, lawyers from several U.S. offices relentlessly advocated to stay his execution—including, in late October 2012, winning a last-minute postponement as Ferguson waited strapped to a gurney in the prison's death chamber. The State of Florida ultimately executed Ferguson in August 2013. The firm's long and tireless advocacy for him is often cited nationally in the debate surrounding the death penalty, mental illness, and the importance of effective indigent defense counsel.

Good Citizenship Program Areas

The combined Hogan Lovells expanded its longstanding citizenship commitments by setting a new, ambitious goal: to be a visible, vocal, and global advocate for good citizenship and corporate responsibility. This commitment encompasses five critical program areas:

Pro Bono: Providing quality legal services to improve the lives of those without access to justice and to meet the legal needs of nonprofits and social enterprises.

Diversity: Fostering a work environment where people of all backgrounds and experiences can reach their full potential.

Community Investment: Supporting and developing projects that focus on local communities, often in partnership with clients and other stakeholders.

Matched Charitable Giving ("Touch"): Using the resources of a leading international law firm to support projects that improve social conditions for the world's poor and disadvantaged.

Environment: Carrying out the firm's business in a sustainable way.

Hogan Lovells lawyers and staff members have embraced this holistic approach to good citizenship. The strength of the firm's geographical reach and practice areas means that the resources of the firm can be employed to effect considerable change. The firm aspires to engage everyone so that business services professionals work alongside lawyer colleagues to improve the lives of the disadvantaged. ■

Hogan Lovells ■ Our Story

ABOVE: May-Elaine Thomson from the Hogan Lovells Johannesburg office, took part in the International CEO SleepOut in 2015 on one of the coldest nights of the year to raise awareness and funds for Girls & Boys Town—a charity working with homeless and vulnerable children in South Africa. Other Hogan Lovells staff also took part by arranging a sympathy sleepout. The event raised a staggering $1.9 million.

RIGHT: Hogan Lovells lawyers brought a class action lawsuit against the District of Columbia on behalf of homeless families illegally denied places in shelters.

The firm also has offered multifaceted support for individuals' and communities' voting rights. Litigation teams based in the Philadelphia office, for instance, defended Pennsylvania voters' rights in two 2012 cases: firm lawyers represented a bipartisan group of voters in a successful challenge to the state's unconstitutional redistricting plan, and a complementary federal lawsuit challenged Pennsylvania's failure to comply with a federal requirement to make voter registration materials available at public benefits agencies. Lawyers from Baltimore, Los Angeles, Miami, New York, San Francisco, and Washington, D.C. supported the Lawyers' Committee for Civil Rights Under Law's Election Protection program by staffing election day call centers, hosting volunteer training sessions, and drafting volunteer training materials.

In recent years, the firm's efforts have resulted in significant victories for lesbian, gay, bisexual, and transgender (LGBT) individuals. Lawyers in Brussels, London, New York, Singapore, and Washington, D.C. offices provide legal support for the Human Dignity Trust, a UK organization that seeks to end government criminalization of homosexual activity. Lawyers based in Washington, D.C. represented multiple advocates in each of several landmark Supreme Court marriage-equality cases. And New York lawyers drafted a first-of-its-kind set of model transgender affirming hospital policies in collaboration with LGBT advocacy organizations. These complementary efforts highlight the ability of Hogan Lovells to harness its lawyers' enthusiasm and resources across all offices to advance a critical human rights movement.

Hogan Lovells has employed a similar cross-office model to protect housing rights and advocate for the homeless. New York-based lawyers, for example, achieved a significant victory in a suit challenging discriminatory housing and exclusionary zoning practices by the Village of Garden City in Long Island, New York. After a lengthy trial, a federal judge ruled that Garden City had violated the U.S. Constitution, the federal Fair Housing Act, and other civil rights statutes, handing the Hogan Lovells client a categorical win. Firm lawyers also volunteer at San Francisco-based Project Homeless Connect, staff a homeless shelter's on-site legal clinic in Alexandria, Virginia, and advise a Denver-based homelessness charity. And in coordination with the Washington Legal Clinic for the Homeless, a team of Washington, D.C. lawyers brought a class action lawsuit against the District of Columbia on behalf of homeless families illegally denied private shelters on cold

LEFT: Hogan Lovells invests in social entrepreneurship. The loans received from the firm's charity of the year, Lendwithcare, enable Marcelline Dohami in Benin to develop her grocery business and, in turn, support her family.

BELOW LEFT: Sidai, the social enterprise arm of Farm Africa, provides animal husbandry and health services to livestock keepers across Kenya.

nights. The team secured a preliminary injunction to force the city to comply with the law and appropriately house homeless families, and Hogan Lovells successfully defeated the city's challenge to that ruling on appeal.

Other offices have secured similar victories for pro bono clients' civil and human rights. The Johannesburg office, for example, secured a significant victory for local street vendors. In 2013, the city removed vendors lawfully operating under local policies and started demolishing the vendors' stalls. A team of lawyers representing the South African National Traders Retail Alliance successfully secured an emergency appeal before the Constitutional Court of South Africa, which permitted the vendors to return to their trading stalls immediately.

Mexico City-based lawyers joined a team of global law firms, corporations, the International Association of Women Judges, and the Thomson Reuters Foundation to research legal and institutional frameworks for prosecuting "Sextortion," or corruption involving sexual exploitation. The research spanned nine jurisdictions across six continents, and generated guidelines for effective laws and practices to strengthen justice systems, protect and empower victims, and ensure victims' access to justice.

Supporting Social Entrepreneurs

Hogan Lovells continues to support social entrepreneurs across industries and regions through the social enterprise and social finance practice created in 2007. Its work spans the globe, for example, a multioffice team provided legal assistance to Farm Africa, which works directly with African farmers to help ensure lasting rural prosperity and to overcome a series of formidable challenges. In 2012, legal changes in Ethiopia threatened Farm Africa's ability to operate there. A partner from the New York office traveled to Addis Ababa to meet with the client, government officials, British Embassy personnel, Ethiopian lawyers, and foreign entrepreneurs, helping to fashion a structure

RIGHT: The social enterprise program has helped start-up businesses such as Rubies in the Rubble based in London. The company, founded by Jenny Dawson, produces jams and chutneys from excess food that would previously have gone to waste and works to combat social exclusion by hiring people struggling to get back into work.

FAR RIGHT: Washington, D.C.'s local Touch charity partner for 2013–2015 was the Wounded Warrior Project that provides rehabilitation opportunities for injured veterans and raises public awareness of the challenges they face. Shown here are participants in the charity's annual "Soldier Ride."

RIGHT: Hogan Lovells lawyers in London and the Royal British Legion have developed a strong pro bono partnership. Their complementary work has resulted, in the provision of assistance with inquests for bereaved service families, and with appeals relating to war pensions and armed forces compensation.

by which Farm Africa's Ethiopian operations would be reorganized into a for-profit business that will operate on a more sustainable basis.

A team in the London office also helped Farm Africa design Sidai Africa Ltd., a tax-efficient social business offering veterinary and livestock services on a financially viable basis through a network of branded franchises owned by qualified personnel. Sidai has now started thirty-six small businesses across Kenya, serving 2,000 customers.

Madrid- and London-based lawyers offered similar assistance to a Peruvian entrepreneur. Plant your Future, a grassroots Peruvian charity, seeks to reduce poverty for farming communities and mitigate climate change by restoring degraded land in the Amazon and selling carbon offsets. Hogan Lovells aided both these efforts.

In 2015, Hogan Lovells took its commitment to social entrepreneurship a step further by establishing the business and social enterprise program (Hogan Lovells BaSE) to train young lawyers in business and finance, promote greater understanding of companies' social impact, and provide direct client relationships. Hogan Lovells BaSE partners with Ashoka and UnLtd, two organizations supporting social entrepreneurs through start-up financing, support services, and global networking. These partnerships build on the organizations' existing relationships with lawyers across several offices, including Munich, Mexico City, Frankfurt, Paris, and Dusseldorf.

Supporting Veterans

London-based lawyers have a long history of partnering with the Royal British Legion to assist hundreds of members of the armed forces with appeals relating to war pensions and armed forces compensation. The firm expanded its commitment to the organization in 2011 by representing families at proceedings to determine the circumstances of their relative's death before a coroner's inquest. The firm supported the Wounded Warrior Project, the Washington, D.C. office's local Touch charity partner from 2013–2015, by raising over $84,000 through office fundraising events, such as an annual Wii Bowling competition. And lawyers from multiple U.S. offices advise Team Red, White & Blue, a veterans' nonprofit organisation, on an array of issues, including corporate partnership and sponsorship agreements, risk management, corporate governance, and privacy-related issues.

Chapter 5 ■ Our Citizenship

Combining Offices and Practices for our Pro Bono Clients

Firm pro bono clients—just like our paying clients—benefit significantly from our ability to harness lawyers' experience across practice groups, industry sectors, and offices. Denver-based lawyers from the corporate group combined with the energy and natural resources group to assist E+Co, which through its fund manager Persistent Energy Partners provides African households living off-grid with affordable renewable energy. Lawyers from Johannesburg, London, New York, and Washington, D.C. supported the Denver team in connection with numerous acquisitions, dispositions, joint ventures, debt and equity investments, restructurings, loan work-outs, and enforcement actions in Tanzania, Ghana, and South Africa.

Industry sector groups often donate their specialized knowledge to address gaps in the local expertise of communities. One notable example: the firm's health practice, in conjunction with the International Senior Lawyers' Project, assists the Liberian Ministry of Health and Social Welfare. Health lawyers played integral roles in establishing the Ministry's General Counsel Office, drafting legislation to create the Liberian Medicines and Health Products Regulatory Authority, and making important revisions to the country's mental and public health laws. These efforts complemented the firm's fundraising efforts for its then global charity partner Action Against Hunger, which works with the Liberian Ministry of Health and Social Welfare to build the country's capacity to detect, treat, and prevent malnutrition.

Hogan Lovells also uses its global reach to tackle tough international problems, such as human trafficking. Lawyers in France, Germany, Hungary, London, and Milan have worked with their U.S. colleagues and nonprofit Polaris to research international jurisdictions' protections for human trafficking victims. The Hong Kong office also supports Liberty Asia, a local charity working to provide a more effective, coordinated response to modern slavery. The firm was uniquely positioned to support each of these pro bono clients—no matter their location—by marshalling resources across offices, practice groups, and industry sectors.

DIVERSITY

Hogan Lovells has long been at the forefront of efforts to improve and promote inclusion of all people from different backgrounds and talents. The firm's diversity efforts have been recognized with a number of global awards, including five consecutive rankings in the Stonewall Workplace Equality Index Top 100 Employers for commitment to LGBT equality in the workplace, two consecutive recognitions as a Yale Law Women Top Ten Family Friendly Firm in the United States, a Dell Legal Diversity Award and the PMN Management Award for the German offices' Women@HL program which supports the development and progression of female lawyers.

> Hogan Lovells uses its global reach to tackle tough international problems such as human trafficking. The International Organization for Migration Ukraine opened an art installation, "Invisible in Plain Sight," in Kiev in 2014 to remember the 120,000 Ukranians who have fallen prey to human trafficking since 1991 and to tell the real stories of trafficked victims who are found around the world, and yet so often remain unseen.

ABOVE: Being a diverse and inclusive place to work is at the heart of the firm's vision and values. An LGBT network has been in place since 2007—it was renamed Hogan Lovells Pride in 2012. Shown here is a LGBT event in the London office with Ruth Grant.

RIGHT: School students taking part in the firm's Ladder to Law program in London.

As one of the first institutions to set targets for the elevation of women to the Board and partnership level, the firm developed a comprehensive strategy to support that aspiration and has signed the CEO Statement of Support for the UN Women's Empowerment Principles. This commitment extends worldwide with the establishment in 2009 by the Hong Kong office of Breaking Barriers, a networking platform for professional women, set up to offer intelligent and thought-provoking lunchtime seminars and evening social events. It also serves as a mentoring platform for young lawyers to gain business and networking skills. Since its establishment, Breaking Barriers has spread across the region to the offices in Singapore and Mongolia and is one of the flagship diversity programs in the area.

Hogan Lovells is committed to open and fair access to the legal profession and works to break down barriers that may deter talented individuals. The emphasis is on early intervention and flexible screening to source talent from a range of backgrounds. To improve the ethnicity and social mobility of the firm's future trainee solicitors, the London office graduate recruitment team focuses on interventions with different groups of students. The early engagement program for school students aims to inspire students to consider careers within the legal sector with support and advice on how to achieve this, and the university engagement program reaches out to talented students interested in becoming lawyers and encourages them to apply to the firm for their training contracts. The Ladder to Law program targets local schools outside the catchment area of the traditional City of London financial district, and reaches out to students of all ethnic backgrounds at schools where a high percentage of the pupils are on free school meals and are likely to be the first in their family to go to university. The aim is to give them an insight into what studying law would be like. The program includes workshops, open day events and work experience placements. In the U.S., lawyers from the New York and Washington, D.C. offices mentor first-year law students through Columbia Law School OutLaws, an LGBT student organization. Mentors are matched based on students' interest in particular legal paths or in certain practice areas and they provide valuable guidance on seeking internship and other career opportunities, and encourage LGBT students to consider a career with the firm.

Hogan Lovells also has a long track record, nationally and globally, of supporting those with disabilities. The firm promotes and supports disability sport as a platform to raise the aspirations of young disabled people; to help them tackle disadvantage; and to change perceptions of people

RIGHT: The opening ceremony of the 2012 Summer Paralympics in London.

BELOW: In 2015 Hogan Lovells extended its commitment to Paralympic sport by appointing the swimmer Ollie Hynd MBE to be its Paralympic Ambassador. Richard Welfare, Hogan Lovells client partner for the British Paralympic Association, commented, "We're delighted to be sponsoring a star of the British Paralympic team. Ollie is a true inspiration and we're very excited to be welcoming him as our Paralympic Ambassador."

Support for Paralympic Sport

Hogan Lovells has provided exclusive pro bono legal advice to the British Paralympic Association (BPA) since 2007. The firm's diverse contributions have included legal support in drafting and negotiating key commercial contracts with the main sponsors of the team and drafting and negotiating agreements for the training facilities for the athletes. This work ramped up considerably in the lead-up to the London 2012 Paralympic Games. Lawyers from our London, Hong Kong, and Beijing offices also provided services during the 2008 Beijing Games.

The firm also supported athletes of Haiti's first Paralympic team for London 2012 and advised a leading charity on the purchase of the television rights to show the games in Haiti for the first time, to an audience numbering in the millions. The momentum Hogan Lovells created to get the Haitian team to the UK for the games, and the subsequent TV coverage, helped to secure UN funding to open a new integrated sports facility in Cap-Haïtien, free to those with disabilities and staffed by the disabled.

In 2013, Hogan Lovells became the BPA's official legal services provider, advising on a range of issues in the lead up to, and during, the Sochi 2014 Paralympic Winter Games in anticipation of Rio 2016.

Following the firm's successful sponsorship of the British Paralympic Association, lawyers in the Johannesburg and London offices were engaged to extend the 2012 Paralympic legacy by supporting the international development of Boccia, particularly in Africa. Boccia is a sport, similar to the British game of bowls, played by athletes with moderate to extreme mobility impairments.

with disabilities. Internship programs also serve the needs of those with disabilities at a more local level. The Madrid office was one of the first offices to offer an internship to those with learning disabilities, raising awareness of the challenges and benefits of integrating people with learning disabilities in an international law firm. The London office too gives young people with disabilities an opportunity to gain work experience. The pro bono representation program also provides access to justice for disabled people around the world.

RIGHT: Haiti's Josué Cajuste competing in the 2012 Summer Paralympics. Hogan Lovells was instrumental in bringing the Haitian team to the games and in negotiating the TV rights. Edward Fennell in the London newspaper The Times wrote: "TV coverage of the Paralympics seems to be changing attitudes towards disability. By bringing it to Haiti, Hogan Lovells may be shaping the perceptions of a generation."

TOP: Hogan Lovells has a long-established relationship with Elizabeth Garrett Anderson School in London. Michelle Obama has visited the school a number of times and Hogan Lovells made it possible for twelve pupils to make a trip to the White House in Washington, D.C. in 2012. Yasmin Waljee OBE commented: "We have been supporting the school for some time now and are pleased to be able to help give the girls this once-in-a-lifetime opportunity."

ABOVE LEFT AND RIGHT: Debate It! is a Hogan Lovells flagship community investment program focused on teaching young people in schools public speaking and debating skills. Shown here are Debate It! participants in Dusseldorf, Germany.

COMMUNITY INVESTMENT

The community investment program applies the vast range of personal and professional skills found in Hogan Lovells for the good of others through a wide range of non-legal volunteer projects, using those skills to tackle social issues within our local communities. The program supports education, employability, social welfare, and the elderly and homeless in the communities on our doorsteps. Projects have included mentoring adults and children, assisting with reading skills, providing new and used clothing, and serving meals at homeless shelters.

The firm is committed to improving the social diversity of young people entering the profession from non-traditional backgrounds. For example, lawyers from the London office developed a pioneering program to build the confidence and soft-skills of young people by teaching the art of debating—something that lawyers naturally identify with. "Debate it!" involves members of Hogan Lovells working alongside teachers to create a program that encourages critical thinking, verbal reasoning, and presentation skills. The program, first introduced in schools across London, was subsequently adapted by offices in Germany and rolled out to schools for students from low-income households in Cologne, Duisburg, Frankfurt, Munich, and Hamburg. In 2015, the German Ministry of Education commended the firm for its leadership in this area, and new internship programs were created as a result of these efforts.

MATCHED CHARITABLE GIVING (TOUCH)

The firm's Touch program provides capped matching of funds raised by offices to support global and local charities selected by firm-wide and regional votes, respectively. Charities are normally supported for a two-year period. The results thus far are impressive.

Between 2011 and 2013, the firm raised and donated over $1.14 million to both the global Touch partner, Action Against Hunger, and to offices' local partners through various fundraising programs, including a 520km bike ride from London to Paris led by a team of partners from the London, Washington, D.C., Singapore, Munich, Hamburg, Miami, and Amsterdam offices. In 2014, over 60 percent of the firm voted to elect Lendwithcare through CARE International as the new global charity partner. Lendwithcare provides microloans to individual entrepreneurs in nine developing countries. Since January 2014, the firm has made over 680 loans to small enterprises.

ENVIRONMENT

The firm has been a founding member and leader of the Legal Sustainability Alliance, an inclusive movement of legal firms committed to working collaboratively to take action to improve the environmental sustainability of their operations and activities. We also complement our commitment to the environment with pro bono activities aimed at assisting environmental nonprofit organizations around the world.

CENTRE: Members from the Alicante office taking part in a Touch charity bicyle ride.

ABOVE: Warming up before a run in support of Action Against Hunger, London 2012.

LEFT: Regan Leahy (left) and Gill McGreevy (right) during a cycle ride to raise funds for global Touch charity partner, Lendwithcare, through CARE International. Shown here with Savan Tob, an entrepreneur funded by Hogan Lovells in Cambodia. Savan was able to repay the loan taken out in 2014 to buy seeds and fertiliser within a year. She uses the extra income to support her six children.

BOTTOM LEFT: Hogan Lovells consistently responds to catastrophic global events. In 2015 a firm-wide fundraising campaign was launched in response to CARE International's Nepal earthquake appeal to provide food, shelter, and other emergency supplies to victims of the tragedy. The firm raised $65,406 including matched funding.

LEFT: Hogan Lovells has reduced the number of plastic bottles it uses by installing water bottling stations, like this one in the Brussels office.

BELOW: In 2011 the Washington, D.C. office unveiled the firm's Ford Transit Connect electric vehicle. An office-wide competition to name the new vehicle came up with ZELDA ("Zero Emission Lawyer Driven Automobile"). ZELDA, among her many errands, delivers used clothing donations to shelters throughout the city—a double benefit that helps preserve the environment while supporting those most in need.

BOTTOM: Nick Cray signing the firm's Environmental Pledge at the partnership conference in Miami.

BELOW LEFT: Volunteers from Hogan Lovells taking part in an environmental cleanup in Canton Waterfront Park, Maryland, 2015.

Improving our Environment

2010: 30 percent reduction in London office's emissions since 2007
2011: 100 percent renewable energy for Munich office
2011: Leadership in Energy and Environment Design (LEED) certification for Baltimore office
2011: 136 metric tonnes of CO^2 saved per year by installing motion detectors for lighting in London
2012: 50 percent reduction in gas usage in London as a result of streamlining heating and cooling to use ambient temperatures
2013: 76,000 fewer disposable bottles used annually as a result of London's in-house bottling plant
2013: 18 percent reduction in copy paper used in U.S. offices
2014: 85,450 kWh of electricity a year saved in twenty-two offices in Europe, Asia, and the Middle East by installing automatic nightly computer shutdown software
2014: 81,000lb (36,740kg) of paper recycled in Washington, D.C. office

Within the firm's offices, the main impact on the environment comes from energy use, the waste generated, travel, and procurement. The firm's environmental policy seeks to raise internal awareness of environmental issues, minimize energy consumption and waste, maximize recycling and reuse, and travel and procure responsibly. Many varied initiatives have been introduced in these areas, including the introduction of movement sensors, automated computer shutdowns, improved video meeting capabilities to reduce or contain travel, and cycle-to-work schemes. Multiple offices have installed water bottling equipment to save on disposable bottles, programmed printers to default to double-sided printing to reduce paper consumption, provided reusable mugs, and encouraged and supported recycling. The collective energy saving and waste reduction has been substantial.

THE YEARS AHEAD

These few examples represent only a tiny snapshot of Hogan Lovells' global good citizenship achievements. There is so much more to come: in 2015, Hogan Lovells launched a new global citizenship policy to take the firm's commitments one step further. All members of the firm—including non-lawyers—are asked to devote at least twenty-five hours per year to citizenship activities across the program's five pillars: pro bono, diversity, community investment, matched charitable giving (Touch), and environment. Hogan Lovells is the first law firm to set an hourly target for each staff member's citizenship activities.

In May 2015, the firm undertook its broadest global initiative yet—as a role model and agent for change in the area of gender equality. The Hogan Lovells Empowering Girls and Women Initiative focuses significant citizenship activities on addressing gender-based violence, enhancing educational opportunities for girls and women, and empowering women to shape society. As signatories of the CEO Statement of Support for the UN Women's Empowerment Principles and a member of the Clinton Global Initiative, the firm launched an ambitious three-year "Commitment to Action" and has already identified more than thirty local, national, and international nonprofits and other organizations with which to partner. Together with all of those groups, at a local and global level, Hogan Lovells will work to narrow the gender gap, which has plagued the economic, social, and political rights of girls and women.

Calvary Women's Services in Washington, D.C. are part of the firm's Empowering Girls and Women Initiative. Hogan Lovells has contributed more than $340,000 to Calvary Women's Services through financial donations, in-kind contributions, and pro bono services. Employees regularly serve as volunteers and provide meals for women in Calvary's transitional housing programs.

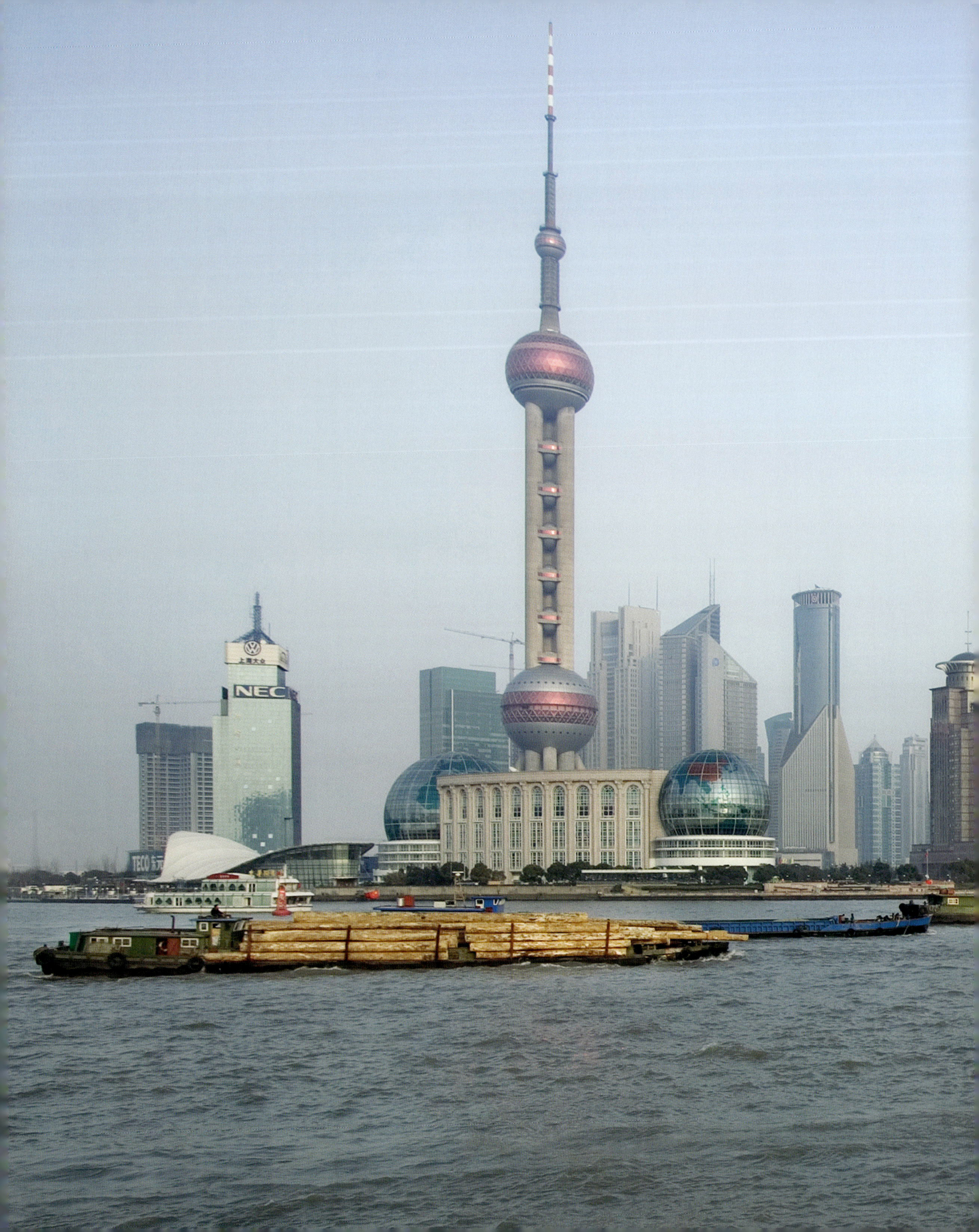
NEC
TECO

Chapter 6

Our Worldwide Team

Chapter 6

Our Worldwide Team

PREVIOUS PAGES: Shanghai's famous waterfront, seen from the Bund. The firm's Shanghai office opened in 2003.

BELOW: Staff at the Hong Kong Spring dinner, 2015.

RIGHT: The firm's first office opened in Hong Kong in 1982 in The Landmark building.

With nearly fifty offices on all five continents, Hogan Lovells is where clients need it to be: the commercial hubs in the U.S. and China; the established markets of Europe and Japan; the booming economies of South-East Asia; the financial power houses in the Middle East; the fast-developing countries in Latin America; and in new routes into new markets in Australia and Africa. As part of its global team, each office plays a particular role in the firm's vision.

A good part of an office's success is due to those who set it up and made it grow. Each office has its own stories that contribute to the firm's history. Stories from Washington, D.C., London, Germany, Mexico, and South Africa have been told in previous chapters, here are some anecdotes from the early years of other offices.

ASIA
Hong Kong (1982)

Following social and economic reforms in the 1970s and 1980s, Hong Kong became a global financial hub—one of the "Four Asian Tigers." At the height of this development in 1982, Lovell White & King sent Andrew Walker, later to become the firm's Senior Partner, to open an office there. Walker, however, returned with empty hands; he was not prepared to

TOP LEFT: The firm's first office in China was set up in the Beijing Friendship Hotel in 1986. Today the Beijing office (bottom left) is in China Central Place in Chaoyang District.

ABOVE AND LEFT: The Japan office in Toyko celebrated its twentieth anniversary in 2010.

agree to a rental agreement within a couple of hours, which at the time was standard fare in the overheated property market. Walker had better luck on his second visit that year and took a lease in the famous "Landmark" building.

In the early days, legal practice and procedure were largely bound to English law. Accordingly, many of the office's first lawyers came from England, including Nicholas Gould and Patrick Sherrington, who during his first stay served as the vice president of the Hong Kong Law Society. For them and for others, Hong Kong was an excellent arena to prove their talent.

In later years, Hong Kong became the "mothership" for many other offices in the region.

Beijing (1986)

In 1986, long before China began to ease its restrictions on foreign trade, Durrant Piesse moved to Beijing together with its client, the London Export Corporation. In those days, the London Export Corporation was among the few foreign businesses allowed to have a trade presence in China. Building on that foundation, Lovell White Durrant was one of the five foreign law firms that obtained a license to practice international law in Beijing when they were first granted in 1992.

One of the office's key achievements was the launch of the Sino-Global Legal Alliance. Devised and orchestrated from Beijing, the alliance combines the experience and resources of Hogan Lovells with a specially selected group of other leading Chinese law firms located in the country's major cities.

Hogan & Hartson also set up an office in the capital. Led by Jun Wei, the office opened with a celebration in the Great Hall of the People in 2002. The event was promoted by the slogan "Practicing at the Intersection of Business and Government Regulation," highlighting the office's competitive edge.

In the years that followed, the Beijing office established itself as the hub for the firm's China outbound investment and related types of work.

Tokyo (1990)

Japanese law for legal practitioners from foreign countries changed fundamentally in 1985; starting in that year, lawyers from countries who guaranteed reciprocity could open an office in Japan. Driven by that opportunity, David Moss went to Tokyo to begin an eighteen-month placement with a local firm, and

ABOVE: The firm's office in Ho Chi Minh City, Vietnam, is situated in the Bitexco Financial Tower, the tallest building in the city.

RIGHT: One of the world's most celebrated sculptures, Auguste Rodin's "The Thinker," greets staff in Singapore as they come and go from the Collyer Quay offices.

eventually opened an office for Lovell White & King in 1990. He secured office space in a building owned by Mitsui, a corporate giant with century-old roots. In order to get the lease, Moss had to undergo an unusual interview; his character and etiquette were tested by Prince Higashikuni of the Imperial Royal Family. Overcoming the challenges of the Japanese recession during the 1990s, the Tokyo partners built strong and lasting ties in the ensuing years with many Japanese corporations to the benefit of other offices across the firm.

Attorney at foreign law (gaikokuho jimu bengoshi) was a rare title to hold for U.S. patent attorneys in the mid-1990s. David Lubitz was one of the few to have qualified. In 2000, he was the obvious candidate to open Hogan & Hartson's Tokyo office. To the present day, patent law is among the office's core areas of work.

Vietnam (1996)

The firm's history in Vietnam reaches back to the Doi Moi reforms of the late 1980s, when Lovell White Durrant began assisting clients with services related to the relaxing of economic policy. In 1994, after some five years of doing business in Vietnam from the Hong Kong office, partner Stephen Hayward formed a team in Ho Chi Minh City with the support of two seconded lawyers from a local firm. The success of this team won it the honor of being the first international law practice to be granted a branch office license there in 1996.

In 2006, activity in Vietnam was re-energized across industry sectors and focus was extended to Hanoi where the firm opened its second office in 2009. These offices grew to include lawyers qualified in Vietnam, the U.S., and UK, who work closely together for clients operating in this fast-growing economy. Both offices are active participants in the Hogan Lovells global citizenship program and work to improve life for people in less developed parts of the country.

Singapore (1998)

The Singapore office serves as the gateway for the firm's work in South and South East Asia. When Lovells first opened in 1998, three partners threw themselves into project finance and corporate work, which were the main focus at the time, essential for the financial restructuring required in the region following the Asian financial crisis in the late 1990s.

In 2000, the Singapore government liberalized the legal market by permitting foreign law firms

ABOVE AND LEFT: Hogan Lovells staff in the office in Ulaanbaatar, Mongolia, and on an outing in May 2013.

FAR LEFT: The firm celebrated ten years of its office in Shanghai with a cocktail party at the Shanghai Gallery of Art in 2013. Its first office in Shanghai was in the Shanghai Kerry Centre.

to partner with local Singapore law firms. Lovells moved swiftly. In 2001, it entered into a joint law venture (JLV) with Lee & Lee, a leading full-service law firm, founded in 1955 by Singapore's first Prime Minister, Lee Kuan Yew, together with his brother, Lee Kim Yew, and his wife, Kwa Geok Choo. The Hogan Lovells Lee & Lee JLV continues today and is the oldest joint law venture in Singapore.

Shanghai (2003)

The preparations for Lovells' second office in mainland China started in a low-key way. In 2000, Doug Clark was seconded from the Hong Kong office to a local firm in Shanghai. While there, he explored the options of opening an office in the city. A few years later, in 2003, the Chinese government relaxed regulations restricting the operation of foreign law firms to one city. That was the starting shot for Clark and Zhen "Katie" Feng to inaugurate the firm's practice in Shanghai, China's commercial hotspot for international trade.

Hogan & Hartson's Shanghai office opened just one year after Lovells—in 2004, the firm's centennial year—and they joined forces following the 2010 combination.

Early success for the office came in the shape of the Schneider Electric case involving claims for multimillion dollar damages from the Chint Group. The case was so prominent that Nicolas Sarkozy, then the President of France, addressed the issue during a state visit to China. Building on this recognition, the firm's Shanghai lawyers handled large parts of the dispute between Qualcomm and Nokia, which was regarded as one of the biggest pieces of patent litigation in the world at the time.

Ulaanbaatar (2011)

In 2009, Michael Aldrich, a Beijing-based partner with twenty-five years of experience in Asia moved to Ulaanbaatar to win work for the firm in this frontier market. Initially, as a liaison between the firm and a local office, Aldrich began to build a Mongolian legal practice aligned with the needs of international clients.

The office formally opened in 2011 with a particular focus on projects and related work. In 2012, Chris Melville, a seasoned practitioner with extensive experience in Russia, joined Aldrich. Their combination of Asian- and Russian-based experience was a significant factor in accelerating the office's development.

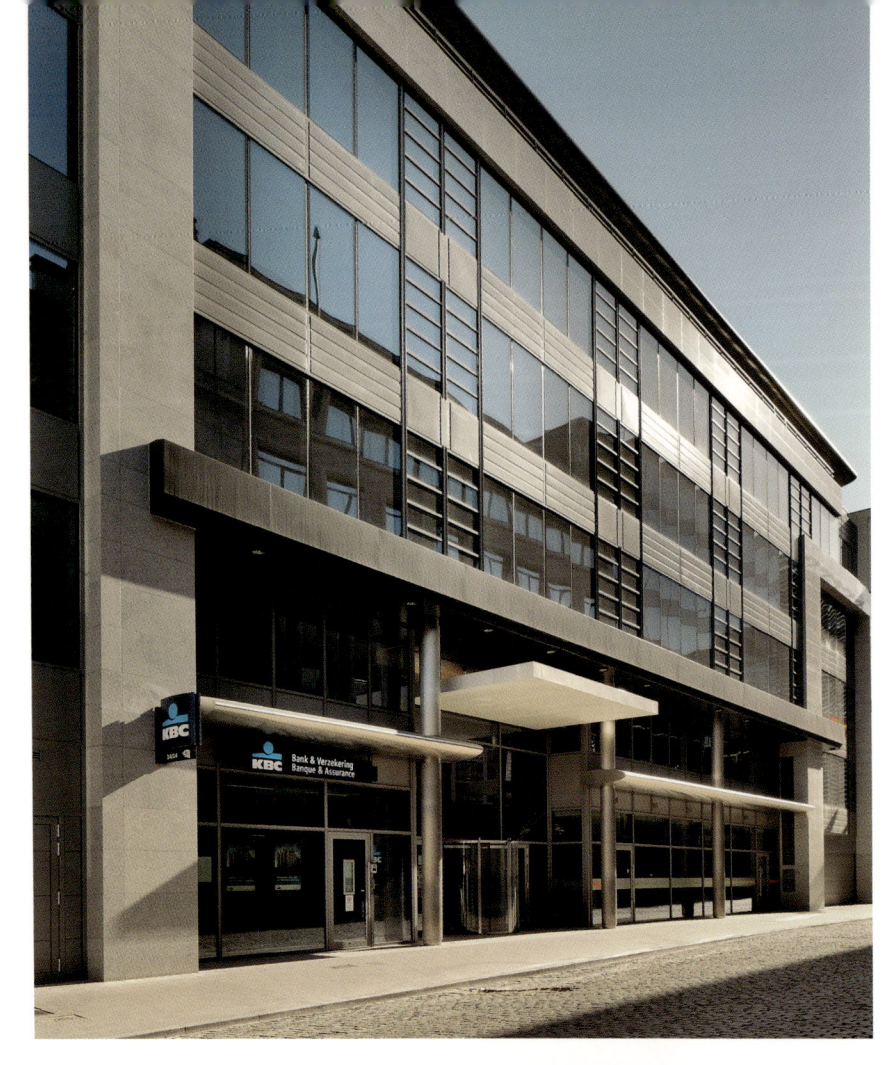

ABOVE: After the combination in 2010 the combined Hogan Lovells Brussels team moved to the Pericles Building.

RIGHT: "La Lutte équestre" or "Le combat des cavaliers" (1899–1909) by Jacques de Lalaing, in front of the Lovells ofice on Avenue Louise, Brussels.

EUROPE
Brussels (1972)

Lovell White & King began its European expansion in the early years of the European Economic Community. In January 1972, the UK joined the EEC. That same year, Andrew White opened the London firm's first overseas office in Brussels. Beginning in 1976, Simon Bullimore started a secondment system for young lawyers from London. This gave the firm wider European experience—and the related introduction and farewell events fuelled the office's reputation as being a very social place to work.

The office focused on competition law and handled some of the first high-profile cases at the heart of European integration, for example the famous "right-hand drive" case for Ford, a case involving the parallel import of cars originally supplied to members of the British army in Germany. The case ran to what was then called the European Court of Justice and put the Brussels office firmly on the map in this area of law. Its reputation continued to grow over the years, with high-profile cases like the Trans-Atlantic Conference Agreement (TACA) cartel fine of €273 million which a Lovells team successfully overturned.

Hogan & Hartson's presence in Europe was backed by Sandy Berger, who believed that a clearly defined niche in Brussels was needed to perform well against other firms. When he opened the firm's Brussels office in 1991, it focused on European regulatory matters and as more partners joined from Washington, D.C. the practice diversified to include competition law as well.

Brussels is officially the most merged office of the firm. Boesebeck Droste's office was first to merge with Lovell White Durrant's. Siméon et Associés then brought a Brussels operation with it and in 2010, Hogan & Hartson's Brussels office was united with the Lovells office.

Paris (1990)

Driven by his work for French clients in the late 1980s, John Cooper laid the foundation of Lovell White Durrant's office in Paris. From the start, Cooper pulled together an exceptionally international team, with Sharon Lewis from the UK, the American-born Russell Sleigh, the French lawyer Robert Follie, and the charismatic Milan Chromecek. (Chromecek, a Canadian-trained lawyer, had escaped from communist Czechoslovakia and endured years of hardship in Austrian refugee camps.)

FAR LEFT: Rooftop event in the Paris office looking over to the Grand Palais.

LEFT: Valentin Ribet, a talented Hogan Lovells Paris litigator, died in November 2015, a victim of the terrorist attack at the Bataclan concert hall in Paris. He was 26.

As the office grew steadily over the years, the intention to merge with an established French firm became stronger. In 2001, Lovells joined with Siméon et Associés, a French firm founded in 1974. With high-calibre partners and a broad practice, the Siméon merger transformed the Paris office fundamentally bringing it on a par with other global law firms in the city.

Hogan & Hartson had a presence in Paris from 1991, which came about from the lateral hire of partner Mark Mazo. Mazo was already a respected specialist in public company mergers and acquisitions, bankruptcy, insolvency, and federal securities law and had built a special relationship with Aérospatiale, a French state-owned aerospace manufacturer. Hogan & Hartson's hands-on support of Aérospatiale during the lateral hire process also persuaded this client to follow. After a joint venture with another firm, Hogan & Hartson moved to its own office in 2004 with lawyers including Winston Maxwell, Mark Mazo, and Bill Curtin, who had substantial client interests in France.

Warsaw (1991)

With the social and industrial unrest of the 1980s and the rise of the "Solidarity" movement, Poland was at the forefront of transformation from a communist to a democratic state. Hogan & Hartson were involved at an early stage of this process when Joseph C. Bell became legal adviser to the Polish Ministry of Finance and opened an office in Warsaw. During his time, he made a considerable contribution to the establishment of free market rules for the Polish economy.

The Lovells Warsaw office developed a strong focus on finance, insurance, real estate, corporate, and tax work when it hired Beata Balas-Noszczyk, Jolanta Nowakowska-Zimoch, Marek Wroniak, and Andrzej Dębiec, as partners in 2000. Now together with Piotr Zawislak and Rafał Grochowski they continue to shape the office to this day. The office has steadily built on the foundations of its early work for financial institutions and its clients are now representative of many other industry sectors as well.

The office building of Hogan Lovells in Warsaw was designed by the distinguished Polish architect Marian Lalewicz, a proponent of academic classicism. The building was commissioned to be the headquarters of Bank Rolny. Lalewicz died during the Warsaw Uprising in 1944.

ABOVE LEFT: The firm has had a presence in Moscow since 1994. Shown here is an office outing to the Sochi Winter Olympic site in 2014.

ABOVE RIGHT: Alicante, home to the European Union Trademark Office, is a key location for trademark and design protection across Europe. The Hogan Lovells Alicante office deals primarily with intellectual property issues around trademarks and designs, and the laws and practices that affect them.

Moscow (1994)

Hogan & Hartson entered the Russian market when Rebecca Bronson opened its Moscow office in 1994. Lovell White Durrant followed in April 1997, led by the Canadian-born dispute resolution and mediation specialist Daniel Gogek. Both offices demonstrated how law and its connection to business can bridge social and political divides. Hogan & Hartson's office, for example, represented various Russian businesses before the United Nations Compensation Commission in relation to claims arising from Iraq's 1990 invasion of Kuwait; they advised on a tender for management of one of the world's largest pipeline systems in Kazakhstan from Russia, and they guided a Hollywood studio on copyright issues for the submarine film *K-19* relating to personal histories of the Russian crew.

A new era of the firm in Russia began in 2005 when Oxana Balayan, a lawyer dual-qualified in Russia and England, took on the management responsibilities of the office. Around this time, Russia's international prominence increased as a member of the newly coined BRIC (Brazil, Russia, India, and China) group. As a result of this, the Moscow office set up a close working relationship with a dedicated Russia team in the London office and started to hire English-qualified lawyers in Moscow.

Alicante (1996)

In the early 1990s a new type of trademark was created: the European Community Trademark. To the great surprise of many, the remote Spanish coastal town of Alicante was picked to host the European office to administer the new trademark regulations. From that time forward, Alicante became a key location for trademark and design protection across Europe.

Hamburg partner Dietrich Ohlgart sensed the importance of Alicante early on, sending a young, Spanish-speaking trademark lawyer to the city to set up an office there. The Alicante office opened in January 1996, with one junior associate, one secretary and, initially, only an ironing board to serve as a desk. In its early days the EU Trademark Office was small, with a staff of around forty. As a result, the firm's lawyers knew all the EU staff well; business was often carried out informally and many discussions on the finer points of law and procedure were held on the soccer pitch or over tapas. Since that time both the EU Trademark Office and Hogan Lovells have grown in size formidably; both are now hubs for all European trademark matters.

Milan (2000)

The new millennium marked the firm's entrance into Italy. All roads may lead to Rome, but for much of Italy's business and finance transactions Milan is the place to be. The Lovells Milan operation got off the ground in October 2000 with client work before there were desks. The team became so busy so quickly that there was no time to discuss the outcome of that year's European soccer championship. (A "last-gasp" equalizer by France in injury time snatched victory from the grasp of the Italian team and forced the game into extra time. France scored a golden goal in the thirteenth minute of extra time to win 2–1.)

The Office Managing Partner, Marco Rota Candiani, remembers this initial period fondly: "There were just a few of us, acting with many 'hats' and with a spirit that combined a sense of adventure with the satisfaction of seeing business rapidly growing from scratch. Everyone should be proud of what has been achieved, but the best is yet to come."

Rome (2000)

In close coordination with activities in Milan, a group of London partners with Italian ties volunteered to establish an office in Rome, then the first truly Latin civil law environment for the firm. Among these was the current Italian Managing Partner Leah Dunlop, an Italian speaker with family ties in Italy. Lateral hires from a well-established Italian boutique firm completed the kick-off team, which was so swiftly assembled that the initial office had to be a one-room, one-telephone facility rented from a temporary office provider.

The office's first major corporate transaction was for the international drinks company SABMiller, in its acquisition of the Italian company Birra Peroni SpA. Over its first decade the Rome office grew quickly to become one of the largest international law firms in the capital, with a truly diversified practice, under Office Managing Partner Fulvia Astolfi.

The Hogan Lovells offices in Milan (above left) and Rome (above right) provide advice to Italian and international companies on a wide range of complex business transactions.

LEFT: The Amsterdam office on the Keizersgracht combines strong local knowledge with international experience, placing a particular emphasis on the integration of corporate, finance, and tax services.

BELOW: In 1998 a special tram trip took place through Amsterdam for staff of Ekelmans Den Hollander to mark its twentieth anniversary. Two years later Ekelmans Den Hollander merged with Lovells.

A number of firms were evaluated for merger; Ekelmans Den Hollander stood out as the favorite. The Dutch firm was founded in 1978 and had established a successful corporate practice as well as a good reputation in intellectual property. The Lovells merger with Ekelmans can be traced back to the initial contact between London partner Nicholas Macfarlane and Bert Oosting during the Merck–Monsanto case. This merger opened possibilities for acquisition of new client work for clients like Merck, Sharp & Dohme, Xerox, GlaxoSmithKline, RWE, ING, Rabobank, Mitsubishi, ScheringPlough, GEM, Mars, and Mitsui.

Madrid (2004)

At the beginning of the new millennium, at the height of Spain's economic boom, the Spanish legal market was in turmoil. A market dominated for decades by a handful of national players now witnessed the arrival of many international law and accountancy firms. In that heated environment, Lovells looked for an individual who had the drive and resilience to build an office from scratch. In 2004 they found the young and ambitious M&A lawyer José Maria Balañá. Balañá persuaded others to join the firm such as the dispute resolution partner José Luis Huerta, and the office was opened in the same year. The office soon attracted additional talented lawyers. Among them was the German intellectual property partner Burkhart Goebel, who transferred his practice from the Lovells Hamburg office to Madrid.

The strong foundations of the Madrid office became apparent when Spain was hit hard by the EU financial crisis. The boom years were over but the Madrid office continued to grow and perform strongly—while many competitors went under or left the country.

Amsterdam (2001)

Following the merger between Lovell White Durrant and Boesebeck Droste in 2000, a presence in the Netherlands was firmly on the agenda as part of the new firm in the Lovells plans for expansion. Since the mid-twentieth century, Lovell White Durrant had strong client relationships there, particularly through partner Oliver Huntley's work for the Dutch government.

Chapter 6 ■ Our Worldwide Team

Birmingham (2014)

Some offices serve a very specific purpose. This is the case for the Hogan Lovells Legal Services Centre, located in Birmingham which started operations in 2014. By carrying out some elements of its UK-based work in a less expensive location, the office enables the firm to make a particularly cost-effective offering to clients and, based on early successes, is looking to broaden its range of services. The Birmingham lawyers work as part of the relevant London team under the supervision of a London partner.

Luxembourg (2013)

In 2013, Hogan Lovells looked to grow the firm's funds and tax practices and expand its capabilities in the corporate, real estate, and private equity sectors. With this goal, in August 2013, investment funds partner Pierre Reuter, corporate partner Jean-Michel Schmit, and tax partner Gérard Neiens, launched the Luxembourg office with the assistance of a team composed of several lawyers, one paralegal, an office manager, a know-how coordinator, and two secretaries.

This founding team attracted work from diverse clients such as asset managers Areca and Pareto, the real estate investment trust Dream REIT, the telecom groups Millicom International Cellular and Nii, the diversified manufacturer group Leggett & Platt, and the privately held electronic supplier group YESSS.

ABOVE: Hogan Lovells Madrid real estate team.

TOP LEFT: An event to celebrate the tenth anniversary of the Hogan Lovells Madrid office in 2014. From left to right: José Maria Balañá, Steve Immelt, Lucas Osorio, and Nicholas Cheffings.

FAR LEFT: In 2013 David Harris commented: "Luxembourg is an increasingly important jurisdiction for investment funds. Our new office will allow us to offer a much fuller funds capability to our clients and it will also be a key to a number of our other practice areas such as corporate, real estate, private equity, and tax."

LEFT: The Hogan Lovells Legal Services Centre is based in Colmore Plaza, Birmingham, UK.

Hogan Lovells ■ Our Story

ABOVE: View from the Hogan Lovells New York office at 875 Third Avenue. The office has more than 210 resident lawyers and is the firm's second-largest U.S. office.

ABOVE RIGHT: Spectators watching the Hogan Lovells Cup during the Virginia Gold Cup Races in May 2013. The Northern Virginia office was established in 1985 and are race sponsors.

UNITED STATES OF AMERICA
New York (1977)

Hogan & Hartson recognized that high-end corporate and litigation work in Manhattan was the domain of a tight network of established firms, but in 1998, the firm decided it needed to be on the ground there and asked Warren Gorrell to lead the effort. Gorrell, Jeff Schneider, Mark Landis, and others carried out the advance planning and groundwork required and the office opened in 1998 with a small team of corporate lawyers including Gorrell, Landis, and Andrew Trubin. The office took a major step toward becoming a full-service practice two years later when it acquired thirty-five lawyers from Davis, Weber & Edwards, a highly regarded litigation boutique. Then in 2002, the firm merged with Squadron, Ellenoff, Plesent & Sheinfeld. With over 100 lawyers, the New York and Los Angeles firm Squadron enjoyed a superb reputation in the media, communications, entertainment, and technology industries. It served national and international clients such as News Corporation, British Sky Broadcasting, Fox Entertainment, and their affiliates in the far-reaching Murdoch empire. Aside from his client work, founding partner Howard Squadron was an activist for human rights and an ardent supporter of many art programs.

Lovells founded its New York office in 1977 to serve as an important link to the London practice for the large number of its U.S. clients such as Woolworth's, Standard Oil (Exxon Mobil), Ford, and Merck & Co., Inc. With the combination in the year 2010, the existing Lovells office was integrated with the Hogan & Hartson office to bring the total number of lawyers in this office to well above 200 with strong practices in all key areas.

The New York office has handled countless significant corporate transactions and litigations over the years. A few examples include the Talisman Energy Alien Tort Statute action, a significant and high-profile case which Joe Cyr and others won on summary judgment and appeal. New York partners Eric Lobenfeld, Ira Schaefer, and Ted Mlynar successfully defended Sprint in a $1.4 billion lawsuit brought by patent troll High Point SARL. And, as restructuring partner Chris Donoho rightly pointed out, "Nothing tops the Kodak experience"—an award-winning transaction, managed between New York and London, saved both Eastman Kodak and the pension plans of over 15,000 former employees.

Northern Virginia (1985)

The opening of the Northern Virginia office in 1985 was a milestone for Hogan & Hartson. Aside from running a support office in Bethesda, Maryland, Hogan & Hartson had been exclusively a Washington, D.C. firm. The economic development in the mid-1980s changed that: Northern Virginia was seeing growth in the technology and defense industries as a result of increased investment under the Reagan administration. As a result, the real estate market in the surrounding area was also picking up fast.

Bob Odle asked Lang Keith to relocate from D.C. and brought technology specialist Raymond Vickery back to the firm to open the office with Jane Roush (who later was appointed to the Virginia Supreme Court), Richard Becker and other partners. Propelled by the rapid growth of technology and internet business during the 1990s, the office quickly established its own identity and expanded as a full-service office with a distinctive position in the thriving Northern Virginia business community.

Baltimore (1988)

Hogan & Hartson's Baltimore, Maryland, office arose from Bob Odle's plans to expand the Bethesda office by hiring Ty Cobb, a former federal prosecutor in Baltimore. By the end of their first interview, however, Odle and Cobb were instead talking about opening a new office in Baltimore with a focus on litigation, white collar defense, and banking. Once all arrangements for the opening of the office had been made, Cobb went to George Beall—the former U.S. Attorney for the State of Maryland and his mentor at his current firm—to tell him about his intention to join Hogan & Hartson. To Cobb's great surprise, instead of showing disappointment, Beall suggested that he would like to follow and help to set up the new office.

The office opened in 1988 with ten lawyers including Cobb and Kevin Gralley with George Beall at the helm. Another former federal prosecutor, Steve Immelt, was originally slated to join the founding team but instead joined a year later. Immelt got his start in management when he succeeded Beall as Office Managing Partner on the Baltimore office's tenth anniversary; he is currently the firm's CEO.

From its origin as a white collar defense, litigation, and finance practice, the Baltimore office diversified into corporate law beginning with the hires of Duke Lohr and Mike Silver in the early

The Baltimore office of Hogan Lovells has grown to nearly 80 lawyers and staff. Key industries served by the office include life sciences, energy, high technology, private equity, financial services, aerospace, defense, and government services. The firm moved to the Legg Mason Tower (on the right), a 24-story glass building in the fast-growing area of Baltimore's Harbor East development, in 2009.

ABOVE: The Hogan Lovells Denver office is due to move to the Union Station area of the city in 2016. Craig Umbaugh, partner in the Denver office, says: "We have enjoyed being in one of downtown's premier buildings and now we look forward to being an anchor tenant in 1601 Wewatta. The redevelopment of the Union Station area has created a great vibe and energy in the city."

RIGHT: The Colorado Springs office is located at Two North Cascade Avenue in the heart of the city.

Denver (1993)

As part of its strategy to expand its corporate and commercial practice across the U.S., Hogan & Hartson opened its Denver office in late 1993 with corporate specialist Donis Walker and a team of public finance lawyers. These partners brought a number of prominent clients to the office and over twenty years later, the United States Olympic Committee (USOC), Denver International Airport, and the University of Colorado remain highly valued clients of the firm.

With the 2007 arrival of Cole Finegan, who had served as city attorney, the office also became more involved in large public projects at the intersection of law and public policy. It played a key part in handling financing and redevelopment of the Denver Union Station, Lowry Air Force Base, and the former Stapleton International Airport.

Craig Umbaugh and David Scott were central to the financing and construction of the three principal sports venues in Denver. Niki Tuttle's work with the cable television industry included her representation of the first out-of-market sports deals with the National Basketball Association and National Hockey League. Steve Cohen, Chris Walsh, and other Denver corporate lawyers also represented the three largest U.S. movie theater chains on multiple matters including a joint venture with major film studios involving the deployment of the first satellite network for the distribution of Hollywood films, directly from the studios to theaters.

1990s and a number of lateral hires since. Project finance and tax practices followed in the mid-1990s and the office has steadily grown through internal advancement and lateral hires.

Colorado Springs (1994)

The Colorado Springs office opened in 1994 with Scott Blackmun spear-heading its commercial practice with Donis Walker, of the Denver office. In 1995, Walker and Blackmun recruited John Cook, an experienced trial lawyer, to lead their litigation practice. Walker and Cook further developed the U.S. Olympic Committee (USOC) client relationship, acting as its outside litigation counsel. The office's construction litigation practice is a key group in this office, which was significantly developed when Jeff George joined, bringing commercial litigation experience from his years in Dallas, Texas. In September 1999, Bill Kubida joined the Colorado Springs office, providing a depth of intellectual property advice to start-up companies as well as Fortune 100 corporations. In 2001, David Isbell, a preeminent real estate lawyer in Colorado, joined the Colorado Springs office. Isbell brings his vast real estate experience to numerous projects in Colorado Springs and throughout the United States.

Los Angeles (1996)

Hogan & Hartson next looked to expand to the West Coast, choosing downtown Los Angeles for its first location in 1996. The firm opened its doors in early April in the Biltmore Tower, which had been constructed in the motor court of the historic Biltmore Hotel. It was traditional in design, with dark wood and an iconic photograph of Frank Hogan and Theodore Roosevelt prominently located behind reception—marking the Washington, D.C. roots of the new office.

Motivated by its strong regulatory practice, the firm hired Marc Bozeman from the federal Food and Drug Administration (FDA) as its first California lawyer and Managing Partner. From the outset, the office had a diverse practice; its lawyers included the former California Commissioner of Corporations, as well as senior members of the California Patent Bar. An early bond with Japanese clients was strengthened by the arrival of a patent prosecution and litigation group.

The 2002 merger with Squadron, Ellenoff, Plesent & Sheinfeld in New York brought to the firm several partners in Los Angeles and clients in the media and entertainment industries such as News Corporation and its affiliates. A high-profile case in this area was the antitrust class action challenging the business relationship between the big motion picture studios and Blockbuster Video. This resulted in a major victory for News Corporation and the other defendants following a lengthy jury trial.

Lawyers in both offices worked together, and a common summer clerkship program was instituted and when leases for both Los Angeles locations were nearing an end the firm decided to combine them. The united team opened at new premises in Century City which was less traditional in design, featuring light woods and modern art.

Miami (2000)

Hogan & Hartson had been developing an international project finance and dispute practice since the mid-1990s. This practice increasingly focused on Latin America, which led the firm to set its eyes on Miami due to the city's geographical and cultural connections. In the year 2000, Mark Sterling opened the Miami office as part of the firm's acquisition of Davis, Weber & Edwards, which had had a small office in Miami in addition to its New York office. Sterling had been with the firm since 1979, but relocated to Miami in 1993 to take on a top position in a leading healthcare company before rejoining Hogan & Hartson.

ABOVE LEFT: The Los Angeles office is located in Century City, along the Avenue of the Stars, in west Los Angeles.

ABOVE: Opening in 2000, the Miami office has lawyers working in areas such as complex litigation and arbitration, healthcare, corporate, and project finance. Located in Miami's financial district at 600 Brickell Avenue, the office has views of Biscayne Bay.

Hogan Lovells ■ Our Story

LEFT: Located in the hub of the U.S. energy industry, lawyers in the Houston office are involved in complex, high-profile, multinational disputes and transactions.

BELOW: Hogan Lovells opened an office in Philadelphia in 2008. Shown here is Independence Hall, built in 1753, where the U.S. Constitution and Declaration of Independence were signed.

Sterling soon established a multidisciplinary team of lawyers with leadership experience in the healthcare industry and in senior government positions. Later, two prominent Florida lawyers, Parker D. Thomson and Carol A. Licko brought with them a nationally recognized litigation practice to serve clients at the local, state, and national levels.

Starting from a solid basis, the Miami office grew fast during its first years. In the early 2000s, the corporate and project finance practice was reinforced by the arrival of Jorge Diaz-Silveira, Luis Perez, José Valdivia, and Miguel Zaldivar. Daniel González and Richard Lorenzo also joined around that time to strengthen the litigation and arbitration practice. The Miami operation is now ideally placed to serve clients in various industries throughout the U.S. and to fulfil its role at the crossroad between Latin America and the U.S., Europe, and Asia.

Houston (2006)

Home to a significant number of Fortune 500 companies, Houston has ascended to the forefront of the global economy. To win business in that demanding environment, Hogan & Hartson opened its office there in 2006. The Houston market quickly embraced the firm's entry, the team outgrowing its original office space in a few short years. The client portfolio grew to include global energy and infrastructure companies; global engineering, procurement, and construction contractors; a large foreign-owned petrochemical refiner; international drilling contractors; major financial institutions; and private equity groups. Under Office Managing Partner Bruce Oakley, the Houston team takes on a broad mix of transactional, regulatory, and disputes-oriented matters for such clients. And the office continues to grow; four new lateral hire partners arrived in 2015, further boosting the office's capabilities.

Philadelphia (2008)

Hogan & Hartson gained its first Philadelphia foothold in 1998, when then D.C. associates Janice Hogan and David Newmann moved there to start a satellite office. Ten years later, in 2008, after reaching a critical mass of Philadelphia lawyers, Hogan & Hartson officially opened its office overlooking the Philadelphia Art Museum and the Schuylkill River. The Philadelphia team came to specialize in the Food and Drug Administration (FDA)/Medical Device practice, with a focus on biomedical devices, representing clients before the FDA. In 2010, the office added a thriving white collar and investigations practice, led by federal prosecutor Virginia Gibson. Its commercial litigation practice became another vital team representing clients before state and federal courts and arbitration panels in Pennsylvania and nationwide.

The office received the Pennsylvania Bar Association's 2012 Pro Bono Award for its successful challenge to the state legislature's decennial redistricting plan—the first such win in forty years of Pennsylvania redistricting litigation.

San Francisco & Silicon Valley (2008)

In 2008, Hogan & Hartson opened offices in both San Francisco and Silicon Valley to extend the reach of the firm's global capacity to serve the growing markets in high tech, biotechnology, medical research, social media, the proliferating sharing economy, and related businesses. The initial offices featured litigators from an established San Francisco firm, including Michael Shepard, a former federal prosecutor, Robert Hawk, a civil litigator, and Megan Dixon, a former Justice Department official.

During the offices' early years their teams have carved prominent profiles in investigations related to laws governing corrupt practices and securities litigation; trials, and white collar criminal defense; cartel cases; antitrust; commercial litigation; consumer class actions; civil litigation; an emerging company corporate practice; and M&A. Areas of focus responsive to California's specific needs have also grown, including the addition of global payments, medical device regulation, intellectual property, and insurance litigation and regulation.

Minneapolis (2015)

Norm Coleman, a former United States Senator from Minnesota, joined Hogan Lovells in 2011, forming the firm's fledgling Minneapolis "presence." In 2012, Coleman teamed with two partners, both former colleagues at Hogan & Hartson, who had also worked together as joint executive vice president and general counsel of UnitedHealth Group, a Minneapolis-based Fortune 20 healthcare company. This team built a respected presence by early 2013, enhancing the Hogan Lovells portfolio in Minneapolis–Saint Paul and beyond. A fourth partner joined the firm in 2015. He shared the winning formula of the team he joined: he was a former associate at Hogan & Hartson, spent some years in public service as an assistant U.S. attorney in Denver, and had served within United Health Group as its senior deputy general counsel.

This group's success was sealed with the announcement in 2015 that Minneapolis would become an official office in the firm's global network.

ABOVE LEFT: The San Francisco office is located in the Embarcadero Center, a few blocks from the historic Ferry Plaza waterfront.

ABOVE: Hogan Lovells opened an office in Silicon Valley, home to many of the world's largest high-tech corporations, as well as thousands of start-up companies, in 2008. Due to rapid expansion the firm moved from Palo Alto to a state-of-the-art office space in the heart of Menlo Park in 2013.

Hogan Lovells ■ Our Story

LEFT: The Hogan Lovells Caracas office serves a broad base of local and international clients and provides a strategic and practical platform for conducting business in Venezuela, or for those entering the Latin American marketplace.

BELOW: Hogan Lovells opened an office in Rio de Janeiro in 2013. As reported in *Latin Lawyer,* Hogan Lovells is "the first full-service international law firm to announce it is opening an office in Rio de Janeiro."

LATIN AMERICA
Caracas (2005)

Miguel Zaldivar and José Valdivia developed the business plan for Hogan & Hartson's first office in Latin America. It opened in Caracas in 2005 with the incorporation of Luis Bottaro and Bruno Ciuffetelli, who brought extensive oil and gas transactional experience and cross-border experience from a wide range of industries. More generally, Caracas served as a launch pad office for further advancement into the region and the choice of Venezuela worked well for the firm, particularly when it came to energy sector work.

The office solidified the firm's relationship with state-owned petrochemical company Pequiven and strategic client Petróleos de Venezuela, S.A. (PDVSA). Representative matters for PDVSA have included: several issuances of bonds in the international market totaling $15 billion; the $4 billion financings for the Puerto La Cruz Refinery; and various financings with Chinese Banks totalling more than $10 billion. The Caracas team has also participated in international arbitrations (treaty disputes claims and commercial disputes) on behalf of PDVSA and the Republic of Venezuela.

Rio de Janeiro (2013) and São Paulo (2014)

Hogan Lovells became the first full-service international law firm to have offices in Rio de Janeiro and São Paulo when Claudette Christian opened the firm's office in Rio de Janeiro in early 2013 and then in São Paulo in early 2014. Christian, who had been working extensively in Brazil since the late-1990s, was joined by a team of experienced, multicultural, and dual-nationality lawyers trained in both civil law and common law and qualified in Brazil and New York.

Given Brazil's global importance, in 2014 Hogan Lovells soon recognized the need for an office in São Paulo; the firm was already serving a number of São Paulo-based clients through its Rio de Janeiro, New York, and London offices. After opening the São Paulo office, Christian was joined by lateral hire partner Isabel Costa Carvalho and additional finance and corporate lawyers.

MIDDLE EAST
Dubai (2007), Abu Dhabi (2008), and Saudi Arabia (2010)

On 1 May 2007, at the height of the boom prior to the global financial crisis, Lovells established its office in the Dubai International Financial Centre with its current Office Managing Partner, Rahail Ali, Imtiaz Shah, Rustum Shah, and two partners seconded from London. The team found permanent accommodation in the Al Fattan Currency Tower. Over the years the initial team of nine (working on just banking and finance and corporate matters) grew to an office of over twenty-five, providing a full range of legal services.

In 2008, Hogan & Hartson established a presence in Abu Dhabi, managed then by four partners who split their time between Abu Dhabi and Washington, D.C. Following the 2010 merger, the combined firm maintained the Abu Dhabi office until the decision to consolidate the UAE presence in the Dubai office, which would act as a hub for the region.

In 2010, the firm expanded its capability and reach into Saudi Arabia, one of the Middle East's largest economies, by seconding one partner and two senior associates to an associated firm with offices in Jeddah and Riyadh.

AUSTRALIA
Sydney and Perth (2015)

In July 2015, Hogan Lovells launched its Australia practice with offices in Sydney and Perth. The initial focus of the practice is on corporate and banking and finance transactions, specializing in deals and projects in the energy, natural resources, and infrastructure sectors within Australia and regionally.

Establishing a presence in Australia further enhanced the firm's commitment to the development of its Asia practice, given the cross-border trade flows to and from Australia, particularly with South East Asia, Japan, and China. It means that the firm can offer increased support to clients investing in Australia; Australian entities extending their operations into emerging markets such as Africa; and in-depth M&A advice to Australian pension and investment funds which are active in the UK, Continental Europe, and in the U.S.

FAR LEFT: The hub of the Hogan Lovells Middle East practice is in Dubai, UAE. An experienced legal team provides advice on a range of finance and business matters to financial institutions, corporates, and governmental entities.

LEFT: The Hogan Lovells offices in Sydney and Perth opened in 2015 with a particular focus on the energy, natural resources, and infrastructure sectors. The Sydney office (left) is located in a new building at 20 Martin Place, in the heart of the business district, and the Perth office (below) is on St. George's Terrace.

Hogan Lovells ■ Our Story

ASSOCIATED OFFICES
Zagreb (1994)
Hogan Lovells is represented in Croatia by associated office Bogdanovic, Dolicki & Partners. The firm advises foreign companies on the taking up of economic activities or investments in Croatia and the enforcement of claims of foreign clients in Croatia. Clients include prominent Western banks, insurance companies, and industrial and commercial enterprises, as well as tour operators.

Budapest (2000)
Hogan Lovells is represented in Hungary by associated office Partos & Noblet, which works in close cooperation with the firm, particularly in Central and Eastern Europe, the United States, and Asia-Pacific. The Budapest team includes lawyers and legal advisers from Hungary and the United Kingdom, including Christopher Noblet, who trained with Lovells in London. Many of its long-standing clients are financial institutions, real estate developers and investment funds, capital-markets and private-equity funds, and participants in the media and telecommunications sectors.

Indonesia (2012)
Indonesia is a survivor of the global financial crisis and one of the strongest growing economies. Hogan Lovells manages its Indonesian operation through an association with a local firm, focusing on corporate, finance, infrastructure, energy, and litigation work.

Budapest, Hungary.

Chapter 6 ■ Our Worldwide Team

Our People, Our Future

Over more than a century, our firm has evolved from modest beginnings to a global enterprise with more than 6,000 people. Numerous lawyers, past and present, have been instrumental in the success of the firm—brilliant litigators, clever negotiators, unstoppable salesmen, straightforward dealmakers, charismatic client-getters, hands-on managers, strategic thinkers, far-sighted visionaries, and many other characters.

But their contributions would not be worth anything without the enduring effort of all the people that work in our offices throughout the world. They are the lifeblood of Hogan Lovells: the trainee lawyers who unearth obscure judgments in support of a case; business development specialists who help develop new client relationships and strengthen old ones; technology specialists who build digital interfaces with our clients and ensure we are able to work each day; the people team looking after the well-being of our employees; researchers and professional-support lawyers helping lawyers find the information they need; the finance team, raising and paying the bills; the personal assistants who work alongside our lawyers; the receptionists who greet our clients when they enter the office; and all of our other essential teams.

All of our people are vital to our shared enterprise. Recognizing their value—and treating each other with the warmth and respect each person deserves—is the single most unique feature of our firm. Without the collegiality with which we treat one another, without showing a real interest in each other's work, without striving to create a diverse and inclusive workplace, without encouraging our people to pursue their passions in life outside of work, and without the courage to fight for those who have no voice, we will lose what sets us apart from other firms.

Long before the combination of Lovells and Hogan & Hartson, we cultivated mutual respect and shared core values. Those intangibles cannot be displayed on a balance sheet or a bottom line, but they are fundamental to our work, our growth, our client service, and our collective professional happiness. They make us the firm we are, and they are the foundation for the firm we can be.

Hogan Lovells

Let's go

How redefining engagement will help us realize our potential

Spring 2015

change   redefine

engage

HOGAN LOVELLS OFFICES
DECEMBER 2015

OFFICE	OPENING DATE
Alicante	1996
Amsterdam	1978
Baltimore	1988
Beijing	1986
Birmingham, UK	2014
Brussels	1972
Caracas	2005
Colorado Springs	1994
Denver	1993
Dubai	2007
Dusseldorf	1951
Frankfurt	1919
Hamburg	1884
Hanoi	2009
Ho Chi Minh City	1996
Hong Kong	1982
Houston	2006
Johannesburg	1892
London	1899
Los Angeles	1996
Luxembourg	2013
Madrid	2004
Mexico City	1948
Miami	2000
Milan	2000
Minneapolis	2015
Monterrey	2004
Moscow	1994
Munich	1960
New York	1977
Northern Virginia	1985
Paris	1974
Perth	2015
Philadelphia	2008
Rio de Janeiro	2013
Rome	2000
San Francisco	2008
São Paulo	2014
Shanghai	2003
Silicon Valley	2008
Singapore	1998
Sydney	2015
Tokyo	1990
Ulaanbaatar	2011
Warsaw	1991
Washington, D.C.	1904

ASSOCIATED OFFICES (with date of association)

Budapest	2000
Jakarta	2012
Jeddah	2010
Riyadh	2010
Zagreb	1994

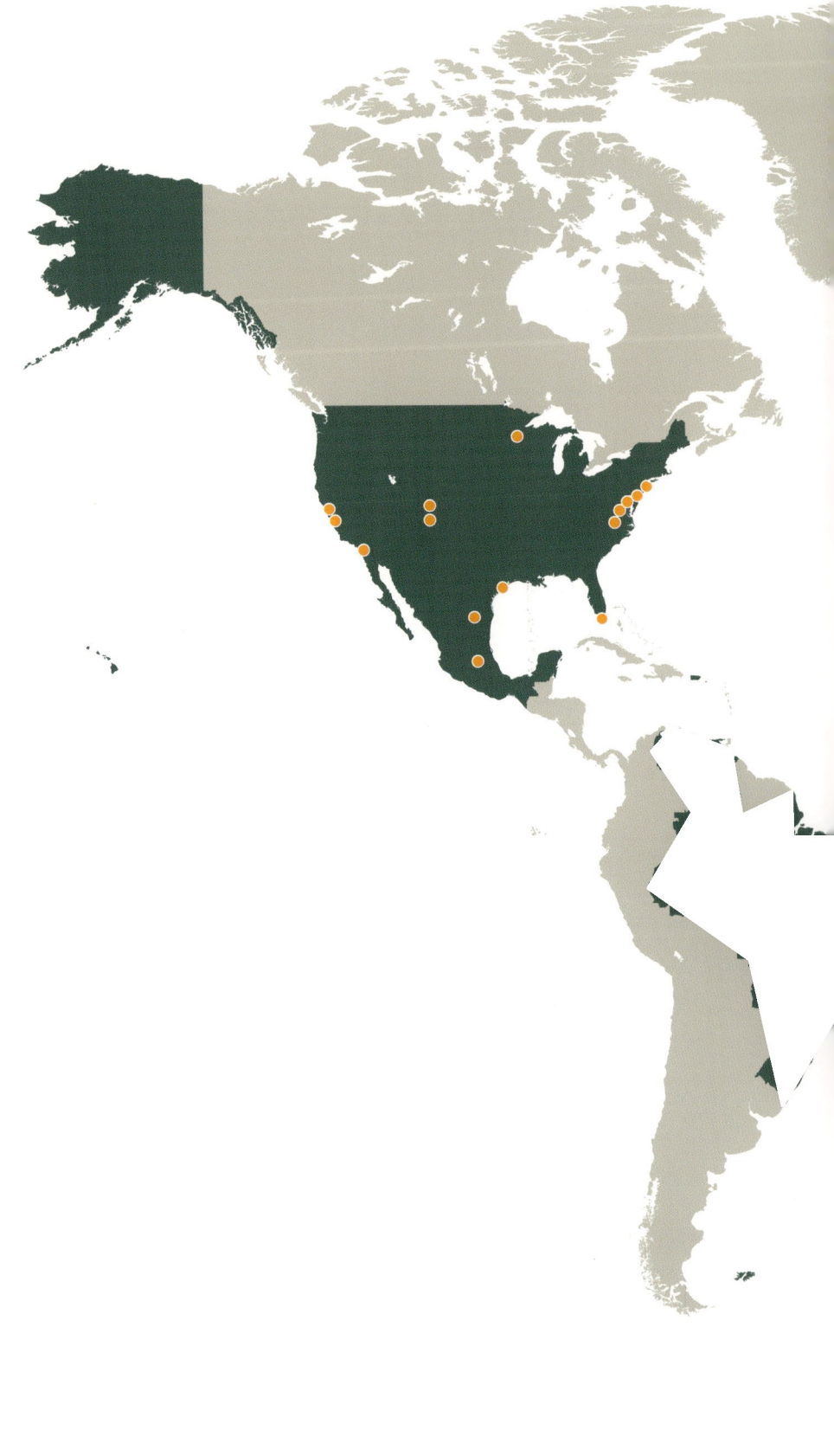

Chapter 6 ■ Our Worldwide Team

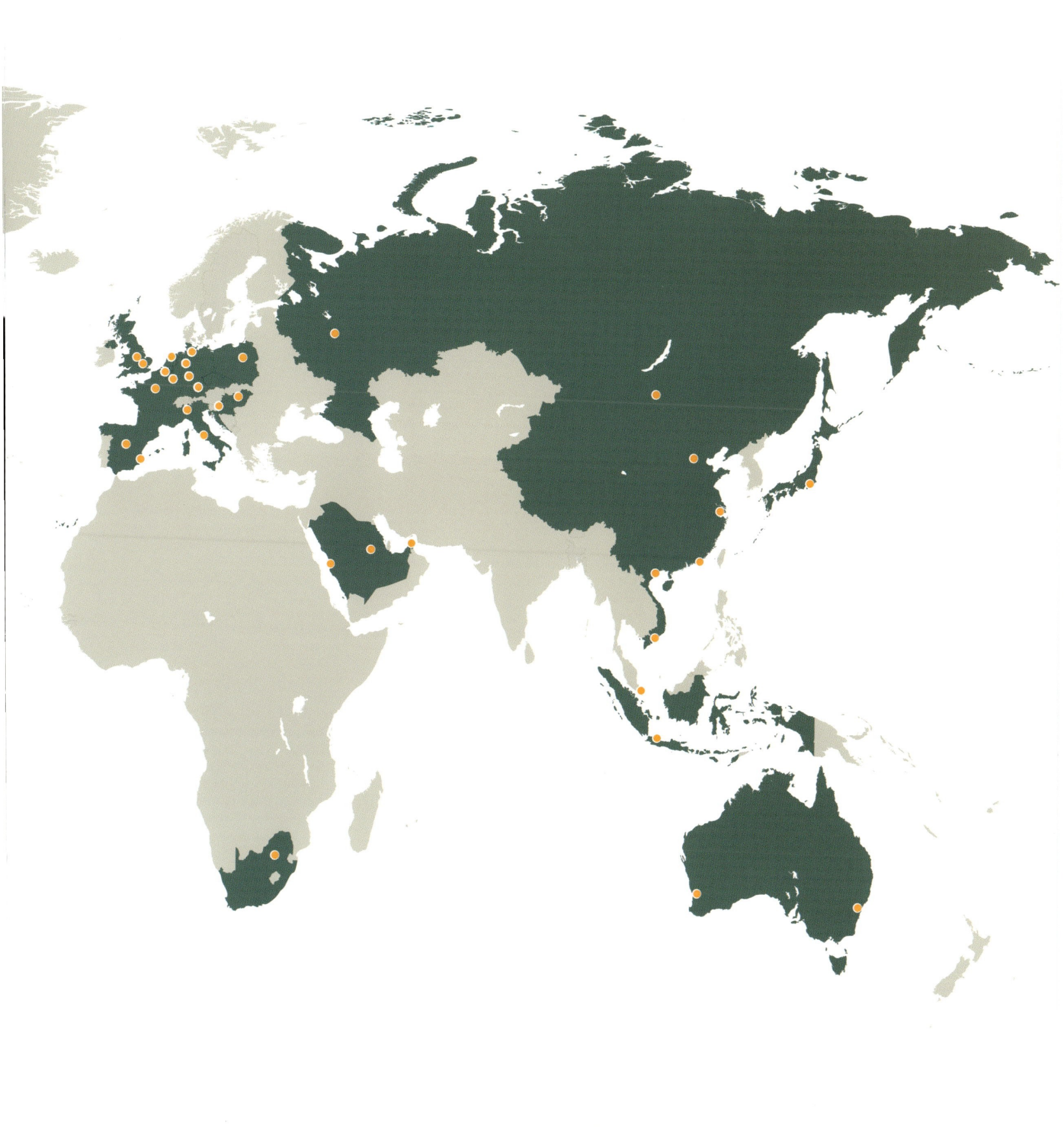

PICTURE CREDITS

The majority of the images come from the Hogan Lovells archives; other sources and copyright holders are listed below. In the case of an inadvertent omission, please contact the publisher.

9 top **Mindy Best**
10–11 **The Image Works**
13 top right **Library of Congress, Prints and Photographs Division Washington, D.C.**
13 bottom right **Mark Rucker/Transcendental Graphics/Getty Images**
14 bottom left, 24–25 **B. Christopher/Alamy Stock Photo**
14 bottom right, inset **Georgetown University Library, Washington D.C.**
15 **Washington Historical Image Collection, Martin Luther King Jr. Library, Washington, D.C.**
16 right, 18 top left **Corbis**
18 inset top **Robbie George/National Geographic Creative/Corbis**
18 middle **Chuck Pefley/Alamy Stock Photo**
20 right **Library of Congress, Prints and Photographs Division Washington, D.C.**
21 top left **Granger Historical picture library**
21 top right **Los Angeles Public Library**
24–25 **B. Christopher/Alamy Stock Photo**
26–27 **Albany Wiseman**
28 top **London Metropolitan Archives, City of London/Bridgeman Images**
29 top **Ian Ribbons**
30 bottom **Chetham's Library**
31 top **Cheshire Military Museum**
32 top **Charles Best**
32 bottom **Angelo Hornack/Alamy**
33 inset **Look and Learn/Peter Jackson Collection**
34 top **Hugh Piesse, photograph by Charles Best**
34 bottom **Paul Harrington**
35 bottom **Topham/AP**
36–37 **Hoberman/UIG/Bridgeman Images**
37 bottom **Dirk Renckhoff/Alamy Stock Photo**
39 top **Ullstein Bild/Contributor/Getty Images**
40 left **Daniel Sambraus/Stock4B/Corbis**
42–43 **David Gentleman**
44, 45 top **Jack Hutchings**
45 bottom **Barry Lewis/Alamy Stock Photo**
46 **Peter Blake**
47 right **National Portrait Gallery, London**
47 bottom **National Maritime Museum, Greenwich, London, Greenwich Hospital Collection**
48 left **Central Press/Stringer/Getty Images**
48 bottom **PA Photos/TopFoto**
49 **National Portrait Gallery, London**
50 **John Sturrock/Alamy Stock Photo**
53 **PA/PA Archive/PA Images**
54 top **Jim James/PA Archive/PA Images**
58 left **1981 DER SPIEGEL**
58 top **Lessing archive**
62–63 **Buyenlarge/Contributor/Getty Images**
64 **Getty Images USA**
65 left **George Skadding/The LIFE Picture Collection/Getty Images**
65 right **Library of Congress, Prints and Photographs Division Washington, D.C.**

66 **Diana Walker/Liaison/Getty Images**
68 top right **Heritage Image Partnership Ltd/Alamy Stock Photo**
69 **Stock Connection Blue/Alamy Stock Photo**
70 **Bettmann/Corbis**
72 top **Jill Freedman/Getty Images**
72 inset **David J. Frent/David J. & Janice L. Frent Collection/Corbis**
72 bottom **Michael Reynolds/epa/Corbis**
73 bottom left **Richard Ellis/Contributor/Getty Images**
73 top right **Getty Images USA**
73 bottom **Washington Historical Image Collection, Martin Luther King Jr. Library, Washington, D.C.**
74 bottom left **Bettmann/CORBIS**
75 top **The National Hospice and Palliative Care Organization, Virginia**
75 bottom **Pictorial Parade/Hulton Archive/Getty Images**
76 top **Everett Collection Historical/Alamy Stock Photo**
78 bottom **Benjamin N. Cardozo School of Law, Yeshiva University**
79 top right **Gary Cameron/Reuters/Corbis**
79 bottom right **Jason Reed/Reuters/Corbis**
80 top **AP Photo/Rajanish Kakade/Press Association Images**
80–81 **AP Photo/Bullit Marquez/Press Association Images**
81 top **AP Photo/Mary Altaffer/Press Association Images**
82 **Blaine Harrington III/Alamy Stock Photo**
84–85, 87 right **Mindy Best**
88 bottom left **Financial Times, Wednesday 17 September 2008, used under licence. All rights reserved**
88–89 **Charles Best**
91 **Jesse Winter**
92 left **Charles Best**
93 **Ingo Bartussek/Westend61/Corbis**
94 top **Carolyn Jenkins/Alamy Stock Photo**
96 bottom **Charles Best**
98 top left, 98–99 **Dave Chidley**
100–101 **Oscar Cid Flores/Jacky Rubalcava**
101 bottom right **Jesse Kraft/Alamy Stock Photo**
102 **Renelle Rampersad**
107 **Justin Sullivan/Getty Images**
109 right **AP Photo/David Duprey/Press Association Images**
110 **Mandel Ngan/AFP/Getty Images**
111 top **Stephane Mahe/Reuters/Corbis**
112–113 **NAMIG/epa/Corbis**
114 **[e]Stringer/Xinhua Press/Corbis**
115 top **Ingram Pinn, Financial Times, used under licence from the Financial Times. All rights reserved**
115 bottom **Feature Photo Service for IBM/PA/Press Association Images**
116 left **Alex Wong/Getty Images**

116–117 **Chris Warham/Alamy Stock Photo**
117 right **Brendan Smialowski/AFP/Getty Images**
118 bottom *Managing Intellectual Property*
119 top **Sam Yeh/AFP/Getty Images**
119 bottom **AP Photo/Darron Cummings/Press Association Images**
121 top right, right **Reproduced with permission of Merck Sharp & Dohme Corp., a subsidiary of Merck & Co., Inc., Kenilworth, New Jersey, U.S.A. All rights reserved**
124 **Sean Dempsey/PA Archive/PA Images**
125 left **Schöning/Ullstein Bild via Getty Images**
125 right **Guibbaud Christophe/ABACA/Press Association Images**
126–127 **Ashley Jones**
127 bottom right, 129 **Renelle Rampersad**
136 **Andrew Lichtenstein/Corbis**
138 top **Alastair Fyfe**
138 bottom left **Darren Filkins**
139 right **Peter Macdiarmid/Getty Images**
140 bottom **SCPhotos/Alamy Stock Photo**
141 top **All rights reserved by Lendwithcare**
142 top left **Fiona Hanson**
142 bottom right **Simon Williams**
142 top right **Olivier Douliery/Pool/Corbis**
143 **Sergii Kharchenko/NurPhoto/Corbis**
145 top right **Phil Searle**
145 bottom **Glyn Kirk/AFP/Getty Images**
146 top left **Jim Young/Reuters/Corbis**
147 bottom left **CARE International/2015/Prashanth Vishwanathan**
148 bottom right **Harvey Bilt**
153 bottom left **Lou-Foto/Alamy Stock Photo**
154 top **Robert Harding/Alamy Stock Photo**
154 bottom **Charles Pertwee/Corbis**
158–159 **Image Source/Alamy Stock Photo**
159 centre **Atlantide Phototravel/Corbis**
159 right **Bernhard Ernst/Alamy Stock Photo**
160–161 **Loop Images/UIG via Getty Images**
161 bottom **Craig Holmes**
162 left **Mindy Best**
162–163 **Matt McClain/The Washington Post via Getty Images**
163 right **Clarence Holmes Photography/Alamy Stock Photo**
164 top **Denver Post Photo by Cyrus McCrimmon/Getty Images**
165 left **egdigital/iStock**
165 right **Felix Mizioznikov/Shutterstock.com**
166 top **Gavin Hellier/Robert Harding/Corbis**
166 bottom **Lester Lefkowitz/Getty Images**
167 top left **ivanstar/iStock**
167 top right **Frank Ramspott/iStock**
168 bottom **Tim Tadder/Corbis**
169 bottom **Rob Tuckwell**
170–171 **dleiva/Alamy Stock Photo**
176 **Mindy Best**